Popular Music and Youth Culture

Popular Music
and Youth Culture

Music, Identity and Place

ANDY BENNETT

Published by
PALGRAVE
Houndmills, Basingstoke, Hampshire RG21 6XS and
175 Fifth Avenue, New York, N. Y. 10010
Companies and representatives throughout the world

PALGRAVE is the new global academic imprint of
St. Martin's Press LLC Scholarly and Reference Division and
Palgrave Publishers Ltd (formerly Macmillan Press Ltd).

Outside North America
ISBN-13: 978-0-333-73228-1 hardback
ISBN-10: 0-333-73228-6 hardback
ISBN-13: 978-0-333-73229-8 paperback
ISBN-10: 0-333-73229-4 paperback

Inside North America
ISBN 0-312-22753-1

10 9 8
10 09 08 07 06

A catalogue record for this book is available
from the British Library.

Library of Congress Catalog Card Number: 99–16789

Printed and bound in Great Britain by
Biddles Ltd., King's Lynn, Norfolk.

To my parents

Contents

Acknowledgements   viii
Introduction   1

Part I Theories of Youth Culture and Popular Music
1 The Sociology of Youth Culture   11
2 Youth Culture and Popular Music   34
3 The Significance of Locality   52

Part II Local Representations: Case Studies
4 Dance Music, Local Identity and Urban Space   73
5 Bhangra and Asian Identity: The Role of Local Knowledge   103
6 Hip Hop am Main, Rappin' on the Tyne: Hip Hop Culture
   as a Local Construct in Two European Cities   133
7 The Benwell Floyd: Local Live Music, Sociality and the
   Politics of Musical Taste   166

8 Conclusion: Youth Culture and Popular Music   195

Bibliography   199
Index   216

Acknowledgements

I would like to say a very special thank you to Simon Frith, whose highly constructive comments on draft chapters of this book were of invaluable help, and to my PhD supervisor, David Chaney, whose studied reflections on cultural life continue to be a great source of inspiration to me. Thanks also to Dick Hobbs and David Morely for their advice on how to develop my PhD research into a book, and to Dave Laing, Les Back, Jason Toynbee and Ben Carrington, who have each read and commented on various papers drawn from material featured in this book.

A big show of thanks is also due to those people who helped make the fieldwork for this book such an interesting, pleasurable and, at times, humorous experience – Tom Müller, the Benwell Floyd, Asher Rashid, Mark Lawton, Dave Rae and the many young people in Newcastle and Frankfurt without whose generous co-operation this book could never have been written. Thanks also to Moni for the German lessons, for sending all those 'essential' pieces of German literature I continually requested and for having patience, and to Beat the Rain for the much needed musical interludes between the days of reading, researching and writing.

Last, but not least, I would also like to express my thanks to the Economic and Social Research Council for providing the financial support for my research in the form of a PhD studentship.

Introduction

Music and style-centred youth cultures are now familiar aspects of everyday life in a range of globally diffuse social settings. Initially restricted to the developed industrial regions of the world – North America, western Europe, Australia and Japan – where the musical and stylistic innovations of the 1950s and 60s had their greatest cultural impact on youth, music and style have gradually become important cultural resources for young people throughout the world. In countries across South America and in parts of Africa and Asia young people collectively embrace forms of popular music and their attendant stylistic images. Similarly, during the 1970s and 80s, music and style-led youth cultures became a powerful form of collective expression in the then 'Communist bloc' countries of eastern Europe and have remained a significant aspect of youth lifestyles in the *glasnost* and post-*glasnost* eras. The globally established relationship between youth culture and popular music has attracted much attention, not least of all from academic researchers; accounts of youth culture and popular music being a major focus of interest across a range of subjects including sociology, cultural and media studies.

The purpose of this book is twofold: first, to consider the various ways in which youth culture and popular music have been theorised by sociologists, cultural and media theorists and to critically evaluate some of the claims that have been made in this wide-ranging body of work; second, to bring a new perspective to some of the more recent work on youth culture and popular music that takes as its starting point those 'local' spaces in which popular music is heard by young people and appropriated as a cultural resource. Such work argues that local appropriations of musical and stylistic resources involve inscriptions of meaning that are inextricably bound up with local experience. As such, it is suggested, music and style highlight rather than obscure localised distinctions between young audiences. Moreover, studies of music and locality have also revealed that it is not simply at national levels that such 'local' distinctions assume cultural significance. Local distinctions are also to be seen in the context of regions and cities where issues of identity are equally if not more readily articulated around notions of space and place. It is with this latter notion of locality that I am primarily concerned in this study. Drawing upon recent social-geographical work, the analytical and empirical approach I apply here views the 'local' as a *contested* rather than *fixed* space – the cultural significance I attach to music being its role in the construction of particular narratives of the local.

My study of popular music and youth culture in a local context takes the form of an ethnographic journey through the musicalised lives of young people in the north of England and, in the case of Chapter 6, central Germany. In each of the four ethnographic chapters that make up Part II of this book, I will illustrate how my research substantiates, or in some cases challenges, observations made by other researchers who are similarly interested in the significance of the 'local' as the cultural space in which music is collectively heard and used by young audiences. The ethnographic approach is, I feel, crucial in gaining an understanding of how popular music features in the lives of young people in the context of their everyday lives. Interviews and discussions with young people, together with observations made through visiting clubs, venues and other locations in which types of music and their attendant stylistic innovations are appropriated and 'lived out' by young people, provide crucial insights into the cultural relevance of music and style within the contextual frame of those localised experiences that collectively inform everyday life.

In adopting an ethnographic approach to the study of youth and music, I also hope to illustrate something of the pluralistic and, in many cases, confrontational nature of musical and stylistic meanings as these inform the daily lives of young people. Thus, if the appropriation of certain musics and styles by young people enables them to articulate collective forms of hegemonic struggle against those individuals, groups and institutions that oppress them in various ways, then such patterns of appropriation also ignite struggles between young people themselves, particularly concerning issues of 'identity' and 'authenticity'. This is clearly demonstrated in Chapters 5 and 6 which respectively consider the contested nature of bhangra and hip hop.

In presenting the results of my research, I have observed May's contention that ethnography 'is supposed to be about the study of people, their interactions and environment' (1993, p. 72). Thus, rather than placing interview and other fieldwork material in an 'Appendix' or 'Ethnography' section, I have chosen to work this material into the body of my own theoretical analysis so that the ethnography becomes a central focus of the study. At the same time, however, I appreciate fully that, in the final analysis, all 'ethnographic discourses are necessarily "partial truths"' (Moores: 1993, p. 4). In response to this often-stated problem concerning ethnographic research, I can say only that in regarding the voices of my fieldwork participants as centrally significant to my analysis, I have attempted to remain as faithful as possible to the fieldwork experience while at the same time giving clear indications of where the research participants' accounts of their everyday experiences finish and my own interpretations of such accounts take over.

The fieldwork for this study was conducted over a 12-month period between October 1994 and October 1995. I began writing while the fieldwork was still in progress, a strategy that I felt would allow for my writing to capture more directly some of the situations and experiences that characterised the fieldwork process. Additionally, I also reasoned that this approach would allow me to remain more objective about my experiences in the field, or, to use Hobbs's words, would remove the danger of 'going native [by] going academic' (1988, p.15). My research in the UK was conducted primarily in the city of Newcastle upon Tyne. The decision to use Newcastle upon Tyne as the UK base for the fieldwork was influenced in part by the city's close proximity to Durham University, my research base at this time, but also because of the relatively scant attention paid to Newcastle and the wider northeast region of England in academic work dealing with youth culture and popular music.

As England's northernmost city, Newcastle has a highly distinctive local culture. Originally a centre for shipbuilding, Newcastle retains a strong sense of its industrial heritage, captured in the preservation of social rituals such as the 'working man's weekend', (Hollands: 1995) where young men, in the tradition of their fathers and grandfathers, divide their weekend evenings between drinking with friends and taking out their girlfriends or wives. Similarly, a great deal of pride continues to be invested in being a 'Geordie', the name given to a native of Newcastle (see Colls and Lancaster: 1992), such pride being readily articulated through the highly distinctive 'Geordie' accent and reputed 'down to earth' attitude of Newcastle people. Articulations of 'Geordiness' also manifest themselves through certain practices of music-making and consumption in Newcastle, particularly in the context of local pub venues. Chapter 7 considers one example of how such aspects of Geordie culture have become infused with live music in local pubs and the types of band–audience relationship that result.

While such expressions of pride in relation to place and identity are given considerable currency in some areas of Newcastle's musical life, this is by no means a standard cultural response. Indeed, among certain sections of Newcastle's youth, the wholesale rejection of those cultural traits typically associated with Newcastle has resulted in highly particularised strategies of resistance in which music and style also play a crucial role. As Chapter 4 illustrates, this is particularly so among those young people involved in the local urban dance music scene for whom music acts as a central cultural resource in determining their 'otherness' from what they collectively deem to be the mainstream 'townie' youth scene. In considering the distinctively 'local' nature of this form of resistance I also refer to other studies of local dance music scenes, in the UK, the US and Germany, where the same musics are seen to resonate with different everyday contexts thus producing further examples of 'localised' response to urban dance music.

Newcastle is also highly distinctive in terms of its ethnic composition. In comparison with many other English cities, Newcastle is almost exclusively white, a fact that presents special problems for the small ethnic minority groups who live in the city. Again, strategies of resistance to the more oppressive features of Newcastle's essential whiteness are often mobilised via music, especially among the city's young Asians. During the course of Chapter 5, I will examine the role of bhangra in relation to the construction of Asian identities in Newcastle and will also consider the way in which such 'local' constructions of Asianess vary between different British cities. In particular, I will consider how local variations in the cultural response of young Asians to bhangra problematise the notions of a new 'Asianess' which certain theorists attach to the significance of bhangra in contemporary Britain.

My UK fieldwork was supplemented with research carried out in Frankfurt am Main, Germany, a city that is culturally very different to Newcastle. The choice of Frankfurt as a fieldwork location in Germany was prompted by my familiarity with the city's music scene and with the diverse cultural composition of the local youth culture. Prior to commencing my research, I had worked with the Frankfurt Rockmobil, a project that encourages young people from Frankfurt's many ethnic minority groups to become involved in collaborative music-making activities in an attempt to promote better ethnic relations in the city (see Bennett: 1998). While working with the Rockmobil, I became involved in some highly innovative projects in which young Turkish and Moroccan people from *Gastarbeiter* (guestworker) families fused African-American rap sounds with traditional Turkish and Moroccan music (indeed, it was this experience that initially motivated me to begin my research). My work with these young people inevitably led to conversations about the wider hip hop scene in Frankfurt. During preliminary fieldwork in Newcastle, I discovered a parallel local hip hop scene and realised that the respective scenes in Newcastle and Frankfurt provided an ideal opportunity for a comparative ethnographic study of local hip hop scenes in an international context. The results of this research and a discussion of the ways in which they relate to and build upon broader debates concerning hip hop's role as a 'glocal' culture (Mitchell: 1998) are presented in Chapter 6.

Methodology

The main methods of research I employed in my study were participant observation, semi-structured 'one-to-one' interviews and focus groups, that is, group discussions on set themes. Interview and focus group sessions were taped and later transcribed. Permission to use a tape recorder was in every instance sought from interviewees/focus group participants before sessions began. On the few occasions when interviewees refused permission for a tape recorder to be used, notes were made during the interview. I also made limited use of question-naires in my research on Asian youth and bhangra. This was done at the suggestion of an Asian youth worker who felt that it might prove a useful way of gaining information from young Asians given the difficulty I initially experienced in gaining access (see below). The questionnaires were distributed to young Asians in schools around west Newcastle. However, the response rate was relatively poor and it was often the case that simple yes/no answers were given where I had indicated the need for a more detailed account. Subsequently, I decided against the use of questionnaires and attempted to gain as much information as possible via direct contact with young Asians.

In her introduction to *Rock Culture in Liverpool*, Cohen comments upon the way in which much useful information concerning Liverpool's popular music scene was gleaned from everyday conversa-tions with local people such as 'taxi-drivers, hairdressers, waitresses and waiters' (1991, p. 1). In many respects, I found that the same was true for my own study. Moreover, being a musician and playing in a local Newcastle band meant that I was constantly meeting or being introduced to musicians and music enthusiasts who gave me a great deal of background information about what types of music were popular in Newcastle, the clubs at which such musics were featured and specialist record shops which were a focal point for particular types of music consumers.

Another source of useful preliminary data on the Newcastle music scene was acquired through interviews with the staff of locally produced youth magazines, such as *The Crack*, and 'zine' projects such as *NE29*. The information gained from these interviews helped me to focus the direction of my field research by giving me a clearer picture of what styles of music were current in Newcastle at the time and which clubs and venues catered for particular musical trends. Similarly, in the summer of 1994, while watching the *Channel Four Goes to Glastonbury* programme, I saw Ferank, a Geordie poet and rapper, who gave an impromptu version of his rap 'Aa dee it coz aa can' (see Chapter 6) as an interviewer and camera crew made one of their regular forays into the festival audience. It was not until a year later that I was able to locate Ferank, after one of his raps had been published in *NE29*. Ferank proved to be a valuable source of information on rap and hip hop in Newcastle, in addition to which he kindly agreed to let me reproduce some of his work in this study.

During the early stages of my fieldwork I also made contact with several local 'City Challenge' initiatives including Dance City, a project established to encourage young people in Newcastle to become involved in dance activities, and the Outreach Detached Centre, a young people's 'drop-in' centre in west Newcastle with sports facilities, a cafeteria and a counselling service. In addition, I made several visits to a community 'drop-in' centre in the Percy Main district of Newcastle and a NACRO music project in Benwell, a district in west Newcastle.[1] Each of these organisations was extremely helpful and gave me initial assistance which proved to be crucial to the overall direction and development of my research. For example, through approaching Dance City, I made contact with a local hip hop enthusiast who proved to be both an important source of information and a principle 'gatekeeper', giving me access to other hip hop enthusiasts and hip hop events in Newcastle. In Percy Main, I was introduced to several urban dance music enthusiasts who gave me a valuable insight into the local urban dance music scene. Similarly, one of the part-time sessional workers at the Outreach Detached Centre in Elswick frequently helped in the organisation of urban dance music 'house parties' in Newcastle and gave me access to this scene. Through my visits to the NACRO music project, I was introduced to the Benwell Floyd, the focus for my study of local pub and club music in Chapter 7. Some of the Benwell Floyd's members were, or had formerly been, involved with the NACRO music project.

More problematic was my research on bhangra in Newcastle. Prior to commencing this aspect of my research, I had been warned by an Asian colleague that trying to conduct interviews and focus groups with young Asians in Newcastle would be difficult because of the constraints placed upon their leisure time by parents. I was eventually able to overcome such problems with the help of an Asian community worker who arranged access to a number of 'structured' groups and events, such as the regular weekly meetings of the Black Youth Collective (held at a comprehensive school in west Newcastle directly after the normal school day had ended), where I could be formally introduced to the young people who would take part. Similarly, I was granted access to a special training group that had been established for those young Asians in Newcastle who wished to contribute to the organisation of the 1995 Newcastle Mela.[2] Problems of access were also resolved to some extent by the approaching summer, which meant that I was able to attend outdoor events such as the Middlesborough and Newcastle Melas and the Stockton Festival, the last attracting many young Asians from Newcastle because of the live bhangra music featured in its programme. By attending such events in the company of an Asian youth worker, who had agreed to act as a gatekeeper, I was able to spend more time talking to young Asians, thus gaining the supplementary information I needed to complete my research on bhangra in Newcastle.

Finally, in selecting interviewees for my research on the Frankfurt hip hop scene, I was able to rely upon the network of contacts established through my work with the Rockmobil. Such contacts in turn introduced me to other young people who were involved in the local hip hop scene either as producers, performers or consumers. I also gained useful information from journalists, record labels and fanzines that I contacted during my fieldwork visits to Frankfurt. In facilitating the Frankfurt-based aspects of my ethnographic research, my former employer, Tom Müller (Head of the Frankfurt Rockmobil Project), was of invaluable assistance in helping me to arrange interviews and meetings so that everything ran relatively smoothly during my short fieldwork visits to Frankfurt. All of the interviews that I carried out in

Frankfurt were conducted in German and have been subsequently translated into English. My references to the German rap group Advanced Chemistry in Chapter 6 are based in part on information acquired from *Lost in Music*, a documentary programme on German hip hop broadcast in Germany in early 1993.

NOTES

1. NACRO stands for the National Association for the Care and Resettlement of Offenders. Although the project was initially established to work with offenders, it now offers a range of skills training programmes for the long-term unemployed and school leavers.
2. A Mela is an annual Asian festival (see Chapter 5).

Part I

Theories of Youth Culture and Popular Music

Chapter 1

The Sociology of Youth Culture

The history of youth culture as an object of sociological study is both long and complex. Just as youth culture itself has undergone a rapid succession of stylistic and aesthetic changes, so the analytical tools and theoretical perspectives that sociologists have employed in attempting to interpret the social significance of youth culture have also varied over time. Early studies of youth tended to focus on issues of crime and delinquency, that is to say, on the issue of youth as a social problem. In the years following the Second World War a proliferation of style-based youth cultures, especially in Britain, led to new explanations of youth that, while maintaining an interest in the socio-economic issues pertaining to young people, began to consider how the deviant responses of the young to such issues were played out on the surface of the body to produce a form of spectacular 'subcultural' resistance. Although it proved to be a highly influential paradigm, the dominance of subcultural analysis during the 1970s and early 1980s closed off a number of other potentially useful avenues for youth research and attracted considerable criticism on the grounds that 'youth had no reality outside its representation' (Cohen: 1986, p. 20). Since the mid-1980s, interest in subcultural theory has declined and the sociology of youth culture has assumed a new direction that, rather than attempting to impose a singular discourse on the stylistic sensibilities of youth, remains receptive to the plurality of issues and circumstances that underpin the identity politics of contemporary youth cultures.

The historical origins of youth culture

A commonly stated point of origin for the phenomenon that we today refer to as youth culture is the period immediately following the end of the Second World War. Certainly, contemporary versions of youth culture have their roots in socio-economic and technological developments that occurred during the late 1940s and early 1950s. The post-war period was a time of increasing economic affluence in Britain and the US. In Britain especially, the temporary absence from the world market of major exporters such as Germany, France, Japan and Italy meant that the nation enjoyed an unprecedented rate of economic growth. Output rose by some 35 per cent between 1951 and 1961, while real average earnings increased by approximately 2.7 per cent a year (Leys: 1983, pp. 60–1). Consequently, consumerism, once a luxury reserved for the wealthier classes, 'began to develop among all but the very poorest groups' (Bocock: 1993, p. 21). Such shifting patterns of consumerism were paralleled by new techniques of mass production which allowed for consumer goods to be produced both in greater quantity and more cheaply than had been possible before the war. The youth market was, in many ways, an inevitable extension of this new consumer-based society. Young people, especially those who were still living with their parents, had the highest amounts of disposable income. During the early 1950s, a range of commodities designed specifically for the young began to appear. Such commodities included fashion clothes, cosmetics and jewellery as well as new goods such as plastic 45 rpm records (which replaced the fragile 78 rpm record of the pre-war years) and portable transistor radios (Chambers: 1985, pp. 15–17; Bocock: 1993, p. 23).

The post-war period, then, gave rise to crucial shifts in the socio-cultural status of youth. However, it is erroneous to presume that youth culture in itself did not exist prior to 1945. References to distinctive youth sensibilities can be traced back to the work of Roman playwrights Plautus and Terence whose 'comedies [centred upon] debauched, pleasure-seeking young men and their conflicts with their fathers' (Boëthius: 1995, p. 39). Other studies reveal a historical lineage of youth groups and gangs exhibiting similar characteristics to those of contemporary youth cultures. Pearson's account of the London 'apprentices' during the seventeenth and eighteenth centuries clearly illustrates the connections between such 'forgotten' youth cultures and their latter-day counterparts both in terms of their collective cultural sensibilities and the reactions of the wider society towards them. Thus, explains Pearson, the apprentices:

> were thought of as a separate order or subculture... Various attempts were
> made to regularize the conduct of apprentices, banning them from partici-
> pation in football games, playing music, or drinking in taverns... The
> length of hair was another focus for periodic conflict between the genera-

tions, and one typical order of 1603 had required that they should not 'weare their haire long nor locks at their ears like ruffians' (1994, p. 1166; see also Pearson: 1983, pp. 190–4).

Roberts provides a similar account of a series of late nineteenth-century youth gangs, known collectively as the Northern Scuttlers, who were located in the neighbouring conurbations of Manchester and Salford in northwest England. Roberts's account is particularly interesting because of the parallels it reveals between the stylistic sensibilities of the Scuttlers and those of modern day youth cultures. According to Roberts, the Scuttler 'had his own style of dress – the union shirt, bell-bottomed trousers, the heavy leather belt, pricked out in fancy designs with the large steel buckle and the thick, iron-shod clogs' (1971, p. 123). There are obvious comparisons between this description of the Scuttler's stylistic image and the way in which contemporary youth cultures choose particular styles of dress as a way of marking themselves out from the wider society, often customising such clothes, for example the studded leather jacket of the heavy metal fan or 'multiple zips and outside seams' of the punk style (Hebdige: 1979, p. 107). Peukert's study of the *Wilden Cliquen* ('wild crowds') of 1920s Germany adds to the picture of youth as a stylistically distinct grouping long before the trappings of the modern youth market were in place to produce and promote youth-orientated fashion commodities. Moreover, it wasn't simply the clothing of such groups that set them apart from the wider society but also their penchant for adorning the surface of the body with 'coloured bracelets, earrings and tattoos' (1983, p. 67).

Similar evidence of pre-war style-based youth cultures is provided by Fowler in a study of teenage consumption patterns in British cities between 1919 and 1939. According to Fowler, 'the leisure habits and spending patterns of teenage wage-earners in the interwar period were similar to those of postwar teenagers' (1992, p. 134). Fowler then goes on to cite music, cinema and teen magazines as among the most popular youth pastimes during the inter-war period. Fowler also notes how dance halls at this time 'served as meeting places for gangs of male youths', one example of which were the Napoo, a Manchester-based gang who wore 'a highly distinctive uniform borrowed from American gangster films [which consisted of] a navy blue suit, a trilby and a pink neckerchief' (ibid., p. 144). Finally, Willet's study of swing music in wartime Europe provides an early example of popular music and its attendant stylistic innovations being used in a politicised and potentially subversive fashion. Although increasingly popular throughout Europe in the late 1930s, American hot swing music was heavily censored by the German Third Reich during the war years. From the point of view of the young, however, such action was unacceptable and, in Germany especially, swing music began 'to symbolise a resistance to authority and non-cooperation with the Third Reich' (1989, p. 157). As Willet explains: 'The *Swing Jugend* (Swing Kids), as followers of swing were known, consciously separated themselves from Nazism and its sentimental, petit-bourgeois culture, greeting each other with "*Swing-Heil!*" and addressing one another as "old-hot-boy"' (ibid., p. 161).

The sociological study of youth

The attempt to study youth from a sociological perspective also predates the post-Second World War period. The foundations of the modern sociology of youth culture were laid during the 1920s and 30s by a group of US sociologists based at the University of Chicago. The 'Chicago School', as this group came to be known, wanted to construct a *sociological* model of juvenile delinquency as an alternative to the individualist criminological accounts that held sway at this time. Criminologists such as Lombroso had suggested the existence of a criminal 'personality', arguing in turn that 'crime [is] an inherited and atavistic propensity towards behaviour which humanity as a species has outgrown' (Sapsford: 1981, p. 310). The Chicago School rejected this explanation of crime, arguing instead that juvenile delinquency, as with other forms of criminal behaviour, when studied in its cultural context could be shown to be a normal response 'determined by cultural norms, and not a symptom of psychological deficiency' (Frith: 1984, p. 40).

One of the most detailed studies to emerge from the Chicago School is Whyte's *Street Corner Society* (1943). The study focuses on an Italian-American slum, which Whyte refers to as 'Cornerville'. In keeping with the other Chicago theorists, Whyte uses *ethnography*, the practice of going out into the 'field' to observe social actors in their day-to-day settings (see Hobbs and May: 1993), as a basis for his research in Cornerville. Whyte believed that the ethnographic method was the key to providing an alternative to the dominant view of the slum as a social problem, a view upheld and propagated by social policy studies and social work reports at this time, and to see it instead as a world within a world where particular rules apply and must be observed if one is to survive. Consequently, Whyte was less concerned with labels such as 'criminal' or 'delinquent' as with illustrating how the social structure of Cornerville produced particular forms of behaviour. In relating this to the behaviour of youth gangs in Cornerville, Whyte argued that such gangs (the 'little guys') were simply a normal part of growing up in the district. By joining gangs and engaging in acts of violence and theft, the youth of Cornerville prepared themselves for adult life by learning the social codes and norms that they would need in order to move up the social structure and become racketeers, whose activities involved such things as dog racing, organised gambling and the trafficking of liquor – this being during the time of the US prohibition.

Subsequent Chicago studies continued to focus upon deviance as a *normal* response when looked at from the point of view of the 'deviant' actors themselves. At the same time, however, emphasis began to shift away from the 'local' as a frame of reference for the acquired deviant sensibilities of youth and towards a new approach which suggested that youth itself was capable of generating a series of norms and values, that youth was, in effect, a 'culture' or *subculture* in its own right. Subcultural explanations of youth deviance became increasingly popular in the US during the years immediately following the Second World War when it was discovered that post-war affluence was not, as expected, resulting in a decreasing crime rate and a higher level of social integration. On the contrary, in addition to rising rates of economically motivated crime, there was also a significant increase in deviant forms of crime such as 'gang-based youth violence [and] new types of drug use' (Chaney: 1994, p. 37).

A number of different models were offered by Chicago theorists to explain how deviant subcultures function to normalise particular forms of deviant behaviour. Becker argued that deviant behaviour is the product of social *labelling*; that 'social groups create deviance by making the rules whose infraction constitutes deviance and by applying those rules to particular persons and labelling them as outsiders' (1963, p. 9). Delinquent subcultures, according to Becker, become locked into a process of deviance amplification in which the initial negative responses of dominant norm-producing institutions, such as the police and the mass media, result in such subcultures committing further acts of deviance which, in turn, reinforces the stigmatisation conferred upon them by the dominant society. Becker's approach was subsequently utilised by Stanley Cohen in his now famous study of the British media's representation of clashes between mods and rockers at seaside towns on the southeast coast of England during 1964. According to Cohen, the media's representation of the mods and rockers as 'folk devils' served to create a 'moral panic', sensitising sections of the general public to the alleged threat of violence and unrest, which the mods and rockers were deemed to pose, while simultaneously alerting agents of social control to the need for vigilance and 'special' measures of law enforcement (1972, pp. 77, 91–2). Becker's concept of labelling was also central to Hall and Critcher *et al.*'s (1978) study *Policing the Crisis* which illustrated how 'mugging', a US term hijacked by the British press to describe a spate of economically motivated street attacks in British cities during the early 1970s, was associated by the media almost exclusively with young Afro-Caribbean males with the effect that they *became* the mugging problem in the public imagination.

Several other 'subcultural' theories of deviance posited by members of the Chicago School have also been utilised in more contemporary sociological work on youth, notably Merton's (1957) model of means and goals. Merton suggested that deviance becomes a solution for those groups who lack the socially prescribed 'means' to acquire material and cultural rewards but who, nevertheless, desire such rewards. According to Merton then, delinquent subcultures are deviant in their means but conformist in terms of their desired goals. An interesting adaptation of Merton's means–goals thesis is employed by Cashmore, who argues that the 'disjuncture between the goals of consumption and the channels through which such goals can be achieved' was a contributing factor in the onset of the British inner-city riots of 1980 and 1981 in which youths battled with police and looted shops, seizing consumer items such as fashion clothes, records and stereo equipment (1984, pp. 81–6, 90). According to Cashmore, during the economic recession of the early 1980s, youth, whose striving for a means of expression was previously realised via the consumer items appropriated from the youth market, were forced to resort to deviant means of acquiring such items.

Two other Chicago theorists, Matza and Sykes (1961), contested the notion that subcultures will in every case resort to some form of delinquent activity. They argued instead that it is also possible to speak in terms of *legitimate* subcultures whose codes of *subterranean* values, while deviant in as much as they offer non-conformist routes to pleasure and excitement, do not challenge the socio-economic order of the dominant society as such. This latter interpretation of subcultures is central to the approach utilised by Willis in his study *Learning to Labour*. Willis follows the progress of a group of male working-class teenagers, the 'Lads', during their final two years of education in a British comprehensive school. During this time, the 'Lads' participate in what Willis terms a *counter-school culture*, employing a strategy of subterranean values which reject the educational demands of school system in favour of 'having a laugh' (1977, p. 29). According to Willis, however, although within the school environment such behaviour is regarded as deviant, it simultaneously mediates to the 'Lads' those working-class cultural values that prepare them 'for the manual giving of their labour power' (ibid., p. 3). Thus, in a wider social sense, the subterranean values of the *counter-school culture* help to sustain the system of class relations underpinning the capitalist mode of production.

Subcultures as resistance

As early as the 1920s then, 'subculture' was a recognised analytical and discursive trope in youth research. It was, however, through the work of the British, Birmingham-based Centre for Contemporary Cultural Studies (CCCS) that the term subculture became most readily associated with the sociological study of youth. As in the US, British studies of youth were originally concerned with studying the connections between collective sensibilities of youth gangs and groups and the localities from which such gangs and groups emerged. Thus, for example, in a study of juvenile delinquency in Liverpool, Mays (1954) echoed Whyte's synopsis of the Cornerville gangs in suggesting that such delinquency was part of a local *tradition* via which young males received and put into practice deviant norms which were a part of everyday life in many underprivileged neighbourhoods of Liverpool. Twenty years later, Howard Parker (1974) advanced this argument claiming that the emphasis placed upon leisure by working-class youth in Liverpool was informed by a traditional system of values transmitted by the parent culture. Central to this, suggested Parker, was an acquired awareness of the limited opportunities offered by the local job market. Similarly, Patrick's (1973) study of Glasgow gangs revealed the longstanding tradition of gang culture in certain parts of the city underpinned by an historical cycle of socio-economic hardship.

With the publication of the CCCS research, however, British studies of youth culture began to change in two significant ways. First, emphasis moved away from the study of youth gangs and towards style-based youth cultures, such as teddy boys, mods, rockers and skinheads, which, from the 1950s onwards, rapidly became an integral feature of everyday British social life. Second, in keeping with the central hypothesis of the CCCS, the local focus of earlier youth studies was abandoned in favour of a subcultural model of explanation. Using the original Chicago premise that subcultures provide the key to an understanding of deviance as normal behaviour in the face of particular social circumstances, the CCCS reworked this idea as a way of accounting for the style-centred youth cultures of post-war Britain. According to the CCCS, the deviant behaviour of such youth cultures or 'subcultures' had to be understood as the collective reaction of youth themselves, or rather working-class youth, the point of origin for style-based youth cultures, to structural changes taking place in British post-war society.

The significance of the CCCS approach lies in its application of a Marxist perspective to the study of youth subcultures. Influenced by the 'new criminology' of the late 1960s, which argued that crime could be interpreted as a direct result of class conflict (see Taylor *et al*.: 1973), the CCCS posited that a version of this interpretation could also be applied to youth subcultures. Hall and Jefferson's *Resistance Through Rituals* (1976), the centrepiece of the CCCS's work on youth culture, combines this explanatory model with a sophisticated critique of the 'classless society' thesis. According to some observers, such as Zweig (1961), post-war economic prosperity and the concomitant consumer boom acted to erode traditional class distinctions as working-class consumers effectively bought into the lifestyle of the middle classes. Post-war youth style was also regarded as an aspect of this process. According to the CCCS, however, far from signifying post-war working-class youth's assimilation into a unified teenage consumer culture, the emergent style-based subcultures, while indeed indicative of newly acquired spending habits, also symbolised a series of responses on the part of working-class youth to the socio-economic conditions of their class position.

The notion of subcultures as a collective symbolic response to the conditions of class was adopted from an earlier CCCS working paper, Phil Cohen's 'Subcultural Conflict and Working Class Community'. According to Cohen, the nature and function of youth subcultures was to be understood in terms of their facilitating a collective response to the break-up of traditional working-class communities as a result of urban redevelopment during the 1950s and the relocation of families to 'new towns' and modern housing estates. Subcultures, suggests Cohen, were an attempt on the part of working-class youth to bridge the gap between life on the new estates and former patterns of traditional working-class community life. Thus he argues:

> It seems to me that the latent function of subculture is this – to express and resolve, albeit 'magically', the contradictions which remain hidden and

> unresolved in the parent culture... [each subculture attempts] to retrieve
> some of the socially cohesive elements destroyed in their parent culture and
> to combine these with other class fractions symbolising one or other of the
> options confronting it (1972, p. 23).

Although Cohen's concept of 'magical recovery' is developed in *Resistance Through Rituals,* it is posited as purely one of a number of themes around which subcultural responses are constructed. Subcultures are seen to form part of an ongoing working-class struggle against the socio-economic circumstances of their existence. This approach is heavily indebted to Gramsci's concept of ideological hegemony which suggests that 'history is a process of conflicts and compromises where one fundamental class will emerge as both dominant and directive not only in economic but also in moral and intellectual terms' (Bennett and Martin *et al.*: 1981, p. 199). However, while the state, under the direction of the dominant class, functions 'as the unifier and arbitrator of diverse interests and conflicts' it is unable to ever resolve the struggles occurring within the social structure in absolute terms (ibid.). Following Gramsci's argument, the CCCS suggest that: 'The subordinate class brings to this "Theatre of Struggle" a repertoire of strategies and responses – ways of coping as well as of resisting' (Clarke and Hall *et al.*: 1976, p. 44).

Subcultural resistance then is conceptualised in a number of different ways in *Resistance Through Rituals.* Clarke's study of skinhead culture echoes Phil Cohen's view in arguing that the skinhead style represents 'an attempt to re-create through the "mob" the traditional working-class community as a substitution for the real decline of the latter' (1976, p. 99). A recent study of skinhead culture in Australia by Moore (1994) develops Clarke's argument through its suggestion that the 'magical recovery' of community takes on a new level of meaning for Australian skinheads, many of whom are first generation Australians with English parents. According to Moore, for many such skinheads England becomes a symbolic homeland and a place that must be periodically returned to.

Jefferson, in a further study from *Resistance Through Rituals,* argues that the style of the teddy boy directly reflects his '"all-dressed-up-and-nowhere-to-go" experience of Saturday evening' (1976, p. 48). The relative affluence of the teddy boys allowed them to 'buy into' an upper-class image – the Edwardian suit revived by a group of Saville Row tailors in 1950 and originally intended for an upper-class market. Jefferson argues, that the teddy boys' 'dress represented a symbolic way of expressing and negotiating with their symbolic reality; of giving cultural meaning to their social plight' (ibid., p. 86). Similarly, Hebdige claims that the mod style was a reaction to the mundane predictability of the working week and that the mod attempted to compensate for this 'by exercising complete domination over his private estate – his appearance and choice of leisure pursuits' (1976a, p. 91).

In accounting for the cultural work performed by style in facilitating such forms of subcultural resistance, two main approaches are put forward by CCCS theorists. According to one school of thought, style-centred resistance depends upon the goodness of fit or 'homology' between the object of consumption – for example a particular type of jacket or pair of shoes – and the range of values or concerns that it is intended to represent. Willis (1972, 1978) suggests that homology encapsulates 'the continuous play between the group and a particular item which produces specific styles, meanings, contents and forms of consciousness' (1978, p. 191). Using the example of biker culture, Willis identifies a homological relationship between the motorbike and the motorbike gang. Primarily, argues Willis, the physical features of the motorbike correspond with certain features of the group themselves: 'The solidity, responsiveness, inevitableness [sic], the *strength* of the motor-bike matched the concrete, secure nature of the bikeboys' world' (ibid., p. 53).

Hebdige, however, rejects the concept of homology, arguing that the latter's central assumption 'of a transparent relation between sign and referent, signification and reality' is oversimplistic (1979, p. 118). According to Hebdige, the problems associated with homology became increasingly apparent with the advent of punk whose 'primary value and appeal... derived precisely from its lack of meaning: from its potential for deceit' (ibid., p. 117). Consequently, Hebdige abandons homology in favour of *polysemy*. Originally developed by the *Tel Quel* group, polysemy relates to the way in which an object or text is seen to generate not one but a range of meanings.[1] Although the *Tel Quel* group applied this mode of interpretation primarily to literature and film, Hebdige argues that the group's 'polemical insistence that art represents the triumph of process over fixity, disruption over unity, "collision" over "linkage"' is mirrored in punk's 'spectacular transforma-tions... of commodities, values [and] common-sense attitudes' on the site of the body (ibid., pp. 119, 116).

Criticisms of subcultural theory

The work of the CCCS offered the first sustained attempt by British sociologists to account for the style-based youth cultures of the post-war period. However, the Centre has not been without its critics, one of the most salient points coming from a writer who was herself formerly associated with the CCCS, Angela McRobbie. McRobbie's criticism of the CCCS relates to the Centre's lack of concern with the relationship of girls to youth subcultures. In 'Girls and Subcultures', the only study in *Resistance Through Rituals* to consider the place of girls in relation to subcultures, McRobbie and co-writer Garber, while conceding the relative absence of girls in subcultural groupings, argue that such absence can be attributed to the stricter parental control and regulation of girls' leisure time. It is further argued that, because of this, 'girls find alternative strategies to that of the boys' sub-cultures' and that a "Teeny Bopper" culture is constructed around the territory available to girls, the home and the bedroom' (1976, p. 219). Just as male subcultures are 'serviced' by consumerism, it is argued, a similar range of consumer goods is made readily available to young female teeny boppers. Therein, however, lies the essential difference between subcultures and teeny bopper culture as, according to McRobbie and Garber: 'The small, structured and highly manufactured space that is available for ten to fifteen year old girls to create a personal and autonomous area seems to be offered only on the understanding that these strategies also symbolise a future general subordination – as well as a present one' (ibid., p. 221).

McRobbie attributes the failure of subcultural theory to acknowledge both this home-centred teeny bopper culture and its long-term implications for girls to the selective bias of the researchers themselves. Thus, she argues:

> while the sociologies of deviance and youth were blooming in the early seventies the sociology of the family was everybody's least favourite option... few writers seemed interested in what happened when a mod went home after a week-end on speed. Only what happened out there on the streets mattered (1980, pp. 68–9).

In later work dealing with fashion and dance, areas that are also strikingly underrepresented in the sociology of youth culture, McRobbie (1984, 1994) provides further illustrations of how female strategies of style-centred resistance have been largely overlooked. Indeed, according to McRobbie, within the related spheres of fashion and dance the ability of girls and young women to use style as a form of resistance has often been much more pronounced than male expressions of style-based resistance. Using the example of US beat culture during the 1950s, McRobbie points to the way in which female beats' appropriation of second-hand middle-class fashions from the 1930s and 40s 'issued a strong sexual challenge to the spick and span gingham-clad domesticity of the moment' (1994, p. 143). Similarly, McRobbie notes how the function of dance 'as a purveyor of fantasy [addresses] areas of absolute privacy and personal intimacy, especially important for girls and women' (1984, p. 134). Taking this argument further and referring to the sexual politics of dance, McRobbie argues that the act of dancing 'carries enormously pleasurable qualities for girls and women which frequently seem to suggest a displaced, shared and nebulous eroticism rather than a straightforwardly romantic, heavily heterosexual "goal-oriented drive"' (ibid.). Significantly, the advent of dance music forms such as house and techno from the late 1980s onwards has provoked a series of changes in attitudes towards dance among both sexes. I will discuss the new significance of dance in the context of contemporary urban dance music cultures during Chapter 4.

A further criticism of the CCCS has been its treatment and interpretation of style which, it is argued, takes no account of the meanings and intentions of young people themselves. Harris, for example, argues that the 'complex' and 'dialectical' features of homology portrayed in Willis's (1978) account ensure that members of a particular subculture remain 'subjectively [un]aware of [the] structural meanings, embedded in the history of [particular stylistic commodities] in previous cycles of provision, transformation and resistance' (1992, p. 90). Stanley Cohen (1987) identifies a similar range of problems with Hebdige's (1979) use of polysemy as a means of interpreting the subcultural significance of style. According to Cohen, polysemy 'may work for art, but not equally well for life. The danger is of getting lost in the forest of symbols' (1987, p. xvi). Cohen then goes on to discuss Hebdige's polysemic reading of the swastika's significance for punk. Thus, argues Cohen, according to Hebdige:

> Displaying a swastika shows how symbols are stripped from their natural context, exploited for empty effect, displayed through mockery, distancing, irony, parody, inversion... But how are we to know this? We are never told much about the 'thing': when, how, where, by whom or in what context it is worn. We do not know what, if any, difference exists between indigenous and sociological explanations (ibid., p. xvii).

Criticism has also been directed at the class-centred nature of the CCCS's explanation of subcultures and subcultural style. Certainly, the CCCS's contention that working-class youth were at the centre of the new style-orientated post-war youth culture is, in itself, unproblematic. During the post-war period working-class youth were the social group with the largest amounts of disposable income and thus the first 'specifically targeted and differentiated consumers' (Bocock: 1993, p. 22). By contrast, middle-class teenagers were at this time still 'constrained in their spending' (Benson: 1994, p. 165). More questionable, however, is the attempt by CCCS theorists to apply the same argument to later youth cultures which were clearly not instigated purely by working-class youth (Benson: 1994, p. 165). Thus as Clarke argues, in Hebdige's (1979) analysis of punk, there is a distinct air of contradiction between its 'metropolitan centeredness [sic]' and the emphasis on 'working class creativity' (1981, p. 86). Clarke then goes on to suggest that 'most of the punk creations which are discussed [by Hebdige] were developed among the art-school avant-garde, rather than emanating "from the dance halls and housing estates"' (ibid).

An equally important, if less well-documented, criticism of the CCCS work is its failure to consider local variations in youth's responses to music and style. Waters, for example, argues that 'geographical specificity is a factor in subcultural studies that cannot be overlooked [and consequently] works need to tone down their stress on the universality of subcultures, and make a concerted effort to focus on... regional subcultures' (1981, p. 32). Indeed, the preoccupation of several CCCS theorists with the notion of 'authentic' subcultures further problematises the Centre's apparent lack of concern with the existence of local variations in the musicalised and stylised sensibilities of youth. This is perhaps most notable in the work of Hebdige where it is argued that subcultures are objects of 'authentic' expression only as long as they remain undiscovered by the market. For Hebdige, at the point when a subcultural style becomes incorporated into the market it is simultaneously stripped of its cultural message and becomes simply another meaningless object of mass consumption (1979, p. 96). To begin with, such a contention involves a fabricated distinction between stylistic innovation and the youth market, the two being regarded by Hebdige as mutually exclusive despite his own observation that, in punk's case, 'the media's sighting of punk style virtually coincided with the discovery or invention of punk deviance' (ibid., p. 93). Moreover, and perhaps more importantly, given that certain styles do originate at 'street level', Hebdige's contention that the market's incorporation of a style renders it culturally meaningless automatically closes off any consideration of the regional variations and local levels of significance that such styles acquire once they become more widely available as commercial products. The four case studies presented in Part II of this book each provide examples of the way in which commercially available musics and attendant visual styles have been inscribed with locally articulated 'authentic' meanings.

Other problems have also been associated with the attempt to identify 'authentic' subcultural responses involving musical and stylistic resources. Murdock and McCron argue that one of the key problems with subcultural theory is that it starts 'by taking those groups who are already card-carrying members of a subculture... and [works] backwards to uncover their class location' (1976, p. 25). If such an analytical process were to be reversed, they argue, starting with the class base rather than the cultural response, then the fact of a common class base eliciting a range of differentiated cultural responses would be obviated. In a similar way, Gary Clarke has argued that 'elements of youth culture (music, dancing, clothes etc.)' are enjoyed and engaged in by the vast majority of youth and not merely by 'the fully paid up members of subcultures' (1981, p. 83). This has led a number of theorists to question the validity of the term 'subculture' itself. Thus, according to Fine and Kleinman the attempt to reify a construct such as subculture 'as a corpus of knowledge may be heuristically valuable, until one begins to give this corpus physical properties' (1979, p. 6). A similar argument is put forward by Redhead, who suggests that '"Authentic" subcultures were produced by subcultural theories, not the other way around' (1990, p. 25). Thornton goes as far as to suggest that subcultures, rather than originating purely at the level of the social, are largely constructed through the representational power of the media. Thus, she argues:

> When [the CCCS] come to define 'subculture', they position the media and its associated processes outside, in opposition to and after the fact of subculture. In doing so, they omit precisely that which clearly delineates a 'subculture', for labelling is crucial to the insiders' and outsiders' views of themselves (1995, p. 119).

According to Thornton then, 'authentic' subcultures are in essence media constructions, members of such subcultures acquiring a sense of themselves and their relation to the rest of society from the way they are represented in the media. Thus, argues Thornton, '"subcultures" do not germinate from a seed and grow by force of their own energy into mysterious movements only to be belatedly digested by the media. Rather, [the] media... are... effective from the start' (ibid., p. 117).

Lifestyles

In their attempt to find an alternative to subcultural theory, a number of youth theorists have begun to use *lifestyle* as a theoretical model via which to examine and interpret the cultural sensibilities of contemporary youth. The concept of lifestyle first appeared in the work of Weber (1919/1978), who argued against Marx's theory of economic determinism by suggesting that status was also a central determinant of the social strata. According to Weber, status manifested itself most readily through the 'lifestyles' of different social groups. Simmel (1903/1971) and Veblen (1912/1953) refined the concept of lifestyle in their work on early patterns of consumerism at the turn of the century. Each of these theorists suggested that lifestyles were actively constructed by particular social groups whose appropriation of particular commodities enabled such groups to mark themselves off from the wider society by establishing distinctive forms of collective identity (Chaney: 1996, p. 51). Lifestyle subsequently became more readily associated with market research. According to Reimer, the concept of lifestyle was of particular use to market researchers as it 'could be used as a more sophisticated instrument than traditional socio-economic background factors to identify segments of buyers' (1995, p. 122). In recent years, however, lifestyle has again become a central theoretical model in social science research on the nature of consumption and its role in the formation of identity.

One of the first contemporary youth culture studies to incorporate lifestyle theory was Jenkins's *Lads, Citizens and Ordinary Kids*. In this study, Jenkins is critical of the fact that subcultural theory tends not only to overlook the essentially interconnected nature of so-called 'subcultures' but also regards them as ideologically separate from the wider society. Thus, he argues, 'the concept of subculture tends to exclude from consideration the large area of commonality between subcultures, however defined, and implies a determinate and often deviant relationship to a national dominant culture' (1983, p. 41). According to Jenkins the term *subculture* imposes a hermeneutic sphere around a series of relations and interactions which cannot, in reality, be so neatly closed off and categorised as belonging to a distinctive and apparently self-perpetuating form of cultural life. The concept of lifestyle, suggests Jenkins, is more suited than 'subculture' as an analyt-

ical framework for the study of youth as it allows for the formation of
distinct social practices while at the same time acknowledging the wider
set of common cultural practices within which such alternative collective strategies are played out.

Two recent Swedish youth studies by Johansson and Miegel (1992)
and Reimer (1995) have also used the concept of lifestyle. In each of
these studies the primary task has been to employ lifestyle as a way of
rethinking the relationship between social class and patterns of taste in
forms of popular entertainment such as music, style and film.
According to Reimer, while certain lifestyle orientations among Swedish
youth are indeed influenced by issues of 'class, gender, education,
income and civil status' none of these appear to be as significant as the
orientation towards entertainment which 'exists almost independently
of socio-economic background' (1995, p. 135). Johansson and Miegel
advance this argument by suggesting that taste patterns in youth
entertainment cannot be reduced to singular class-based or subcultural
explanations but 'must be related to a wider spectrum of individually
held values, attitudes and actions' (1992, p. 103).

Such an interpretation of youth leisure-forms as a more fluid and
reflexive aspect of contemporary social life is also central to Chambers's
study *Urban Rhythms* which effectively re-maps the history of British
post-war youth. Although Chambers does not refer directly to the
concept of lifestyle, his approach fits very comfortably with the central
assumptions of this approach. Moving away from the class-based
interpretations of the CCCS, Chambers focuses upon the importance
of music and style as a form of instantly won creativity for young
people; as a means of temporarily escaping, rather than reinforcing,
one's class position. According to Chambers, the appeal of
consumerism lay in the power that it gave the young to construct
alternative lifestyles which could be lived out in and around the
traditional class-based social institutions such as the family, the school
and the workplace. Thus argues Chambers: 'In contrast to the
anonymous drudgery of the working week, selected consumer objects
provide the possibility of moving beyond the colourless walls of routine
into the bright environs of an imaginary state' (1985, p. 17). A similar
view is expressed in a more recent study by Willis in which he abandons
the structuralist assumptions that informed his earlier work and focuses
instead on the emancipatory effects of consumption for young people.
Willis introduces the term 'grounded aesthetics' as a means of
illustrating the various ways in which young people appropriate,
redefine and particularise the '"raw materials" of cultural life, of

communications and expressions' (1990, pp. 21, 20). Grounded aesthetics, writes Willis, 'are the specifically creative and dynamic moments of the whole process of cultural life' (ibid., p. 22).

Lifestyle theory also places new emphasis on the role of the local as a means of understanding how collective cultural meanings are inscribed in commodities such as music and fashion. The stories that such cultural commodities tell, both to and about those who consume them, are in part determined by the industries that produce such commodities but are in each instance completed by consumers themselves. Youth culture provides a particularly dynamic example of such late modern lifestyles. Young people take the cultural resources provided by the popular culture industries and use the prescribed meanings attached to such resources as templates around which to construct their own forms of meaning and authenticity. Although the resulting variations in musical significance obviously retain a sense of connectedness – for example, hip hop enthusiasts possess essentially the same sensibilities of commercially communicated style, musical taste and 'street-talk' irrespective of their location on the globe – at the same time they become infused with distinctive knowledges and sensibilities which originate from the particular region in which they are lived out.

Such a process is an inevitable aspect of the use of mass cultural commodities in the formulation of what Chaney refers to as lifestyle 'sites and strategies' (1996, p. 91). According to Chaney, lifestyle *sites* refer to the 'physical metaphors for the spaces that actors can appropriate and control', while *strategies* denote the 'characteristic modes of social engagement, or narratives of identity, in which the actors concerned can embed the metaphors at hand' (ibid., p. 92). Through their use as symbolic markers in the lifestyle sites and strategies of individuals, mass cultural products, the primary cultural resources of contemporary social life, assume a form of dual significance. Thus, on the one hand, they are instantly recognisable as global commodities, which connect with common stylistic and aesthetic preferences of individuals throughout the world, while on the other hand, their precise meanings become bound up with the local scenarios within which they are appropriated and the local circumstances which they are used to negotiate. This aspect of contemporary consumer culture and its particular bearing on the musical and stylistic lifestyle sensibilities of youth will be explored in depth during Part II of this book.

Youth and ethnic identity

The move away from subcultural theory as a focus for youth culture research has also given rise to new directions in the study of the relationship between youth and ethnic identity. During the 1970s, references to the youth of ethnic minorities were, for the most part, incorporated into accounts of white appropriations of the latter's stylistic innovations. Hebdige (1976b), for example, considers 1960s ska music and the rude boy image of Afro-Caribbean youth living in Britain mainly in the context of their influence upon the white mod and skinhead cultures which modelled themselves closely on the rude boy style. Similarly, Chambers argues that the common social experience of black ethnic minority groups and white working-class youth – a widely held belief in sociological studies of youth during the early part of the 1970s – enabled the easy translation of black musical and stylistic resources into white terms resulting, for example, in 'Skinheads rewriting "black pride" lyrics as "white pride" [lyrics]' (1976, p. 165).

Later work on youth and ethnic identity has focused more closely on the experiences of ethnic youth themselves and the strategies that such young people devise for negotiating the various forms of racism, racial exclusion and indifference that they encounter in their daily lives. In a study of South Asian youth in Britain, Kaur and Kalra use the term 'Br-Asian' as a way of attempting to culturally situate young South Asians in Britain who, it is argued, occupy a new cultural territory which has been fashioned out of necessity by South Asian youth who no longer feel they must strictly adhere to the traditional norms and values of their parent culture but are also prevented from fully integrating into British society because of the racist stereotypes that are imposed upon them. A significant property of the Br-Asian youth culture is the way in which the cultural and religious divisions between the different parent cultures of young Asians in Britain are crossed. Thus, according to Kaur and Kalra:

> Br-Asian is intended of the centre-margin relationship and to destabilise fixed notions of Asian identities, stressing their contingency on historical and spatial moments. As a hyphenated form of identification, 'Br-Asian' contains possibilities for splintering as it does for other alliances. The question of regional affiliation and the degree of religious and cast consciousness act as breakable joints in this categorization; common subjection to racist oppression and criticisms of mainstream society serve as platforms to align with other marginalised groups (1996, p. 221).

In a similar way, David Parker, in one of the very few studies to have focused on the experiences of Chinese youth in Britain, illustrates how white Britain's stereotypical associations of Chinese minorities with the 'take-away' trade combined with the portrayal of Chinese people in films such as *The World of Suzy Wong* has, in turn, affected the way in which 'non-Chinese people interact with the British Chinese population' (1998, p. 69). According to Parker, however, in the same way that new South Asian cultural forms, particularly music and cinema, are beginning to facilitate new ways of being 'South Asian' in Britain, cultural formations based on film, style and music from the Far East are giving rise to new forms of British-Chinese identity.

This notion of ethnic identity as something that embraces aspects of the popular and fuses them together with an imagined traditional culture and the vernacular knowledges of the local urban/regional settings in which ethnic minority groups are situated now forms a major part of many studies into the nature and significance of ethnic identity in late modern society. Hebdige (1979) began to explore this process in his work on the significance of the Rastafarian style for young Afro-Caribbeans living in Britain during the mid-1970s. In Jamaica, Rastafarianism's place of origin, the style symbolises a belief, based upon African slaves' readings of the bible, that Haille Selassie's accession to the throne of Ethiopia in 1930 represented the fulfilment of the Biblical prophecies relating to the downfall of 'Babylon' and the deliverance of the black races back to Africa (Lewis: 1993). In the early 1970s, Rastafarianism became synonymous with reggae music, reggae artists such as Bob Marley using their music to voice Rastafarian beliefs. According to Hebdige, Afro-Caribbean youth in Britain borrowed the Rastafarian style of Marley and other reggae artists to produce 'a refracted form of the Rastafarian aesthetic... inflected to suit the needs of second-generation immigrants' (1979, p. 43). Thus, Rastafarianism in Britain became a localised form of resistance to the various forms of racism and racial exclusion experienced by Afro-Carribean youth.

Jones develops this argument by reframing the issue of locality to reflect the more micro-social politics of inner-city districts and neighbourhoods, using this analytical framework to consider anew white appropriations of black style. Focusing on Birmingham, a multiracial city with a high percentage of Afro-Caribbean residents, Jones notes how in certain districts 'the cultural lives of both black and white communities have become harmonised around the shared spaces and cross-cutting loyalties of street, pub and neighbourhood' (1988, p. 128). According to Jones, the result of this, particularly among the young, is that racial distinctions become much less important, such distinctions being replaced by a shared feeling of community between black and white residents. Jones then goes on to note how, in such local settings, affiliation between black and white youth will often be emphasised through white youth adopting the style of their black peers. Thus, black style, in addition to its function as a means via which Afro-Caribbean youth can mark themselves out stylistically also acquires a localised meaning as a symbol of community into which local white youth are included.

A useful device for attempting to come to terms with the apparent contradictions inherent in this dual function of black style is Back's concept of *community discourse*. According to Back, community discourse allows for the construction of a given community and those living within it in specifically 'local' terms. Thus the existence of inter-racial tolerance in a particular area or community might be explained in terms of the fact that people have lived together there for a long time, know each other well and get on with each other. Back illustrates this in relation to an area of London, which he refers to as Southgate, where community discourse 'acts as a resource that banishes "racial things" from everyday experience' (1996a, p. 112). At the same time, however, such tolerance is not extended to those groups living outside the area, the types of discourse being used in relation to the latter relying much more on media representations and stereotypes.

Youth culture in an international context

A final aspect of the move away from subcultural theory as a theoretical model for the study of youth culture has been the growth of interest in examples of youth cultural activity outside the Anglo-American world. The limitations of an exclusively Anglo-American focus for youth culture studies were first pointed out by Brake in a comparative study of youth culture in the UK, the US and Canada. Thus, in his discussion of youth culture in Canada, Brake suggests that:

> If there is a tradition of resistance in Canadian youth culture, it is at an individualistic rather than a collective level. The vast size of the country acts against any distinct yet common themes, as in the folk devil traditions of Britain, or the specific ethnically developed subcultures in America... Further, at a more banal level, the long and severe winter which covers most of Canada localises youth cultures to the cities, and even there public spaces tend to be shopping malls, which do little to generate collective gatherings and are easy to control (1985, p. 145).

Brake's study highlights the importance of considering the way in which local factors both limit and shape the types of cultural resource available to youth and the sensibilities inscribed within such resources. A further dimension of this localising process is demonstrated in Pilkington's study of youth culture in Moscow. This study offers an effective illustration of how western musical and stylistic resources have been reworked in a such a way that the meanings which they assume are inextricably bound up with the local socio-economic context. Pilkington refers to the *stilagi*, a local Moscow youth cultural group, which first emerged in the 1950s, appropriating western rock 'n' roll music and its attendant visual style. From the point of view of the wider Soviet society, the *stilagi*'s endorsement of western popular culture was considered 'ideologically reprehensible' (1994, p. 226). Indeed, according to Pilkington, 'the term *stilagi* was [itself] invented by [the media] in order to indicate the negative traits of these young people' (ibid.). From the point of view of the *stilagi* themselves, however, their acquired status as the spectre of westernisation, together with the fear and disgust which this appeared to generate among the wider society, simply enhanced the group's desired image as outsiders.

A somewhat different merging of western youth styles with the socio-political characteristics of the Eastern bloc is noted by Smith in her study of youth culture in the former East Germany. Thus, as Smith explains, during 'the communist period youth cultures always stood in tension between western inspiration, primarily through music and style, and the lived experiences of the period for young people' (1998, p. 290). Smith then goes on to explore some of the experiences of East German youth cultural groups, who modelled themselves on western styles and images, and the responses of such groups to the socio-political sensibilities that held sway in the East Germany at this time. Punks, she states, were seen to symbolise the malaise of youth and were stigmatised because of their allegedly antisocial image and appearance. East German skinheads, on the other hand, despite the neo-Fascist ideology shared by many of them, earned a more respectable reputation due to their smarter appearance and involvement in party activities, for example the Society for Sport and Technology. As Smith points out: 'It was therefore precisely the sites which the state designated as showing commitment to the communist order... which right wing young people used to subvert the meaning of the state' (ibid., p. 292).

Another significant insight into the localisation of popular cultural resources from the west is provided in Liechty's study of youth culture in Kathmandu, Nepal. This study is particularly interesting as, according to Liechty, Nepali youth culture is 'a cultural space that is still being created and genuinely contested between young people, parents and commercial interests' (1995, p. 170). Moreover, as Liechty points out, in addition to being based around 'the consumption of a host of transnational "pop" images', the creation of modern youth identities in Kathmandu is also being achieved via recourse to 'a variety of local goods and services' (ibid., pp. 170, 172). Thus, the developing youth culture of Kathmandu occupies a tenuous space between the mediated cultural territories of western popular culture and the realities of Nepal life or, as Liechty puts it, 'between village and external, modern metropole' (ibid., p. 191). Youth in Kathmandu must somehow learn to reconcile western popular culture's 'images of a modern future with the realities' that they face in Nepal (ibid.). At the same time, however, the new cultural territories that Nepali youth are discovering are serving as a source of power in that youth itself is actively involved in creating a new cultural space and a new identity.

Liechty's study effectively illustrates the dynamic interplay between local and global forces in the construction of cultural meanings around popular cultural commodities manufactured and marketed by Anglo-US culture industries. A recent study by Klitgaard Povlsen on the reception of US soaps by youth in Denmark further illustrates the extent to which the meanings that popular cultural commodities are intended to carry in their countries of origin loosen, and in some cases completely disappear, as these commodities come into contact with groups in different parts of the world who have very different cultural backgrounds and day to day experiences. Klitgaard Povlsen uses as an example of this process the novelty value of the popular teen soap *Beverly Hills 90210* among Danish students, many of whom have formed 'Beverly Hills clubs' which involve dressing up like characters in the show and trying to act like them as well as taking part in '[beer] drinking rituals' (1996, p. 8). In effect, the original intention of the US producers of *Beverly Hills 90210* to sell it as family entertainment has been overturned, the show taking on a form of cult status among Danish students who have inscribed *Beverly Hills 90210* with their own localised meanings.

During the course of this chapter I have been concerned to do two things. First, I have considered the development of youth culture research as an aspect of sociological interest and examined some of the key theoretical perspectives that have been applied in the sociological study of youth. Second, I have begun to contextualise the focus of my own research by highlighting the increasing sociological interest in the role of the 'local' as both a space in which youth cultures operate and a cultural frame of reference for the collective knowledges and sensibilities shared by youth cultural groups. Undoubtedly, a major stylistic resource for young people since the immediate post-Second World War period has been popular music. In Chapter 2, I will begin to consider the significance of popular music in the everyday lives of young people by examining some of the key theories that have been developed to account for the cultural impact of popular music upon contemporary youth cultures.

NOTE

1. *Tel Quel* was a French literary magazine, established by novelist Sollers in 1960, which became influential upon the development of structuralism and semiotics during the 1960s.

Chapter 2

Youth Culture and Popular Music

In many different parts of the world popular music is a primary, if not *the* primary, leisure resource for young people. Popular music features in young people's lives in a variety of different ways and in a diverse range of contexts. From nightclubs, live concerts, cinema films and TV commercials to what Japanese music theorist Hosokawa refers to as the 'autonomous and mobile' form of listening facilitated through the invention of the personal stereo, for a great many young people, popular music is an omnipresent aspect of their day to day existence (1984, p. 166). The significance of popular music as an aspect of youth culture can be traced back to the advent of rock 'n' roll in the early 1950s. Prior to rock 'n' roll popular music comprised, to use Middleton's description, 'a relatively narrow stylistic spread, bounded by theatre song on the one side, novelty items deriving from music hall and vaudeville on the other, with Tin Pan Alley song, Hollywood hits and crooners in between' (1990, p. 14). With the arrival of rock 'n' roll, however, not only did the stylistic direction of popular music radically alter but it also acquired a distinctly youth-orientated and oppositional stance. This manifested itself during 1956 with the release of *Rock Around the Clock*, a feature film scripted around live performances by artists of the day such as Bill Haley and the Comets, the Platters and Tony Martinez (Denisoff and Romanowski: 1991). Early screenings of the film in the US and Britain resulted in unruly behaviour in cinemas as young audiences danced in the aisles and ripped out seats (Street: 1992, p. 304). Across Europe *Rock Around the Clock* sparked off reactions that were, in some cases, even more extreme than those witnessed in Britain and the US. In the West German city of Hamburg cars were overturned and shop fronts and street signs vandalised by young people as police used water cannons in an attempt to quell the unrest (Krüger: 1983). In Holland, where *Rock Around the Clock* was banned in several major cities, 'young

people took to the streets to demonstrate for their right to see the film'
(Mutsaers: 1990, p. 307).

If rock 'n' roll music and the sensibilities that it had apparently
inspired were incomprehensible to the parent culture, then the development of subsequent genres, such as psychedelia, punk and, more
recently, acid house, has continued to drive a wedge between the generations and to mark off youth from the parent culture ever more dramatically. The cultural impact of post-war popular music on young people
has also posed a series of questions for popular music theorists. Indeed,
the continuing centrality of popular music in youth culture since the
1950s has underlain much of the theoretical debate about how to
approach the study of popular music and the various stylistic sensibilities to which it has given rise. In this chapter, I want to both examine
and critically assess some of the theoretical approaches that have been
put forward in an attempt to explain popular music's socio-cultural
significance for youth. I will begin by considering the contrasting views
of Adorno and Benjamin, whose work on mass culture during the first
part of the twentieth century continues to inform much of the research
on popular music in the related fields of sociology, cultural and media
studies. This will be followed by a review of some of the most important
contemporary popular music studies with particular reference to the
ways in which these studies have attempted to deal with what continues
to be a highly problematic issue, that is, how to reconcile popular
music's position in the marketplace with its function as a potentially
counter-hegemonic cultural resource. In addition to drawing upon
examples from Britain and the US, I will also consider aspects of music
production and consumption in Holland, Germany, Japan and
Australia. Similarly, the chapter will also look at how popular music has
featured in key moments of social change in countries such as Russia,
China and the former East Germany.

Popular music and the work of Adorno and Benjamin

Much of the current debate concerning the socio-cultural significance
of popular music derives directly from a polemical discussion on the
nature of mass culture between Adorno and Benjamin during the
1920s and early 1930s. In order to properly understand the ideas of
Adorno and Benjamin it is necessary to briefly relate their work back to
the theoretical tradition with which it is most strongly associated, the
mass cultural critique of the Frankfurt School. Founded during the
1920s, the Frankfurt School, whose leading theorists also included

Horkheimer, Marcuse and Habermas, was chiefly concerned to study
the negative social effects that, they argued, were produced as a
consequence of modern society's increasing reliance upon mass cultural
commodities. According to the Frankfurt School, the mass cultural
profile of modern society signalled the fate of individual autonomy, this
being steadily replaced by a 'scientific-technological rationality'
(Bottomore: 1984, p. 41). The implication here is that with the rise of
mass culture the individual is denied any possibility of creative participation in leisure activities and becomes simply a cultural 'dupe'. Thus,
as MacDonald argues, expounding a view clearly inspired by the
Frankfurt School's approach: 'Mass Culture [sic] is imposed from
above. It is fabricated by technicians hired by businessmen; its
audiences are passive consumers, their participation limited to the
choice between buying and not buying' (1953, p. 60).

Each of the Frankfurt School theorists varied in their account of the
way in which mass culture served to suppress individual autonomy.
Adorno was particularly concerned with the fetishising effects of mass
culture upon art. In the case of music, argued Adorno, because it 'had
been invaded by the capitalist ethos, its fetishisation was almost total'
(Jay: 1973, p. 190). At the centre of Adorno's argument lies a distinction between serious 'art' music and commercial 'pop' music. The social
reception of music, he suggests, is essentially pre-programmed, musical
composition and production following precise guidelines which are
calculated to produce a specific and uniform response among listeners.
However, according to Adorno, in the case of art music, meaning
becomes apparent to the listener only after a considerable degree of
listening skill has been applied, this being essential if the essence of a
given musical piece, its 'concrete totality', is to be properly understood
(Adorno: 1941, p. 303). In the case of popular music, however, no such
listening skill is necessary as, according to Adorno:

> The composition hears for the listener... Not only does it not require effort
> to follow its concrete stream; it actually gives him models under which
> anything concrete still remaining may be subsumed. The schematic build
> up dictates the way in which he must listen while, at the same time, it
> makes any effort in listening unnecessary. Popular music is 'pre-digested' in
> a way strongly resembling the fad of 'digests' of printed material
> (ibid., p. 306).

Adorno goes further in his critique of popular music, suggesting that
it also plays a role in maintaining the social relations of capitalist
production. According to Adorno, popular music does this in two main

ways. First, it acts as a form of distraction, in unison with other forms of mass-produced leisure, ensuring that working-class consumers remain oblivious to the mechanisms of oppression that underpin the capitalist mode of production. Second, the 'patterned and pre-digested' nature of the music offers relief 'from both boredom and effort simultaneously' with the result that periods of leisure can be tailored to provide maximum relaxation and refreshment for the workforce (ibid.).

Adorno's work poses a number of problems for contemporary theorists seeking to explain the cultural impact of popular music since the post-Second World War period. In particular, by concentrating on the alleged regulating and standardising effects of popular music, Adorno closes off any possibility of social actors themselves playing a part in determining the meaning and significance of popular music genres and texts. Consequently, the work of Adorno has been taken to task on a number of occasions. Middleton, for example, argues that 'the reception of cultural products' cannot, as Adorno contends, be taken to 'represent a direct appropriation of the consumer into a pre-given framework but is *mediated* by other, varied interpretative assumptions associated with other social institutions and values' (1990, p. 60). Similarly, Frith argues that Adorno's theory of consumption reduces 'a complex social process to a simple psychological effect' (1983, p. 57). In attempting to rethink Adorno's interpretation of the effects of mass culture upon the individual, some theorists have turned to the work of Benjamin. In contrast to Adorno, Benjamin argues that 'technological *re*production gives back to humanity that capacity for experience which technological *production* threatens to take away' (Buck-Morss: 1989, p. 268). Although none of Benjamin's work focused upon music as such, his ideas can be easily applied to the study of music, especially mechanically reproduced music. A particularly effective demonstration of this is offered by Middleton, who compares Benjamin's thesis on the film audience to the listener's reception of a piece of recorded music. Thus, observes Middleton:

> Benjamin sees the film audience, detached from the moment of production, as being in the position of a *critic*, identifying with the analytical work of the camera rather than with the experience of the characters. The transparency of technique and the ubiquity of the reproductions turns everyone into an *expert*, hence a potential *participant*... This approach has enormously suggestive potential for analysis of listening, for it fully accepts the significance of new perceptual attitudes and situations while by-passing or at least putting into question the usual, too easy Adornian assumptions of passivity (1990, pp. 65–6).

To some extent the ideas of Benjamin, as interpreted by Middleton, enable popular music theorists to overcome the more restricting aspects of Adorno's work by awarding the music listener a degree of participation in the construction of musical meanings. The problem remains, however, to determine the degree of freedom that individuals have in constructing meanings around a form that '[subsists] within the nexus of capitalist production processes' (ibid., p. 66).

The contested nature of popular music

In tackling this issue, the starting point for many popular music theorists has been the music industry itself, or rather the opposing interests around which the modern music industry is constructed. Again, the cultural impact of rock 'n' roll on young people in the 1950s serves as a useful introduction to this issue. Thus, while music 'was a commercial product long before rock 'n' roll', the arrival of the latter together with its pronounced cultural effect upon young people created a number of problems for the music industry (Frith: 1983, p. 32). Of these, the crucial problem was how to market a music that was clearly viable as a commercial product but at the same time highly controversial. In particular, the nature of its partly African-American roots[1] made rock 'n' roll vulnerable to a range of accusations, particularly in the USA, its place of origin. The Reverend Albert Carter of the Pentecostal Church, Nottingham, for example, expressed the view that: 'Rock 'n' roll [was] a revival of devil dancing... the same sort of thing that is done in a black magic ritual' (Street: 1992, p. 305). Likewise, rock 'n' roll was criticised by the parent culture because of the damage it was perceived to be causing to the moral fabric of white US society, allegedly inciting teenagers to unruly behaviour (Hill: 1992, pp. 52–3). Indeed, such antagonisms were shared by the industry itself. Thus, the initial reaction of record companies was to attempt to clean up rock 'n' roll for white teenage consumption. However, this move on the part of the music industry proved contrary to the wishes of white teenage audiences themselves. Thus, as Gillett explains:

> The implication was that people didn't want their music to be as brash, blatantly sexual, and spontaneous as the pure rock 'n' roll records were. But although the position was maintained through to 1963, the success in the United States around this time of British groups with similar qualities suggested that the audience still did prefer this kind of music, if it knew about its availability (1983, p. 41).

A parallel example of this music industry response to rock 'n' roll is illustrated in a study by Mutsaers on the Dutch rock 'n' roll scene of the late 1950s and early 1960s. As Mutsaers points out, rock 'n' roll music in Holland was performed largely by Indonesian immigrants (Indos) whose 'apparently natural musical abilities' and affinity with the guitar – which was used in traditional Indonesian music – enabled them to monopolise rock 'n' roll music in Holland (1990, p. 308). Indobands were, however, very hard to work with in the recording studio; their inability to read music meant that they could not follow music scores and, consequently, were unable to produce the clean, predictable three minute *takes* that studio producers were looking for. Similarly, there were concerns over reactions of audiences to the live shows of Indobands. At dance halls where the groups played there were often violent clashes between white Dutch boys and 'Indo' boys, who, it was alleged, were 'stealing' the girlfriends of the white boys (ibid., p. 310). The point remained, however, that Indobands were extremely popular and thus highly lucrative, both in Holland and in neighbouring Germany, with the result that they continued to play a central role in the Dutch music industry up until the 1960s when their appeal was eclipsed by Merseybeat.

The way that rock 'n' roll music crucially differed from earlier forms of popular music was in the reflexivity of the discourse that was established between rock 'n' roll and its newly emerging youth audience. Indeed, despite the apprehension of the culture industries regarding the potential threat of rock 'n' roll, the visual representation of rock 'n' roll stars in film and on TV also did much to tie the cultural bond between artists and audience. Moreover, it wasn't simply the visual representation of artists themselves that counted in this respect. Thus, as Shumway explains with reference to the early TV appearances of Elvis Presley:

> When Elvis is featured on national TV programmes, the audience becomes part of the show... the film cuts between shots of Elvis and shots of the audience, not as a large mass of indistinguishable faces, but of particular faces whose response tells us of the excitement the performer is generating... These pictures showed other fans how to respond appropriately to rock acts (1992, p. 127).

Ehrenreich *et al.* (1992) have noted a similar process at work with the arrival of the Beatles in the US where fans already knew how to respond to the group having watched TV footage of the Beatles performing in Europe, such footage being similarly intercut with scenes from the audience. The meaning of rock 'n' roll then could not be separated from the contexts in which it was consumed and this has been a continuing feature of subsequent post-war and contemporary popular music styles. This aspect of popular music's cultural significance is particularly well summed up by Grossberg, who argues that the latter 'involve[s] more than just the relationships between logics of production and logics of consumption [but] define[s] particular ways of navigating the spaces and places, the territorializations of power, of daily life' (1994, p. 48). Like other forms of post-war popular culture then, popular music has become an increasingly contested medium. Thus, as Garofalo points out, popular mass culture is:

> one arena where ideological struggle – the struggle over the power to define – takes place. While there is no question that in this arena the forces arrayed in support of the existing hegemony are formidable, there are also numerous instances where mass culture – and in particular popular music – issues serious challenges to hegemonic power (1992a, p. 2).

The ability of popular music to serve as an effective platform for the delivery of such challenges is, in turn, further enhanced by the uncertainty of the music market itself. If the music industry was relatively unprepared for the arrival of rock 'n' roll, then this scenario has since been repeated on numerous occasions, for example by punk rock in the mid-1970s and acid house in the late 1980s. In his study *Sound Effects*, Frith suggests that: 'Record companies by nature don't much care what forms music takes as long as they can be controlled to ensure profit – musics and musicians can be packaged and sold, whatever their styles' (1983, p. 32). Another way of stating this argument would be to say that all the recording industry can maintain with certainty is that it is in place to package and market forms of popular music. Beyond this assertion, however, the trajectory of popular music's stylistic development and its impact upon audiences becomes rather less of an exact science. Indeed, as Attali has pointed out, the music industry occupies a particularly precarious position situated 'on the borderline between the most sophisticated marketing and the most unpredictable of cottage industries' (1985, pp. 102–3). Thus, while record companies would like to think that they are able to predict which artists and musical styles will prove to be the most commercially viable this remains largely an erroneous game of intuition.

Herein lies the central contradiction in modern music marketing, for in attempting to work as closely as possible within the 'organisational conventions [and] commercial logic of capitalism' the music industry is at the same time forced to exercise a looser control over the commodities that are marketed, the performing artists themselves (Negus: 1992, p. vii). In the final analysis, it is the stylistic or ideological appeal of performing artists and their music that generates profit for the industry. Harron, for example, has stated that in the wake of the 1960s hippie movement 'record companies... were confused and even alarmed by the strange groups whose music was so profitable [and had to] bring in young outsiders to tell them what would make a hit' (1988, p. 184). This tendency on the part of record companies to hire in 'street wise' youngsters in order to keep up with the rapidly shifting nature of the youth music market has continued. Thus, for example, Negus relates a discussion with an executive from a top record company who had launched a new 'dance label' and brought in 'dance specialists' on the grounds that he didn't 'know that market' (1992, p. 54).

Perhaps more than any other mass-produced commodity then, popular music is a contested form. While successful artists may generate vast amounts of income for the record companies to which they are signed, at the same time they frequently utilise the mass dissemination of their music or the magnitude of their public profile to communicate a variety of socio-political issues 'that have implications beyond their immediate impact on mass media entertainment' (Ullestad: 1992, p. 37). This aspect of popular music performance has manifested itself at regular intervals during the last fifty years. I have already discussed the socio-cultural impact of rock 'n' roll upon young people from the mid-1950s to the early 1960s. During the late 1960s, popular music became increasingly controversial as artists aligned themselves with a variety of socio-political issues. In the US this was evidenced for example in James Brown's 'Say it Loud, I'm Black and I'm Proud', a tribute to the Black Power movement, and Country Joe and the Fish's 'Fixin' to Die Rag', a powerful anti-Vietnam War song which contained the line 'You can be the first ones on the block to have your boy come home in a box' (Gleason: 1972, pp. 139–40). As Gleason points out, this song was 'heard and understood by millions' with the effect that there was no 'comparable medium' for the anti-war message (ibid., p. 139).

The subversive quality of popular music has also been witnessed in Britain, the possibilities for pop expression having been further enhanced by the art school training of many leading exponents of British pop. Since the 1950s, art schools have produced a succession of musical innovators, such as John Lennon, who, according to Frith and Horne, 'inflected pop music with bohemian dreams... and laid out the ideology of "rock"' (1987, p. 73). The artistic training of such musicians prompted them to experiment with different musical styles and to begin using the medium of song as a means to communicate a whole new range of sentiments, feelings and viewpoints. Thus, as Frith and Horne suggest, 'pop rhetoric – once concerned solely with sentimentality, the language of love, dancing and having a good time' suddenly acquired a whole new level of significance (ibid., p. 66).

In other parts of the world popular music has become a key medium in the articulation of socio-political causes and the fight against forms of political extremism. Wicke, in a study of music's role in the political disintegration of the former East Germany, argues that East German popular music groups and artists 'helped prepare the ground for the heightened popular political consciousness' that resulted in the fall of the Berlin Wall in November 1989 (1992, p. 196). Similarly Easton's study of the Soviet 'rock community' during the mid-1980s suggests that rock groups such as Aquarium played an important role in articulating the disillusionment of Soviet youth with the communist system. Moreover, according to Easton, attempts by the Soviet government to outlaw the performance of rock groups merely 'created a sense of confinement and repression in which underground movements flourish[ed]' (1989, p. 58). Ching-Yun Lee also examines the potential of popular music for political comment in her study of Cantopop, a mainstream style of Cantonese popular music in Hong Kong. As Ching-Yun Lee points out, in the period immediately following the violent military oppression of the Chinese student uprising in Beijing's Tiananmen Square during May 1989, Cantopop lyrics became increasingly supportive of the Chinese student movement, for example, by ridiculing the Chinese government, mourning the students who died in the uprising and pledging support for the democracy movement (1992, p. 129).

A further example of popular music's potential for the articulation of socio-political statements is provided in Davies's study of Aboriginal rock music in Australia. According to Davies, much of this music is linked with the Aborigines' attempt to recover their cultural homelands from white landowners. As Davies explains: 'Cultural survival for the Aboriginal Australians is tied to land rights, to origins, to a cultural integrity beyond contemporary industrial arrangements' (1993, p. 253). As such, argues Davies, Aboriginal rock music performs two main functions above and beyond its status as a commodity form. First, the music represents a form of empowerment through its 'reversal and decentering of colonial social relations' (ibid., p. 256). Second, when the music of Aboriginal rock bands is distributed through mainstream channels such as national radio and MTV, the usually marginalised Aborigine community is given the opportunity to voice its discontent through a central and highly strategic medium (ibid., p. 257).

Between the mid-1980s and early 1990s, the relationship between popular music and socio-political issues took a new turn as pop became the focus for a series of 'mega-events' beginning with Live Aid in July 1985 (Garofalo: 1992b). Live Aid was a globally televised live music event – in aid of the famine in Ethiopia – that brought together 'stadium acts' of the day, such as Queen, Elton John and David Bowie, with a view towards using the medium of a live music performance as a way of simultaneously increasing public awareness of the famine and raising funds to fight it. The success of Live Aid as a media spectacle led to a series of similar events including Farm Aid, which aimed to raise funds for small independent farmers in the US after the Regan administration withdrew its subsidisation of small farming concerns, and the two Nelson Mandela concerts – the first held in 1988 to mark the imprisoned ANC leader's seventieth birthday and the second in 1990 to celebrate his release from prison. The Mandela concerts were also intended to promote human rights issues on an international scale (Garofalo: 1992c).

Audience reception

If the ideological views of performers are one way in which popular music's commodity function is problematised, then audience reception is another. In an account of the cultural significance of progressive rock, Frith argues that, from the point of view of the audience, how the music is actually 'made' and distributed becomes rather less important than how it 'works... the question of *how* music comes to represent its listeners is begged' (1981, p. 159). According to Frith, in the case of late 1960s and early 1970s progressive rock, it was the aesthetic discourse established between audiences and performers that became centrally important in that it combined folk and art ideologies. Thus, argues Frith, 'as folk music rock is heard to represent the community of youth, as art music rock is heard as the sound of individual, creative sensibility' (1987, p. 136). In this way, maintains Frith, the apparent contradictions between progressive rock's status as a commodity and an authentic art form dissolve as, from the audience's point of view, it is the music's deemed 'authenticity' that assumes central importance. In a similar fashion, Negus has argued that: 'It is an irony of consumption that, as audiences, we acknowledge that our favourite artists, whether Bob Dylan, Public Enemy or Madonna are studied, calculated and hyped in various ways, but at the same time we accept them as "real"' (1992, p. 70). Again, Negus's argument suggests that, from the point of view of the audience, the processes that underlie the production and distribution of popular music are rather less important than its value as a cultural resource, that is, as a form that can be appropriated and reworked to serve particular collective purposes.

By the same token, however, it is important not to overstate popular music's utility in this respect. In the process of producing and marketing pop, the music industry clearly imposes structures of meaning on particular genres and sounds which in turn serve to frame audiences' uses of popular music. Thus, as Frith argues 'we are not free to read anything we want into a song... music is obviously rule-bound. We hear things as music because their sounds obey a particular, familiar logic, and for most pop fans (who are technically, non-musical) this logic is out of our control' (1987, p. 139). Similarly, a number of theorists have pointed to the role of the music industry in the construction of male and female gender identities through its promotion of particular styles and images. A particularly illustrative example of this is provided by Frith and McRobbie, who argue that:

> Not only do we find men occupying every important role in the rock industry and in effect being responsible for the creation and construction of suitable female images, we also witness in rock the presentation and marketing of masculine styles. And we are offered not one definitive image of masculine sexuality, but a variety of male sexual poses which are most often expressed in terms of stereotypes (1978, p. 374).

More recent work has served to challenge such observations, suggesting that as public perceptions of gender and sexuality have changed this has, in turn, prompted changes in the ways in which they are represented through the popular music medium. Thus, for example, in her study of MTV, Kaplan argues that: 'The plethora of gender positions on the channel is arguably linked to the heterogeneity of current sex roles and to an imaginary constructed out of a world in which all traditional categories, boundaries, and institutions are being questioned' (1987, p. 90). Similarly, Geyrhalter's study of contemporary British groups the Cure and Suede points to the way in which the male frontmen in each of these groups 'challenge gender stereotypes [and] flirt with the sexually ambiguous without declaring a fixed sexual identity' (1996, p. 217). Hill makes a parallel observation in relation to the gender experimentation of Eurythmics' singer Annie Lennox in promotional videos such as that which accompanied the song 'Love is a Stranger' where Lennox is seen with short cropped red hair and wearing a business suit. According to Hill: 'Annie's haircut made a big contribution to the vogue for gender confusion. Most participants were men who looked like women. Lennox was the reverse' (1986, p. 32).

Despite such shifting perceptions of gender, considerable emphasis continues to be placed by the music industry on the promotion of traditional gender stereotypes. An effective example of this is provided by recent work on the cultural significance of heavy metal music. According to Walser, heavy metal music acts to 'reproduce and inflect patriarchal assumptions and ideologies' which underpin late modern western society (1993, p. 111). Walser suggests that heavy metal groups produce tactics for the legitimisation of male power and control in society through 'misogyny as well as "exscription"' (ibid., p. 110). Misogynistic themes, according to Walser, are often present in heavy metal lyrics and in the promotional videos of many heavy metal groups. Exscription is a broadly opposite strategy to misogyny in that it involves the creation, through music, album covers and videos, of 'fantas[y] worlds without women' where male heroes battle against monsters and superhuman villains (ibid.). In Walser's view, such forms of female exscription in heavy metal result in a form of male bonding which 'excludes the threat of the feminine' (ibid., p. 115). This is not to suggest that heavy metal is an exclusively male concern. Indeed, Arnett's ethnographic research on young heavy metal audiences in the US has located a firmly established female fan base for the genre. However, as Arnett explains, many female followers of heavy metal 'become involved in it through a boyfriend or because of the sexual attraction they feel for the performers or fans [and] struggle to reconcile their enthusiasm for heavy metal with their sense of being not quite welcome in that world' (1995, pp. 139–40).

If the construction of gender and sexuality in popular music continues to promote notions of male dominance and superiority, then it is also a fundamental truism that the music industry continues to be male dominated. Certainly, the ratio of women who become successful in the music industry, both as performers and employees, remains low compared with that of men. In his comprehensive study of the music industry, Negus notes the 'subordinate position' occupied by the majority of female employees, who typically worked as secretaries, while those women with more high-profile careers were very much in the minority and had to deal with working relationships 'based around a bantering male camaraderie' (1992, p. 58). Similarly, in commenting upon the limited career opportunities for women as popular music performers Bayton observes that:

> Women have been largely excluded from popular music-making and relegated to the role of the fan. Women performers have been more prominent in commercial 'pop' than in 'rock', but their place in all these worlds has been that of vocalist rather than instrumentalist (1993, p. 177).

Moreover, even as the presence of all-female pop groups becomes more widely accepted such groups must still contend with and learn to negotiate a number of problems relating to the male-dominated nature of the music business. Thus, as Gottlieb and Wald point out:

> Women performers go through complicated contortions as they both appropriate and repudiate a traditionally masculine rock performance position which is itself premised on the repression of femininity, while they simultaneously contend with a feminine performance position defined primarily as the erotic object-to-be-looked-at (1994, p. 260).

The music industry, then, plays a substantial role in determining how music is heard and responded to by consumers. At the same time, however, consumers of popular music are not, as has sometimes been suggested, cultural dupes but are also active in creating musical meanings. Consumers take the structures of meaning – the musical and extra-musical resources associated with particular genres of pop – and combine them with meanings of their own to produce distinctive variations in patterns of consumption and stylistic expression. It is with such processes of appropriation and the factors deemed to underlie the social uses of popular music that sociological studies of pop have been chiefly concerned.

Subcultures

One of the first attempts to consider the role of the audience in ascribing meaning to popular music forms was the work of the Birmingham CCCS. As has already been noted in Chapter 1, it is the contention of the CCCS theorists that music and style-based youth groups, such as teddy boys, mods, rockers and skinheads, served as visual statements for pockets of working-class resistance to structural changes taking place in post-Second World War British society. The implication here is that such youth cultures took the musical and stylistic commodities produced by the culture industries and constructed their own meanings around them.

Problematically, however, if popular music is considered to be central to the post-war youth phenomenon, little attention is paid in the work of CCCS theorists to its actual function as a cultural resource. For the most part, CCCS accounts focus on the issue of style with occasional, cursory, references to music being made. Thus, as Laing, whose own work on the social significance of punk rock will presently be considered, has pointed out in relation to Hebdige's treatment of punk in *Subculture: The Meaning of Style* (1979), 'for Hebdige, music is only one part of a stylistic ensemble called 'punk', and judging by the limited space he devotes to it, not the most important part. That role is reserved for the visual display of... the "punk look"' (1985, p. x).

The only subcultural theorist to have made any sustained attempt to study the social meaning of popular music is Willis (1974, 1978). In keeping with the central tenets of subcultural theory, Willis presents an interpretation of popular music's social significance that is essentially class-based. Reading the working-class motorbike boys' and middle-class hippies' uses of music in terms of their contrasting structural circumstances, Willis relates the former's preference for rock 'n' roll singles, with their straightforward musical arrangements and 'good strong beat' for dancing, to the group's need for a readily accessible 'antidote to boredom' (1978, p. 68). At the same time, argues Willis, the hippies' preference for the more melodically and rhythmically complex progressive rock reflected their desire for music that 'demanded serious listening and attention' (ibid., p. 157). Similarly, Willis argues that the hippies' desire to restructure '"normal" time' also attracted them to progressive rock, its LP format together with featured electronic effects, such as 'echo, feedback, stereo [and] loudness itself... [giving] the impression of space and lateral extension', especially when listened to under the influence of mind expanding drugs such as LSD[2] (ibid., pp. 168, 167).

Bradley's study *Understanding Rock 'n' Roll* is an interesting departure from subcultural theory in that it serves both to rethink the class-based argument of the subcultural theorists while simultaneously paying much greater attention to the role of popular music itself as a mode of youth expression. While retaining the notion of resistance, Bradley argues that the resistance that rock 'n' roll music offered to its consumers took the form of a reaction against 'the norms of privacy and "modesty" involved in... music use' adding that rock 'n' roll 'involved loudness, showing off, getting together in crowds to do uninhibited things: it even had the glamour of being widely banned in the clubs until around 1960' (1992, pp. 127, 126). Moreover, Bradley also makes the important point that participation in such forms of collective expression was not purely restricted to followers of particular stylistic fashions. On the contrary, argues Bradley, 'this resistant element was also involved in music-use *beyond* the youth culture, among non-participants, and among ex-participants as the years went by, with the youth culture acting as a cultural example for others to follow in their musical lives' (ibid., p. 107).

A similar observation is made by Laing (1985) in his study of the social reception of punk rock. Moving beyond Hebdige's (1979) reading of punk as a working-class phenomenon, Laing suggests that the appeal of punk was rooted in 'the contrast between [its] private accessibility and its public invisibility' (1985, p. 37). The 'authenticity' of the original punk movement, suggests Laing, was unwittingly created by the broadcasting and retailing industries themselves, the latters' censorship of certain records conferring upon punk '"exclusivist" tendencies' and an outsider status thus 'consolidating a special community of punks, to whom punk rock [had] special meanings' (ibid.). Moreover, according to Laing the symbolic messages implicit in the censorship of punk were not only open to interpretation by followers of the punk style but also by the wider record buying public, this being demonstrated by the banning and boycotting of one particular punk rock song, the Sex Pistol's 'God Save The Queen'. Thus, as Laing explains:

> By defining 'God Save The Queen's' difference from the norm as total... the music industry's institutions... virtually instructed anyone with access to it that its effects on them would be totally different from the leisure pleasure provided by the context of daytime radio or *Top Of The Pops*. And of course, most of the 250 000 purchasers of the disc were not 'punks', and nor did buying it confer that status upon them. But the role offered to the listener to 'God Save The Queen' was set apart from both the established music industry and the official royalist celebrations. It was an independent and oppositional role (ibid., p. 38).

Laing's study is important for several reasons. First of all, it signifies a further break with the class-based interpretations of musical taste posited by subcultural theorists. Laing demonstrates how, as opposed to becoming a vehicle for the expression of class consciousness, the fact of musical taste can become a form of opposition which dramatically cuts across class distinctions. Thus, in endorsing the marginalised status of punk rock, audiences were assured of a ready-made source of antagonism which could then be used, if so desired, to articulate a variety of themes and issues relating not simply to issues of class but to a whole range of collectively shared and inter-class sensibilities. Thus, to take again the example of 'God Save The Queen', it is possible that this song's message became incorporated into the sensibilities of a diverse range of disaffected social groups. The frustrated adolescent, the political activist, the atheist and anti-royalist would all have comprehended the message in 'God Save The Queen' in a similar fashion, but the significance they attached to it would have been very different. Indeed, even within the more immediate punk movement, it is arguable that a number of different sensibilities were patched together by the media to suggest a coherent 'subcultural' affiliation. During the original 'punk summer' of 1977, punk in Britain came to symbolise everything from a bizarre form of street-corner society that aimed to poke fun at the establishment, to organised anti-Fascist and Rock Against Racism events (Frith and Street: 1992).

The plurality of meanings that can be read into the punk style is further in evidence when one considers the different forms of cultural significance that the genre and its attendant visual style have acquired outside Britain. Szemere (1992) notes how the Hungarian punk scene of the early 1980s borrowed the ideology of marginalisation from the punk movement in Britain but added new dimensions to this ideology. What the Hungarian punks brought in to their reworking of the punk idea was, as Szemere puts it, 'a particular view and experience of history' (ibid., p. 95). Like youth in the USSR, during the late 1970s and early 1980s, young Hungarians watched the socialist dream collapse under the weight of its own unfulfilled promises. There was a widespread economic recession coupled with a growing sense of insecurity which was felt right across Hungarian society. The youth of Hungary were particularly affected by this. There was a commonly shared feeling among Hungarian youth that the socialist system had let them down and seemed not to care that they were left struggling in a void. For many, the punk movement represented a way in which they could begin to negotiate the situation of anomie that arose from Hungary's socio-economic decline. At first the Hungarian authorities tried to play down the punk movement in the country as right wing and fascist, a feature that was, they argued inevitable given punk's western origins. However, the Hungarian punk movement soon developed its own avant-garde, the latter possessing, as Szemere points out, 'the intellectual and political resources to challenge the official representations of the Western punk movement as fascistic [sic]' (1992, p. 99).

In Germany too, where punk continues to have a large following as evidenced by national success of German-language punk rock groups such as Die Toten Hosen and the Chaos-Tage (chaos days), an annual punk gathering in Hannover (see Geiling: 1995, 1996), the style has become an increasingly localised form of cultural expression. Studies of the German punk movement by Müller-Wiegand (1990) and Hafeneger *et al.* (1993) begin to illustrate how the relationship between punk style, locality and notions of collective identity can take on significantly different meanings even within the same country as musical and stylistic sensibilities become intertwined with the vernacular knowledges of different cities, towns and rural communities. In their comparative study of the punk scene in Frankfurt am Main and Fulda, Hafeneger *et al.* illustrate the differing forms of cultural significance that being a punk assumes in each of these settings. In Frankfurt, a major city, punks are considered by non-punks to be 'old fashioned' not only stylistically but also ideologically (1993, p. 26). Frankfurt punks react to such accusations by becoming totally committed to the punk style, placing great emphasis on the need to both behave and look like an 'authentic' punk as allegedly defined by the British punk scene of the late 1970s. Consequently, in the context of the Frankfurt youth cultural scene, punks represent, according to Hafeneger *et al.*, a culture trapped within its own 'conservatism' (ibid.). The experience of punks in Fulda, a small city approximately fifty miles to the northeast of Frankfurt, is considerably different. Here punks are ostracised not because they are considered out of step with current fashions and youth sensibilities, but because they are believed to be socially deviant. Thus, the local punk culture must learn to deal with a rather different set of social circumstances which deem that they are 'outsiders' who must keep their distance and are not to be trusted (ibid., p. 69).

Arguably, such localised instances of youth cultures and the highly particularised sets of circumstances that govern their attachment to given forms of music and visual image call for an analytical approach that is more sensitive to the role of locality in informing the cultural relationship between youth, music and style. This view is supported by Lewis (1992), who suggests that musical taste and the collective sense of identity to which such taste often gives rise may grow out of a shared sense of experience or the aesthetic and political values that members attach to a particular popular music genre resulting from circumstances encountered in specific localities.

During the course of this chapter, I have been concerned with the social meaning of popular music for young people as this has been theorised and interpreted in the related disciplines of sociology, cultural and media studies. Beginning with an overview of the ideas of Adorno and Benjamin, I have illustrated how the opposing interpretations of mass culture expounded by these theorists have continued to inform contemporary popular music researchers as they attempt to work through and resolve the highly problematic issues surrounding the cultural significance of popular music. The final section of the chapter has centred around the contention that musical meaning, if this is to be seen as a socially constructed phenomenon, must be related to the everyday contexts in which music is heard and collectively responded to. In this respect, the argument presented here builds on that put forward in Chapter 1 by calling for a more systematic address of the local in shaping the cultural relationship between youth culture and popular music. In Chapter 3, I want to look more closely at the significance of the local as a way in which to approach the study of popular music and interpret its meaning as a cultural resource in the everyday lives of young people.

NOTES

1. Although rock 'n' roll is often supposed to have originated directly from African-American folk music, it is actually a hybrid between African-American folk and white American country and western music.
2. LSD is the popular abbreviation for lysergic acid diethylamide, the synthetic hallucinogenic drug widely used by the hippie movement during the psychedelic era of the mid to late 1960s.

Chapter 3

The Significance of Locality

Over the last decade there has been a growth of interest among sociologists and cultural theorists in the 'local'. Ironically, much of this interest stems directly from the insights provided by the 'accelerating processes of globalisation' (Smart: 1993a, p. 129). Thus, as Featherstone argues, a 'paradoxical consequence of the process of globalization, the awareness of the finitude of the boundedness of the planet and humanity, is not to produce homogeneity but to familiarize us with greater diversity, the extensive range of local cultures' (1993, p. 169). In the context of popular music studies too, a number of theorists have begun to focus upon the local as a basis for the study and interpretation of popular music's cultural significance. During the course of this chapter, I want to consider the various ways in which the local has been conceptualised in relation to the production and consumption of popular music and to establish the theoretical basis for my own analysis of the relationship between popular music, identity and locality.

Within the existing literature on popular music and locality there are two main ways in which the term *local* is applied. Thus, in some cases *local* appears to be interchangeable with *national*, reference to the 'local' denoting a focus upon national rather than international or 'global' aspects of popular music production and consumption. In other cases *local* is used as a means of conceptualising such processes of production and consumption in the context of specific urban and rural settings. While both uses of the term *local* in popular music studies have provided valuable information on the significance of music in everyday life, at the same time each approach perceives the local as a 'fixed' space underpinned by commonly acknowledged social discourses. However, more recent work on the relationship between space, place and identity challenges such perceptions of the local as an essentially uncontested territory arguing instead that, as different social groups appropriate and mark out social spaces within a particular place, the local becomes a highly contested territory that is crossed by different forms of collective life and the competing sensibilities that the latter bring to bear on the interpretation and social realisation of a particular place. It is to these ideas that I turn during the final part of this chapter when establishing a theoretical basis for my own study of the significance of locality in framing the relationship between popular music and identity. In the first instance, however, it is necessary to consider in more detail why the local has in recent years become an increasingly important focus in the study of popular culture.

The global and the local

As noted above, much of the current interest in the local stems directly from the globalisation process and its impact on nations and peoples around the world. Although it is difficult to tell precisely when the process of globalisation began, it gathered considerable momentum in the years immediately following the Second World War when, as pointed out in Chapter 1, economic prosperity in the west resulted in a drive towards increased mass production of consumer goods. The subsequent consumer boom was spearheaded by the US with the effect that, in a relatively short space of time, a proliferation of mass-produced goods originating from the US were available in many different countries around the world. This was accompanied by a wave of US-produced popular entertainment forms, notably popular music and cinema films.

The initial response of social and cultural theorists to the apparently one-sided flow of goods and information from the US was deeply pessimistic, especially in Britain where US popular culture had already made significant inroads into British cultural life because of the large numbers of US servicemen stationed in the country during the Second World War (Hebdige: 1988, p. 53). British cultural theorist Richard Hoggart was particularly critical regarding what he saw as the 'Americanisation' of British society and particularly British youth, whose appropriation not only of US popular cultural forms but also the social sensibilities portrayed in such forms served, according to Hoggart, to transform young Britons into 'hedonistic but passive barbarian[s]... who spend their evenings listening in harshly lighted milk-bars to the nickelodeons' (1957, pp. 250, 247). Hoggart's summation of US popular culture and its effects on British youth was to be echoed seven years later by Johnson in his scathing account of the Beatles, who, in Johnson's view, graphically illustrated US popular

culture's steady infiltration of British cultural life. Johnson refers to the
Beatles as 'grotesque idols' before going on to describe the audience at a
Beatles' performance as 'a generation enslaved by a commercial
machine... [their] hands mindlessly tapping in time to the music'
(1964, p. 327).

Raymond Williams (1965) presented a slightly more optimistic
account of post-war massification's effects on British society. Thus, he
argued, the mass culturalistation of British life would not be a straightforward process but would take the form of an ongoing struggle, or a
long revolution, in which individuals would resist the alleged blandness
and facelessness of mass culturalisation by holding onto the vestiges of
'traditional' life or, alternatively, using such forms of traditional life in
order to raise new structures of meaning for mass-produced items.
Williams developed this view through the concept of *residual* and
emergent cultures, which he used to represent the collective practices 'of
some previous cultural formation', together with the 'new meanings and
practices [which] are continually being created' and which may act as
forms of opposition to massification (1980, pp. 41–2). Again, however,
there is in Williams's work a clear implication that mass culture has an
essentially negative effect in that it threatens always to erode 'traditional'
cultures thus subsuming once distinctive local cultures throughout the
world into a single, homogenised global culture.

In more recent years, a number of theorists have begun to readdress
the issue of globalisation suggesting that, far from destroying local
differences between national and regional cultures, globalisation may in
fact work to enhance such differences. This argument is central to a
study by Lull, which introduces the term 'cultural reterritorialization' as
a means of illustrating how global commodities and resources are
'reworked' by local audiences in such a way that their meanings become
inextricable from the everyday settings in which they are experienced
(1995, p. 160). Thus, argues Lull:

> the foundations of cultural territory – ways of life, artifacts, symbols, and
> contexts – are all open to new interpretations and understandings...
> Because culture is constructed and mobile, it is also synthetic and
> multiple... Reterritorialization, therefore, is a process of active cultural
> selection and synthesis drawing from the familiar and the new (ibid.,
> pp. 160–1).

A similar observation is made by Thompson in a study of the effects
of globalisation upon the dissemination and reception of mass media
products. According to Thompson:

The appropriation of media products is always a localized phenomenon, in the sense that it always involves specific individuals who are situated in particular socio-historical contexts, and who draw on the resources available to them in order to make sense of media messages and incorporate them into their lives. And messages are often transformed in the process of appropriation as individuals adapt them to the contexts of everyday life (1995, p. 174).

Both Lull and Thompson are concerned to illustrate how national and regional audiences, although exposed to the same global flow of commodities, images and information, appropriate and inscribe meaning into the latter in highly distinctive ways which are based on the forms of local knowledge underpinning their everyday lives. Such a view in turn opens up new ways of understanding the interpretative power of audiences. Traditionally, cultural theorists have considered audiences to be both powerless and unreflexive recipients of cultural products, a sentiment that is clearly evident in both Adorno (1941) and MacDonald's (1953) studies of mass culture examined in Chapter 2 and in the observations of Hoggart and Johnson considered above. A number of contemporary theorists, however, place much more emphasis on the notion of audiences as 'active' participants in the production and inscription of meaning in the products of the culture industries. Thus, as Ang argues:

'The audience' no longer represents simply an 'object of study', a reality 'out there' constitutive of and reserved for the discipline which claims ownership of it, but has to be defined first and foremost as a discursive trope signifying the constantly shifting and radically heterogeneous ways in which meaning is constructed and contested in multiple everyday contexts of media use and consumption (1996, p. 4).

This new approach to the study of media audiences also serves to challenge the contrast pair of 'tradition' and 'innovation' evident in earlier examples of cultural studies writing. The implication in this contrast pair is that 'traditional' culture, which is deemed to have a positive and liberating and positive influence on the quality of human life, is eroded away by a mass culture that is seen as inherently negative and repressive. Clearly, however, if we are to accept the claims of contemporary cultural theorists such as Lull, Thompson and Ang that, in appropriating mass cultural products, audiences simultaneously acquire new ways in which to both address and negotiate the systems and structures that govern their everyday lives, then we must also accept the potentially emancipatory effects of mass culture. It is with the latter interpretation of the audience in relation to the construction of cultural meanings and value of such meanings that Part II of this study is concerned. The four ethnographic studies presented in Part II offer a series of insights into the role of popular music and its associated stylistic innovations in the cultural emancipation of young people. Thus, in my respective accounts of urban dance music, bhangra, rap and progressive rock there are clear instances of mass cultural resources being used to an emancipatory effect in the face of local cultures and vestiges of tradition which are unequivocally oppressive. Having examined some of the key issues underlying the current interest in the role of the local as a place in which the meanings of popular culture products are both constructed and subsequently lived out by individuals, I want now to consider how the significance of the local is being represented within the field of popular music studies.

Popular music as a local resource

Much of the research focusing on the significance of popular music as a local resource has dealt with the issue of music-making. Sara Cohen, whose work will be considered more extensively in Chapter 7, has produced a particularly effective ethnographic reading of the local music-making culture in post-industrial Liverpool. As Cohen illustrates, in addition to its creative and economic functions in an area with high levels of unemployment, music-making appears to be a deeply ingrained feature of everyday life in Liverpool. Indeed, when reading Cohen's study, it is interesting to note the varied and overlapping range of discourses concerning life in Liverpool which locally produced music was deemed to articulate by local musicians and consumers of locally produced music. Thus, according to Cohen, in attempting to account for the music's 'melodic, lyrical style':

> Some attributed it to the influence of the Beatles or to the absence of students from the music scene, who tended to favour more 'alternative' types of music. Some suggested that the lack of 'angry' music or music of a more overtly political nature reflected the escapist tendency of the bands that produced instead music of a 'dreamy' and 'wistful' style. Others pointed out that Merseysiders had understandably grown cynical about politics and therefore avoided writing about it (1991, p. 15).

If Cohen's study is geared principally towards the issue of music-making, there is at the same time a clear awareness within her work that local music-making practices involve far more than the actual process of composing and performing songs and musical pieces. Indeed, Cohen effectively demonstrates how music-making forms part of what she terms a 'rock culture', the latter being simultaneously the product of local knowledges and sensibilities and a form of independent cultural territory which is removed from the cultural space occupied by significant others such as girlfriends, parents, siblings and non-music-making peers. A number of other researchers looking at local music-making practices have also drawn upon this concept of a rock culture. In a recent study of three young rock groups in Sweden, Fornäs *et al.* suggest that playing in a band serves as an important form of escapism from the more mundane aspects of everyday life. Fornäs *et al.* argue that, through their musical activities, young bands are able to mark themselves off from both the parent culture and the school culture and the demands that the latter impose upon young people. Playing in a group, it is suggested, gives young people a chance to distance themselves from those aspects of life that they least like and to envisage a different kind of life for themselves which is based not upon school-work and subsequently a job or career, but rather upon musical creativity and artistic expression (1995, p. 203). Similarly, Bennett's (1980) US study of local bands and the rehearsal process reveals a strong feeling among certain of the young musicians who took part in the study that complete dedication to the music is the thing that ultimately separates the 'musicians' from the 'non-musicians', that is, those who are prepared to compromise their time spent rehearsing with a band because of other commitments such as part-time jobs, sporting activities or girlfriends (Stith Bennett's study dealing exclusively with male musicians).

Another highly useful series of observations relating to the broader cultural world that forms around local music-making practices is provided by Finnegan in her study *The Hidden Musicians* (1989). Thus, as Finnegan points out, while it 'is true that local music-making in the sense of direct participation in performance is the pursuit of a minority... [such] musical practices... involve a whole host of other people than just performers' (1989, p. 6). Finnegan's work is useful in that, through its account of extra-performance related participation in local live music events (forms of participation that might, for example, include the designing of posters, selling tickets or helping to assemble staging or lighting equipment), it begins to examine the wider dimensions of music-making's function as an occasion for 'sociality' (Shields: 1992, p. 107). I will return to this issue in Chapter 7 where I develop Finnegan's argument further by considering how local live

music events also give rise to what I have called occasions of 'extra-
musical' sociality.

A somewhat different perspective on the social significance of local
music-making is presented in Wallis and Malm's *Big Sounds From Small
Peoples*. Through their investigation of local music industries in
different parts of the world, Wallis and Malm provide a valuable insight
into the social circumstances from which such industries emerge and
the communities which they serve. A pertinent example of this is
Recordiau Sain, a small Welsh recording label established in 1969 to
promote Welsh language popular music. According to Wallis and
Malm, Recordiau Sain was the first of a small number of local labels
established by Welsh language enthusiasts, 'people who felt that they
were losing part of their cultural identity with the demise of the
language their parents spoke' (1984, p. 140). Wallis and Malm go on to
illustrate how, using the medium of the phonogram, such enthusiasts
are able to 'communicate with fellow Welsh-speakers and tease the
establishment' (ibid., p. 141).

A parallel example of the way in which a music can be authenticated
as a local cultural form owing to its particular representation of a nation
and its people is seen in Regev's study of Israeli rock and *Musica
mizrakhit*. Indeed, Regev advances this perspective on music's cultural
significance by demonstrating the plurality of national identities made
possible through different musical genres and the sensibilities of
consumption constructed around such genres. According to Regev,
there exist in Israel two competing notions of national identity based
around the consumption of Israeli rock and *Musica mizrakhit*. Israeli
rock, because of its perceived cultural significance 'as a sign of being
progressive and cosmopolitan', has for a long time been cast in a
discourse of 'national achievement' which has essentially ensured its
place in the recognised national culture of Israel (1996, p. 280). *Musica
mizrakit* on the other hand, owing to its incorporation of elements
from traditional Middle Eastern and Mediterranean musics and the fact
that it is performed by 'native Israelis', has been excluded 'from the
dominant "Israeliness"' (ibid., p. 277). However, through the efforts of
performers such as Haim Mosche and Ofer Levi to increase the
popularity of *musica mizrakhit* by reinforcing the music's connection
with 'the feelings of a large, culturally discriminated sector of Israeli
society', the genre has slowly begun to gain acceptance as an 'authentic'
form of Israeli music with a place in 'the national context' of Israeli life
(ibid., pp. 279, 283).

The power of political expression, which marginalised social groups can often harness through the creation of a 'home grown' grassroots music culture, is further examined in Rose's work on rap and hip hop. Focusing upon the origins of the latter as a form of African-American street culture in inner-city districts of New York, Rose argues that rap and hip hop accurately reflect 'the tensions and contradictions in the urban public landscape' (1994a, p. 72). Thus, according to Rose:

> Even as today's rappers revise and redirect rap music, most understand themselves as working out of a tradition of style, attitude and form which has critical and primary roots in New York City in the 1970s. Substantial postindustrial shifts in economic conditions, access to housing, demographics and communication networks were crucial to the formation of the conditions which nurtured the cultural hybrids and sociopolitical tenor of hip hop's lyrics and music (ibid., p. 73).

In addition to the medium of music itself, Rose also stresses the importance of a number of extra-musical resources associated with hip hop culture. Particularly important, she argues, is the need to visibly impress the nature of the hip hop mission on the face of the local environment: 'Graffiti artists spray-painted murals and [name] "tags" on trains, trucks and playgrounds, claiming territories and inscribing their otherwise contained identities on public property' (ibid., p. 71). The cultural significance of hip hop graffiti as a means of redefining urban space is also discussed in two further studies by Lachmann (1988) and Brewer and Miller (1990). Thus, Lachmann notes how particular graffiti designs are used by hip hop gangs as a way of 'mark[ing] off their territory' (1988, p. 239). Similarly, Brewer and Miller argue that:

> HHG [hip hop graffiti] is an expression of power... In the case of individual writers and crews, HHG lays a personal claim to the surfaces written upon, typically those either seemingly controlled by no one (for example, abandoned buildings, cement walls, neglected property) or apparently never to be controlled by writers (for example, schools, public transportation, businesses, municipal properties) (1990, p. 360).

Another notable instance of a home-grown musical style being used to articulate a specific range of local knowledges and issues is Algerian raï music. According to Schade-Poulsen the development of raï is linked with the massive influx of people from rural areas of Algeria to the country's western cities after the Second World War. Although originally an acoustic folk music, modern raï music is generally performed on electric guitars, synthesisers and drum machines. These instruments have, in turn, 'open[ed] up new possibilities' for the development of raï music – 'the guitar can enter on the upbeat (as in reggae), the drum machine can create a complex mixture of rhythms and sounds' – with the effect that modern raï is essentially a hybrid between a traditional folk form and western popular music style (1995, p. 84). The cultural reception of raï music by Algerian youth represents a further meeting of western popular culture and traditional cultural forms. Schade-Poulsen suggests that raï can be regarded 'as an expression of an ambivalent or fundamental duality in the identity of Algerian youth' (ibid., p. 85). The music reflects the attempts of Algerian youth, having become accustomed to the images of modern western lifestyle inscribed within products such as music and cinema, to balance their desire for these things with the social, cultural and religious institutions that restrict their access to such forms of leisure. Raï also helps young Algerians to negotiate the restrictions placed upon their sexual and emotional desires. According to Schade-Poulsen, the themes of love which are often contained in raï lyrics 'indicate the need for youth to create a sphere for their concerns, independent of the parent generation' (ibid., p. 107).

Music consumption and the local

Thus far, I have considered a number of studies that suggest ways of understanding local music-making practices and related forms of cultural activity as facilitating the construction of local forms of identity. Clearly, however, if we are to fully comprehend popular music's local significance, then we must go beyond issues of music-making and production and consider the wider meanings attached to popular music in the context of everyday life. For much of the time, popular music's relationship to the local has rather less to do with its being a local 'product' than with the way in which commercially available musical products are appropriated and reworked within the context of a given locality. Thus, what becomes important here is a consideration of the way in which patterns of music consumption in particular urban and rural locations are simultaneously *products* of the local and *creators* of particular forms of local knowledge and the sensibilities to which such knowledge gives rise. A useful illustration of this process is provided by Shepherd who argues that music 'does not "carry" its meaning and "give it" to participants and listeners. Affect and meaning have to be created anew in the specific social and historical circumstances of music's creation and use' (1993, p. 138).

The salience of Shepherd's argument is effectively demonstrated in some of the more recent work dealing with the issue of music and ethnic identity. Thus, for example, in charting the reception of reggae in Britain by ethnic minority groups of Afro-Caribbean origin, Gilroy argues that the latter 'ceased... to signify an exclusively ethnic, Jamaican style and derived a different kind of cultural legitimacy both from a new global status and from its expression of what might be termed a pan-Caribbean culture' (1993, p. 82). A similar argument is put forward by Lipsitz, who suggests that 'musical syncretisms disclose the dynamics of cultural syncretisms basic to the process of immigration, and acculturation in contemporary societies' (1994, p. 126). Assessing this observation within the context of modern Britain, Lipsitz goes on to argue:

> Immigrants leaving the Caribbean and Asia... became 'Black' in Britain, an identity that they do not have in their home countries, but which becomes salient to them in England as a consequence of racism directed at them from outside of their communities as well as from its utility to them as a device for building unity within and across aggrieved populations... Popular music in Britain [also] plays an important role in building solidarity within and across immigrant communities, while at the same time serving as a site for negotiation and contestation between groups (ibid.).

Such a process is a clear example of what Stokes refers to as 'cultural relocation' (1994, p. 3). According to Stokes, as notions of cultural identity are threatened by patterns of migration and the forms of social change and readjustment experienced by migrant populations, such populations look for ways in which they can culturally 'relocate' themselves. One way in which this might be achieved is through music. Thus, as Stokes points out:

> The musical event, from collective dances to the act of putting a CD into a machine, evokes and organises collective memories and present experiences of place with an intensity, power and simplicity unmatched by any other social activity. The 'places' constructed through music involve notions of difference and social boundary (ibid., p. 4).

It could also be argued that the concept of musicalised cultural relocation is becoming increasingly relevant for indigenous populations of countries whose national cultures have been augmented and significantly altered by the presence of immigrant groups. One way in which indigenous populations may seek to culturally relocate themselves is by constructing *idealised* versions of national culture based upon an imagined past. At one level, this might explain the rise across Europe of Far Right or Neo-Nazi rock groups whose song lyrics often reflect a felt need to restore what such groups and their followers perceive to be the *traditional* culture of their home nation (Matthesius: 1992; Farin and Seidel-Pielen: 1994; Funk-Hennings: 1998). Similarly, Bjurström argues that the rise of 'Viking and white rock groups' in Sweden relates closely to 'the increase in immigration to Sweden during the last four decades' and the felt need among certain sections of white youth 'to define a Swedish identity' (1997, p. 54).

Another route to cultural relocation for white youth has been to effectively reinvent their ethnicity by appropriating the music and style of local ethnic minority groups or by using globally available resources, typically of African-American or Afro-Caribbean origin, but also in recent years from other parts of the world such as Africa and the Aboriginal territories of Australia. I have already noted several examples of white British youth's borrowings from both the youth of local Afro-Caribbean communities and the culture of African-Americans in my discussion of the work of Hebdige (1976b), Chambers (1976) and Jones (1988) during Chapter 1. Significantly, however, such cultural borrowings can no longer be identified simply with the stylistic experiments of white youth. Bricolage, first discussed by Hebdige in relation to the cut-up style of the punk, has become standard fare in youth cultures throughout the world not only stylistically but also musically; the introduction of new techniques such as sampling enabling fragments from existing musical styles to be borrowed from their original sources and reassembled to produce new hybridised musical forms. Perhaps the most culturally significant hybridised musical style to emerge from such new technologies is rap which, despite its origins and continuing importance within African-American ghetto culture, has found widespread appeal among youth of all races in different parts of the world (Mitchell: 1996). I will go on to examine the implications of such musical hybridisation for our understanding of local music cultures in more detail in Chapter 5, which focuses on the significance of bhangra for South Asian youth in Newcastle upon Tyne, and in Chapter 6 where I present a comparative analysis of the cultural significance of hip hop among white youth in Newcastle and the youth of ethnic minority groups in Frankfurt am Main, Germany.

The contested space of the local

> If it is now recognized that people have multiple identities, then the same point can be made in relation to places. Moreover, such multiple identities can be either, or both, a source of richness or a source of conflict (Massey: 1993, p. 65).

Thus far during the course of this chapter I have begun to consider how popular music functions as a local cultural resource by looking at a number of studies that focus on music-making practices and consumption patterns in a local context. Each of the studies examined suggests particular ways in which musicalised identities take part in a perpetual dialogue with the particular social spaces in which they are lived out, that is to say, with the social and spatial organisation of a given locality. In all of the work considered so far interpretations of the local are formulated upon the premise that the term *local* is unproblematic; that it refers to a fixed territory and a population who are broadly consensual in their perception and definition of what *local* means both in terms of place and the collective identity attached to that place. In the remainder of this chapter I want to reconsider the term *local*, the relationship between locality and identity and the role of popular music as a resource in the construction of local identities. In doing so, I will suggest that by conceptualising the 'local' not as a definite space but rather as a series of discourses, which involve ways of picturing the local and one's relation to it, it becomes possible to see the local as a contested space, as a place that is both real and, to use Chaney's (1993) terminology, *fictionalised.*

In recent years a new approach to the conceptualisation of space, referred to as 'social geography', has begun to rethink more traditional geographical definitions of space and place. While the latter concentrate upon the physical dimensions of space, which in turn leads to the interpretation of spatial meanings as essentially fixed and unchanging, social geography moves beyond this definition by illustrating the changing and highly contested meanings of space as it is appropriated by diffuse and conflicting interest groups (see Shields: 1991; Smith and Katz: 1993). This argument is developed by Keith and Pile, who argue that:

> simultaneously present in any landscape are multiple enunciations of distinct forms of space [and that, consequently the term 'spaciality' may now be used] to capture the ways in which the social and spatial are inextricably realized one in the other; to conjure up the circumstances in which

society and space are simultaneously realized by thinking, feeling, doing individuals and also to conjure up the many different conditions in which such realizations are experienced by thinking, feeling, doing subjects (1993, p. 6).

One of the ways in which individuals make such simultaneous realisations of society and space is through the act of musical consumption. Indeed, musical consumption has proved to be both a particularly distinctive and enduring medium for the collective reconstruction of public space. To map the public spaces of any industrial or post-industrial conurbation in terms of the patterns of musical consumption which exist there is to discover a series of shifting and overlapping territories. Slobin's (1992) study 'Micromusics of the West' offers one way of understanding the role of music in the collective appropriation and redefinition of public space. Slobin argues that modern western societies are increasingly becoming collections of 'supercultures', typically comprising new or recently settled immigrant populations, whose direct physical relation to a city or region is augmented by a felt relationship to an alternative version of social reality which draws upon the traditional notions cultural life that such groups carry along with them when they relocate to new homes in the west. According to Slobin, music provides a key resource through which such 'supercultures' define themselves and their relationship to the new social environments into which they are placed.

Slobin's work significantly enhances the notion of the local as a multiply articulated space. Indeed, one could adapt and extend Slobin's argument to include indigenous taste groups and 'alternative' communities, who also draw upon music as a way of marking out their own cultural space within cities and towns. This aspect of contemporary musical life is addressed by Straw's study of popular music scenes. According to Straw, a scene is a 'cultural space in which a range of musical practices coexist' (1991, p. 373). Straw's observations are borne out by Shank's (1994) study of the music scene in Austin, Texas, which effectively illustrates something of the variety of different musics, crowds and venues that invariably 'coexist' within a local 'music scene'. It follows that such a diverse range of musics and the sensibilities of style that grow up around them will involve different picturings of the cultural space in which they operate. This in turn suggests that, in attempting to define notions of locality and local identity, one must begin to perceive individuals not simply as authors of collective identities but also as authors of those spaces and places in which such collective identities are lived out.

Werlen has argued that all social action is organised around 'spatial frames of reference... whose definition establishes particular character-istic dimensions which coincide with the ontology of the (physical, social or mental/subjective) object to be located' (1993, p. 144). If, as Werlen appears to be suggesting, such spatial frames of reference are social constructs, then it follows that different social groups using the same space may apply varying and, in many cases, conflicting defini-tions to that space. This is clearly illustrated, for example, in Hether-ington's account of the two competing 'social spatializations' attached to Stonehenge as a festival site and a place of heritage (1992, p. 88). Stonehenge, an ancient megalith in the southern English county of Wiltshire, has long been regarded as a significant archaeological site. The unique physical shape of Stonehenge, its function as a Druid temple and the belief among experts that it is an ancient astronomical instrument attracts tourists from around the world. During the 1970s and 80s, Stonehenge also became the site of a free music and crafts festival until increasing pressure from the local police, combined with the placing of a perimeter fence around the monument, forced the festival organisers to find another location for the festival. According to Hetherington, both the tourist and festival-goer's interpretations of Stonehenge draw upon the same basic knowledge of the monument, but each interpretation works this knowledge in different ways to 'legitmize different sets of practices and individualized lifestyles' (ibid., p. 89). For the tourist, the significance of Stonehenge lies in the clues it is seen to provide concerning the culture and customs of Ancient Britain. For the festival goer, Stonehenge's perceived links with Ancient Britain feed into and help to maintain a 'neo-pagan spiritual revival' (ibid., p. 88). In both cases, Stonehenge is being partly fiction-alised, the tourist and the festival-goer both constructing a particular narrative of the monument based upon their own opinion of what Stonehenge represents.

A further important analysis of space as a focus for plural and conflicting interpretations is offered by Massey, whose work also demonstrates how such contests over the meaning of space have been further complicated by patterns of migration. Drawing upon the example of Kilburn in London, Massey points to the way in which the various ethnic groups who have settled in the district and made it their home have at the same time introduced aspects of their own cultural identity into the everyday life of Kilburn. Thus, concludes Massey, 'while Kilburn may have a character of its own, it is absolutely not a seamless, coherent identity, a single sense of place which everyone shares. It could hardly be less so' (1993, p. 65). As Massey's study illustrates, the increasing movement of people between countries and the various forms of cultural baggage that they carry along with them also have significant implications for the basic nature and definition of urban spaces. As these people settle in new towns and cities and begin a process of acculturation, they also become a part of the social fabric of their new environment, colouring the day to day life of a particular place with aspects of their own cultural reality. In doing so, such groups join in the process of redefining and marking out social space in order to accommodate their own collective needs. A useful model for mapping this process is Appadurai's concept of *ethnocscapes*. Appadurai uses this concept to describe 'the landscape of persons who constitute the shifting world in which we live: tourists, immigrants, refugees, exiles, guestworkers and other moving groups and persons' (1990, p. 297). Smart, in addressing the concept of *ethnoscapes*, has suggested that they 'allow us to recognise that our notions of space, place and community have become much more complex, indeed a "single community" may now be dispersed across a variety of sites' (1993a, p. 147).

It should now be clear that in referring to the 'local', we are in effect speaking about a space that is crossed by a variety of different collective sensibilities each of which imposes a different set of expectations and cultural needs upon that space. In doing so, such sensibilities also construct the local in particular ways, a process which ensures that terms such as *locality* and *local identity* are always, in part at least, subjective elements, which begin by utilising the same basic knowledges about the local, its social and spatial organisation, but supplement such knowledges with their own collectively held values to create particular narratives of locality. From the point of view of the young, one of the key resources in the facilitation of such narratives is popular music and its attendant stylistic resources. For young people, the struggle to win and mark out urban spaces turns principally on music and style. Disused inner-city factories and warehouses become dance music venues; student houses in residential areas become locations for 'sound-systems'; the fronts of closed-down shops become poster boards advertising local gigs and club nights; city squares, car parks, building forecourts and pavements become meeting places for skateboaders and breakdancers. In appropriating and reworking urban spaces in such ways, young people construct new urban narratives – narratives that enable them to view the local in particular ways and apply their own solutions to the particular problems or shortcomings that they identify with their surroundings and the policies and practices that shape these surroundings. However, such narratives do not, as has often been suggested, involve the formation of a separate *subcultural* identity. Indeed, such an interpretation of young people's collective uses of music and style imposes, in my view, too narrow an interpretation on instances of collective youth action which are in reality characteristically diverse. The same music and style will often produce not one but a variety of responses on the part of young people to the particular local circumstances in which they find themselves, each response being underpinned by a common set of base knowledges relating to the local but using this knowledge in different ways and to different ends. This aspect of the relationship between music, youth and local identity will be explored more thoroughly in Part II of this study.

Writing 'local' cultures?

Clearly, in any study that investigates the local in the way I propose to do here there is a danger that one will, to use Clifford's words, become 'caught up in the invention, not the representation, of cultures' (Clifford: 1986, p. 2). Indeed, it might be argued that such a problem intensifies when one begins to consider the role of a highly subjective activity such as music consumption in relation to the construction of the 'local' and the formulation of local identities. How can the researcher ensure that the interpretation that he or she makes of such consumption patterns is accurate and not simply a value judgement or fabrication? While such problems may also figure in studies focusing on music-making, the physical fact of the music itself at least acts as a touchstone via which the researcher is able to test particular ideas concerning the relationship of music to the local. Indeed, as is evidenced by Cohen's (1991) study of music-making in Liverpool, instances of local music production clearly imbibe a strong and easily discernible conscious, emotional investment in particular representations of local spaces. It is, however, difficult to make the same claims of the nuances present in local patterns of music consumption. Nevertheless, on the strength of my own ethnographic-based research into local patterns of music consumption, it does seem to me that consumers are in general more aware of the local arrangements around which their musical worlds are arranged than is generally acknowledged. At the most fundamental level, individuals will often identify their motives or offer justification for preferring a particular music and its attendant sensibilities of style using a characteristically local frame of reference. Making a similar point, Pickering and Green have argued that social actors:

selectively and creatively adopt and adapt particular songs according to
their own criteria of how they can serve their own 'way of thinking and
feeling'... Songs constitute ways of handling the empirically experienced
world, as do all imaginative acts and relationships... supporting or
challenging 'how things are', or how they are represented ideologically
(1987, p. 3).

Pickering and Green's observations effectively illustrate the close
relationship between musical experience and the everyday lives of music
consumers. Indeed, as subsequent chapters of this study will endeavour
to show, in some instances musical tastes and accompanying consumption patterns are quite deliberately fashioned in such a way as to enable
the clear articulation of collective attitudes or statements that respond
directly to everyday situations experienced in specific localities.
Moreover, while such messages are sometimes transmitted in a publicly
visible and audible fashion through the mediums of dress and musical
preference, they are also frequently circulated only in the context of
closed communication systems existing between those who choose to
participate in specific events. This is clearly illustrated, for example, in
Chapter 4's study of contemporary urban dance music forms such as
house, techno and *jungle*. With reference to ethnographic research on the
urban dance music scene in Newcastle upon Tyne, England, I illustrate
how, through their participation in select 'club' events and privately
arranged 'informal' house parties, the members of this scene celebrate a
shared underground sensibility that is designed to challenge the
perceived oppression and archaism of Newcastle's official night-time
economy and the coercive strategies of the local police force. The
chapter also draws upon examples from other studies of local dance
music scenes in Britain and Germany and examines some of the parallel
musical and stylistic sensibilities identified by these studies.

In Chapter 5, I consider how the Asian folk–pop fusion style
'bhangra', said by both journalists and academics to be the soundtrack
for a new Asian youth 'subculture' in Britain, is actually being used in a
complex and often contradictory series of ways by young Asians in
Britain whose perception of bhangra's social significance is grounded in
the local circumstances of their everyday lives. Referring again to
ethnographic material collected in Newcastle, I illustrate how local
circumstances are shaping the social use of bhangra by local Asian
youth in two main ways. On the one hand, bhangra is used by young
Asians in the city to articulate forms of identity which orientate around
notions of 'tradition' in a local environment that remains largely

indifferent to ethnic minority groups and where racist stereotypes are often used. On the other hand, certain forms of response to bhangra signify the attempt by many young Asians to break away from the restrictions placed upon them by their respective parent cultures. Again, the material presented in this chapter is supplemented by the findings of studies that have considered the social significance of bhangra in other British cities, notably, Birmingham and London.

Chapter 6 presents a comparative study of how the globally established culture of hip hop has been appropriated and adapted by young people in Newcastle and in Frankfurt am Main, Germany. In the case of Frankfurt, hip hop is seen to provide a powerful soundtrack for statements concerning issues of racism and citizenship while in Newcastle local hip hoppers deliver cutting social statements on what they perceive as the 'narrow-mindedness' of the local mainstream 'townie' youth. During the course of Chapter 6, I also examine work on other local hip hop scenes in Italy, France, Southern Ireland, Sweden, Australia and Japan and consider the various forms of local significance that hip hop has assumed in these countries. Finally, Chapter 7 looks at the issue of live music in a local context. Focusing on the Benwell Floyd, a Pink Floyd 'tribute' band from Newcastle, I consider how through the live performances of the Benwell Floyd Pink Floyd music is becoming interwoven with the pub and club culture of the Newcastle and the wider northeast England region. The music of the Benwell Floyd, I will argue, plays an important role in the maintenance of kinship and friendship networks while simultaneously being used as a way of celebrating local identity in the face of deindustrialisation and economic hardship.

During this chapter, I have begun to consider the significance of popular music as a local cultural resource. Beginning with an overview of the various ways in which the relationship of popular music to the local has been conceptualised in existing sociological work, I then began to establish the theoretical basis for my own study. Using concepts of space and place drawn from the socio-geographical work of writers such as Slobin, Straw, Massey and Hetherington, I have begun to argue that the *local*, rather than constituting a 'fixed' space, is in fact a highly contested terrain. I have further argued that, from the point of view of the young, forms of popular music and their accompanying stylistic innovations are one of the key ways in which local spaces can be appropriated and made habitable. Music and style, I have suggested, function as mediums via which young people can negotiate those aspects of the local that they find least appealing while at the same time fashioning new forms of local identity that simultaneously draw upon the global and the vernacular. In Part II of this book, I will attempt to map out in more detail the relationship between locality and the social uses of popular music which I have begun to consider here – beginning with an exploration of the cultural significance of urban dance music in a local context.

Part II

Local Representations: Case Studies

Chapter 4

Dance Music, Local Identity and Urban Space

The term 'urban dance music' refers to contemporary forms of DJ-orientated music, such as *house* and *techno* (see Redhead: 1993a), which since the late 1980s have broadened the sphere of dance music culture considerably, removing its 'disco' and 'mainstream' connotations and elevating it to the status of a 'serious' music in which debates concerning issues of authenticity (Thornton: 1995) are comparable with those that characterised the progressive rock and punk scenes of the 1970s (see Frith: 1983; Laing: 1985). In many respects, the issue of contemporary urban dance music provides an ideal starting point for an empirical investigation of the relationship between youth, musical taste, locality and identity. Initially characterised by a series of illegal mass gatherings in disused inner-city industrial buildings and, on occasion, remote rural locations, concentrated media attention and police intervention, culminating in the implementation of the Criminal Justice and Public Order Act 1994, have resulted in the original urban dance music scene fragmenting into a number of smaller club-based scenes which spill over into low-key DIY events centred around house parties. Similarly, the general diversification of urban dance music, as new styles have been developed and promoted in different cities and regions around Britain, has also contributed to the fragmentation of the original dance music scene into smaller, more localised scenes. Furthermore, if urban dance music has always involved the appropriation of urban space, such an appropriation has in turn given rise to a highly nuanced form of discourse between the music, its spaces of consumption and the collective identities of urban dance music enthusiasts.

My analysis of urban dance music covers three main issues. In the first instance, I examine the origins of urban dance music, its introduction into British clubs and its reception, both by young clubbers and the media. I will then go on to consider some of the stylistic qualities that underpin urban dance music, particularly its bricoleurist quality, which, as will be demonstrated, is the result of relatively recent technological advances in the process of music production that allow for the borrowing and reworking of musical fragments from a variety of sources. In further considering this characteristic of urban dance music, however, I will argue that, while it has given urban dance music a broad appeal, as indicated by the range of different style groups that converged at some of the early urban dance music events, it does not, as has been suggested, signal the break-up of a former 'subcultural tradition' but rather serves to highlight the shifting and eclectic sensibilities of style and taste that have increasingly characterised the appropriation of popular music styles since the formation of the post-Second World War youth market. In putting forward this argument, I will draw on Maffesoli's (1996) concept of *tribus* (tribes). I will then consider how the 'tribalised' identities that I identify in the context of urban dance music culture work within the context of the particular local settings in which they are lived out. With reference to empirical examples drawn from my own study of the local urban dance music scene in Newcastle, I will endeavour to demonstrate how the sensibilities that inform this scene are infused with forms of local knowledge and experience shared by those individuals who participate in it. In particular, I will be concerned to illustrate how local urban dance music enthusiasts use their acquired musical taste as a way of resisting the felt oppressions of particular cultural and authoritative institutions that combine to shape the character of Newcastle nightlife. My analysis of the relationship between dance music and local space will also draw upon the findings of similar studies carried out in London, Berlin, Leipzig and Chicago.

Acid house and the 'second' summer of love

The urban dance music scene in Britain is generally argued to date back to 1987 with the beginnings of 'acid house' and the series of illegal festivals or *raves* that followed in its wake, the so-called 'Second Summer of Love'.[1] 'House', the music from which 'acid house' acquires its name, is a style pioneered by DJs in Chicago gay clubs during the late 1970s (Rietveld: 1997) in which original music – composed using state-of-the-art digital technology (see Negus: 1992) – is 'mixed' together with existing dance records, typically on vinyl, to produce entirely new sounds and tonal textures. Young Britons first experienced house music during the mid-1980s in dance clubs on the island of

Ibiza. According to Melechi, young British holiday-makers wishing to escape the over-anglicised character of the island's main resort, San Antonio, travelled 'beyond the brochure to Ibiza Town... where the tourist could enjoy anonymity whilst settling into [a] twelve hour cycle of clubbing [in which an] eclectic mishmash of Peter Gabriel, Public Enemy, Jibaro and the Woodentops [was] fused together' (1993, p. 31). House's introduction into British clubs coincided with the arrival in Britain of a new amphetamine-based stimulant known as Ecstasy or 'E' (Rietveld: 1993, p. 42).[2] The ensuing association of house music with Ecstasy resulted in the coining of the term *acid house* by media journalists, who immediately saw comparisons with the psychedelic movement of the mid-1960s (Russell: 1993).

As a direct consequence of the media attention that was focused upon it, acid house and the rave scene that it was inspiring became the centre of a new moral panic (Thornton: 1994). Nightclubs that featured rave events were subject to random spot checks by the police and in some cases had their licences revoked (Redhead: 1993a). Similarly, in 1991, Graham Bright MP's Entertainments (Increased Penalties) Act outlawed the staging of large-scale unlicensed raves and warehouse parties. Further restrictions were placed upon the rave scene with the implementation of the Criminal Justice and Public Order Act 1994, particularly section 63 of the Act which gives the police authority 'to remove persons attending or preparing for a rave' (p. 44). According to the Act, a rave may be classed as any 'gathering on land in the open air of 100 or more persons (whether or not trespassers) at which amplified music is played during the night' (ibid.). The Act further states that '"land in the open air" includes a place partly open to the air' while '"music" includes sounds wholly or predominantly characterised by the emission of a succession of repetitive beats' (pp. 44–5).

While the imposition of such legal sanctions has effectively put an end to large-scale rave events and 'warehouse parties', the musical styles that rave helped to establish have continued to flourish. Indeed, since the early 1990s, the term *rave* has become increasingly redundant as urban dance music has fragmented into a number of distinctive substyles, a scenario that is effectively captured by *The Face* magazine in an article entitled 'A Bluffer's Guide to Dance Music in the 1990s' (1993). Contemporary urban dance music now includes forms such as *techno*, *garage*, *ambient* and *jungle* in addition to house, which has itself became fragmented into a range of different forms including *deep house, piano house, happy house* and *hard house*. Moreover, this fragmentation of the urban dance music scene is occurring on a scale previously unwitnessed in the history of post-war popular music, a fact that continues to puzzle the mainstream music industry. Thus, as John Preston, former chairman of BMG (Bertelsmann Music Group), which owns Arista and RCA records, pointed out in an interview during 1993: 'We'd all love to find a new punk, a new unifying movement, but rock is continually rebelling against itself with more sub-categories' (Wittstock: 1993). The rapid and diversifying evolution of dance music is largely a result of new techniques in recording which have enabled a much greater manipulation of sound sources.

'It's all in the mix': urban dance music and technology

A major breakthrough in the commercial sound recording process came during the 1960s with the invention of multitrack recording which facilitated the layering of independently created sounds over the top of each other. As Frith explains: 'Producers could now work on the tape itself to "record" a performance that was actually put together from numerous, quite separate events, happening at different times' (1988a, p. 22). As a consequence, the recording studio, which up until this time had been used as a means of capturing an essentially 'live' performance on tape, was viewed increasingly as a central resource in the art of music-making itself. This was accompanied by the realisation that music produced in a studio 'need no longer bear any relationship to anything that can be performed live' (ibid.). Among the first commercial records to utilise the potential of the recording studio in this way were the Beach Boys' album *Pet Sounds* (1966) and the Beatles' *Sergeant Pepper's Lonely Heart's Club Band* (1967).[3] For a period during the late 1960s, these albums set an important trend as many rock bands became more studio orientated in their approach towards songwriting. In the context of rock music, however, this trend was relatively short lived, many bands subsequently reverting back to more *live* sounding albums or, alternatively, utilising parallel developments in PA[4] and sound processing techniques to re-create their studio-crafted albums in a live context. 'Studio-music' increasingly became the domain of electro-pop exponents, such as Giorgio Moroder and Vangelis, and experimental avant-garde artists, notably Kraftwerk, Tangerine Dream and Brian Eno, who continued to expand the limits of recording technology during the 1970s. Significantly, many contemporary urban dance music producers and DJs claim to have been heavily influenced by such artists (Laing: 1997, p. 129).

It was with the invention of digital recording during the early 1980s, however, that the crucial foundations were laid for the current urban dance music scene. Digital technology altered the nature of the recording process in two important ways. First, it allowed for sound to be stored in a computer memory thus eliminating the earlier problem of 'white noise'[5] as well as enabling a more accurate level of synchronisation between instruments and sounds recorded at different times. Second, digital technology also facilitated the development of a computerised 'triggering' system referred to as MIDI (Musical Instrument Digital Interface). MIDI enables a musical instrument or sound to be interfaced, that is electronically connected, with an infinite number of *samples*[6] with the effect that when the instrument is played or the sound produced the sampled sounds are also simultaneously triggered. Thus, as Negus points out, MIDI allows for music to be made 'within a computer's memory without the need of an acoustic environment in the studio. Hence, a composition could be produced in a confined space via the technology and the mixing desk. "Studio" quality recording can now [therefore] take place in any location' (1992, p. 25).

In addition to its influence upon modes of music production, digital recording has also had a considerable impact upon the nature of music itself. Digital recording techniques allow for a much wider manipulation of sound sources than was previously possible. Thus, bass lines, drum patterns, vocal and instrumental passages from existing records can now be sampled and seamlessly recombined into entirely new musical pieces (Beadle: 1993). In the following extract, an amateur dance music composer and producer, whom I interviewed in the course of my research, describes his own particular approach to composition:

> When I start to write I try to get a rhythm track down first and then work from there. Sometimes I can get something together myself and sometimes I just take someone else's drum loop. For example, the thing that's playing in the background at the moment is taken from a Black Sabbath song. So, I'm using that drum loop to trigger some of my own samples. Then I'll programme in my own bass line. After that I might add some brass stabs into the track, let's say for argument's sake from an old Motown track. Then I might sample some pan pipes or a good sixties guitar break from somewhere and use that a couple of times in the track as well.

Interestingly, many popular music theorists have considered urban dance music, or rather the recording and sampling techniques upon which it is based, primarily in terms of the challenge that this is seen to pose to notions of authorship. Thus, for example, Frith has argued that 'what is going on here is the systematic dismantling of the belief system that sustained rock 'n' roll, the idea that a recognizable person (or group of persons) made a specific noise' (1988b, p. 124). It seems to me, however, that what is at issue here is not the origins or ownership of a piece of music. Indeed, as will be demonstrated shortly, for the most part urban dance music consumers continue to associate the musical fragments heard in urban dance mixes with their original composers or performers. Rather, urban dance music prises open the whole issue of musical taste and what it signifies for young people.

Urban dance music forces a similar questioning of the relationship between musical taste and visual style, particularly the way in which this relationship has been conceptualised in the work of the Birmingham Centre for Contemporary Cultural Studies (CCCS). A central contention of the CCCS was that music and style were bound together in a homological relationship which served as a medium for the articulation of particular 'subcultural' values (see Chapter 1). As noted in Chapter 1, a great deal of criticism has been directed against the CCCS's use of subcultural theory, much of which has been concerned with the empirical validity of the concept of 'subculture'. In the early 1990s, however, a different type of challenge was made against subcultural theory. Thus, in noting the visual style-mixing that occurred at some of the early raves, several theorists suggested that the arrival of urban dance music had led to a break up of the 'subcultural' tradition' as young people were seen to become far less concerned with the *fit* between visual style and musical taste. Redhead, for example, in discussing the impact of *acid house* upon youth observed how it involved a 'mixing [of] all kinds of styles on the same dance floor... attracting a range of previously opposed subcultures from football hooligans to New Age hippies' (1993b, p. 4). Similarly, Muggleton (1997) suggests that dance music culture is indicative of a new form of 'post-subcultural' youth.

It seems to me, however, that, rather than signalling the end of a subcultural 'tradition', urban dance music opens up entirely new ways of understanding how young people perceive the relationship between musical taste and visual style. This negates the notion of a fixed homological relationship revealing instead the infinitely malleable and interchangeable nature of the latter as they are appropriated and realised by individuals as aspects of consumer choice to be woven into a personal system of identity politics. While this is not to completely dismiss the idea that a form of symmetry can exist between an individual's image and the nature of his or her taste in music, what it does serve to illustrate is that the relationship between musical taste and visual image is much less rigidly defined than was once thought. Such a view is given added weight by the following extract from an interview with a former heavy metal fan and biker, whose account suggests that rather more fluid notions of musical taste and attendant visual image were in place long before the appearance of contemporary urban dance music forms. Thus, explains the interviewee:

> in the town where I grew up we were all rockers. We were leather clad, we were rockers. But it was during the punk thing and I used to like the Clash... eh and I clearly remember Donna Summer's 'I Feel Love' being one of the best songs of '76 or whenever it was and really, really liking it... and a lot of my friends liking it a lot as well, although it was actually still a bit weird to admit it... because we were all into Zep [Led Zeppelin] and Sabbath [Black Sabbath] and Thin Lizzy and all the rest. But now you've got people like Leftfield or the Chemical Brothers who are quite happy to pick up very heavy metal guitar riffs and throw that into a dance mix... or Primal Scream come along and they do a rock album and then other people get hold of that and remix that stuff and eh, people will go and listen to it and they're quite happy to dance to it... I think dance music culture has allowed people to be quite open about the fact that they actually quite like a lot of different stuff. I've never been able to understand the divisions in music. I'm quite happy to go from Orbital to Jimi Hendrix.

As this interview extract serves to illustrate, the relationship between musical taste and visual style, rather than assuming a quintessentially fixed character, has typically been understood by young people as a rather more loosely formulated sensibility. In consuming popular music the individual is free to choose, not only between various musical styles and attendant visual images, but also how such choices are lived out and what they are made to stand for. Moreover, in choosing certain musical styles and visual images, the forms of association and social gatherings in which young people become involved are not rigidly bound into a 'subcultural' community but rather assume a more fluid, neo-tribal character.

Urban dance music and neo-tribalism

Young men with shaved heads and pigtails, stripped to the waist, are executing vaguely oriental hand movements. Freeze-framed by strobes in clouds of dry ice, revivalist hippies and mods are swaying in the maelstrom. Rastas, ragga girls, ravers there is no stylistic cohesion to the assembly, as there would have been in the (g)olden days of youth culture. So what is this noise that has united these teenage tribes? (Willis: 1993).

In attempting to understand the relationship between musical taste, visual style and identity as this manifests itself in urban dance music culture, Maffesoli's concept of *tribus* (tribes) provides a particularly useful theoretical model. Coincidentally, within urban dance music itself there is a heavy reliance upon the use of tribal images and terminology. Hesmondhalgh (1995), for example, has drawn attention to the images of tribalism and primitivism evident in the names of urban dance music artists such as Loop Guru while one of the leading 'rave affiliations [of] the early nineties' called itself Spiral Tribe' (McKay: 1996, p. 109). Similarly, in May 1995, a commercially organised outdoor dance party held near Oxford in the south of England went under the title UK Tribal Gathering 95 (Smith: 1995). Maffesoli's work on *tribus*, however, conceptualises the term *tribe* in a rather different sense to the more familiar anthropological usage that informs its various appropriations and applications within the urban dance music scene.

Maffesoli uses the concept of *tribus* to illustrate the shifting nature of collective associations between individuals as societies become increasingly consumer orientated (1996, pp. 97–8). Thus, according to Maffesoli, the tribe is 'without the rigidity of the forms of organization with which we are familiar, it refers more to a certain ambience, a state of mind, and is preferably to be expressed through lifestyles that favour appearance and form' (ibid., p. 98). Hetherington has further suggested that tribalisation involves 'the deregulation through modernization and individualization of the modern forms of solidarity and identity based on class occupation, locality and gender... and the recomposition into 'tribal' identities and forms of sociation' (1992, p. 93). Shields adds to this description of tribes in arguing that tribal identities serve to illustrate the temporal nature of collective identities in modern consumer society as individuals continually move between different sites of collective expression and 'reconstruct' themselves accordingly. Thus, according to Shields: 'Personas are "unfurled" and mutually adjusted. The performative orientation toward the Other in these sites of social centrality and sociality draws people together one by one. Tribe-like but temporary groups and circles condense out of the homogeneity of the mass' (1992, p. 108). Despite their common acknowledgement of *tribus* as a model for the explanation of the collective lifestyle orientations that characterise contemporary society, there is some disagreement between Shields and Hetherington as to how *tribus* should be framed in this context. Shields argues that *tribus* are 'best understood as 'postmodern tribes' or even pseudo-tribes' (see Maffesoli: 1996, p. x). Hetherington (1992), however, prefers the term neo-tribes. For the purposes of this study, I too refer to *tribus* as neo-tribes as this seems to me to most accurately describe the social processes with which Maffesoli was concerned.

In my view, processes of neo-tribalism are particularly well illustrated by urban dance music. As I have already shown, through its use of new types of technology, urban dance music has both radically altered approaches to musical composition and challenged existing notions of musical style. Indeed, such compositional trends no longer pertain merely to the urban dance music scene but are now seen to routinely inform artists working out of a range of other genres. New Age folk group the Levellers combine Irish folk sounds with heavy metal and punk guitar styles and blues harmonica, as well as incorporating more exotic instruments such as the Aboriginal didgeridoo. Similarly, a review of contemporary arranger and film scorer Anne Dudley's 1995 album *Ancient and Modern* comments upon the way in which the album combines the influence of the English choral and pastoral traditions with 'an eclectic mix which fuses elements from the world of commercial music'.[7]

Such shifts in compositional techniques are deemed by certain theorists to have elicited parallel shifts in the consumption patterns of music listeners. Thus, it is argued, the increasing eclecticism of contemporary music and the sampled soundtracks of urban dance mixes are breaking open and redefining conventional notions of musical taste as the individual enters a 'technological dreamscape of... reconstituted sound' (Melechi: 1993, p. 34). It seems to me, however, that such new compositional techniques, rather than radically altering the way in which consumers respond to music, are themselves rooted in the consumption habits of late modern music consumers. Sifting through various types of music, artists and sounds made available by the popular music industry, consumers characteristically choose songs and instrumental pieces that appeal to *them* with the effect that the stylistic boundaries existing between the latter become rather less important than the meaning that the chosen body of music as a whole assumes for the listener. Arguably, with the development of digital recording technology such forms of musical appropriation have been more forcibly demonstrated as contemporary composers and DJs, who are themselves working out of such eclectic consumer sensibilities, redirect the latter back into the processes of composition and performance.

Thus, rather than signifying the onset of a form of postmodern fragmentation in the tastes of music consumers, a view exemplified in Polhemus' notion of a 'Supermarket of Style' (1997, p. 150), it could be argued that urban dance music, as with other forms of contemporary music, draws upon and thus serves to underline an established and fundamental aspect of popular music consumption. Significantly, when the first urban dance music tracks began to appear there seemed to exist a ready made audience who displayed no apparent objections to the music's transcendence of conventional style boundaries. Indeed, a major aspect of urban dance music's continuing appeal appears to revolve around the consonance of its blatant appropriation and reassembling of stylistically diffuse hooks, riffs[8] and melodic phrases with the musical knowledges of its consumers. This latter observation is supported in the following extracts taken from interviews that I conducted with urban dance music enthusiasts:

Extract One

Rick: There's this club night thing once a week in Glasgow where they have some really good music on, it's more like a kind of acid house kind of thing. I've been there a couple of times. I was up there the other week and they dropped Bob Marley's 'Exodus' in the middle of this fast rave thing... it was like 'boom' [stamps foot to indicate a change in music's tempo and sings 'Exodus'] and everybody went 'whoa'... and it lasts for a couple of seconds and then the other stuff blasts right back in again. And it's like 'great, what's happening next?'.

Extract Two

A.B.: Dance music DJs put snatches of well-known pop songs into their mixes don't they?
John: Yeah, such as they'll be playing something quite hard and then they'll put something like Michael Jackson in... you know what I mean... and it's not like people think 'oh no' you know 'Michael Jackson' and clear the dance floor... it's just like 'oh yeah I recognise that, it's Michael Jackson'.
Susan: If it's done well, if it's chosen well [by the DJ] and it fits in with the music then it's really excellent.

To return to the concept of neo-tribalism, what comments such as those presented above begin to reveal is that musical taste is rather more loosely defined than has previously been supposed. The nature of musical taste, as with music itself, is both a multifaceted and distinctly fluid form of expression. Music generates a range of moods and experiences which individuals are able to move freely between. Urban dance music, because of the genre mixing involved in its production, serves to provide a series of 'snapshot' images of such fluid expressions of musical taste being exercised by consumers. Indeed, in many of the larger clubs that feature urban dance music nights, the desire of the consumer to choose from and engage with a variety of different musical moods has been further realised by using different rooms or floors as a means of staging a number of parallel events with club-goers free to move between these events as they please. Consequently, the nature of the urban dance music event is becoming increasingly a matter of individual choice, the type of music heard and the setting in which it is heard and danced to being very much the decision of the individual consumer. Significantly, such factors in turn have a marked influence on the way in which urban dance music enthusiasts talk about the actual process of clubbing. Thus, for many enthusiasts, clubbing appears to be regarded less as a singularly definable activity and more as a series of fragmented, temporal experiences as they move between different dance floors and engage with different crowds. This is clearly illustrated in the following extract from a discussion in which I asked a group of dance music enthusiasts to describe their experience of a particular club to me:

A.B.:   How would you describe 'Pigbag'? What kind of an event is it?
Diane: Well, I would say um, it's a different experience depending upon...
Shelly: Upon what's on...
Diane: What music's on and what floor you're on as well.
A.B.:   I know there are different things going on on each floor.
All: Yeah.
Rob: There's three types of thing going on actually. There's like the sort of café room which plays hip hop and jazz and then downstairs there's more singing sort of house music... and upstairs there's eh... well how could you describe that?

Debbie: Well it's quite sort of eh... the more housey end of techno
           music with sort of like trancey techno... the sort of easier,
           comfortable side of techno.
Diane: Yeah and then you'll get people moving between all three
           floors and checking out what's going on.

In my view, the patterns of music consumption shared by this group
of clubbers feed into and illustrate wider patterns of popular music
consumption, revealing the distinctly fluid, neo-tribal characteristics of
such forms of collective expression as these have been developing
during the past fifty years. If, however, such neo-tribal forms of
musicalised expression represent highly fluid and transient modes of
collective identity, at the same time they are not so fluid and transient
as to cancel out any form of meaningful interaction with the local
environments from which they emerge. On the contrary, neo-tribes
represent a means of engaging with and negotiating forms of everyday
life as these are encountered in given local settings. Thus, as Shields
points out, neo-tribes 'embrace... the "local" authority of what is "close
to home", based on local territoriality; dependable and micro-social'
(1992, pp. 108–9). With this in mind I want now to consider how the
neo-tribal sensibilities associated with urban dance music map onto
and are acted out in the context of particular urban locations.

Tribes of the underground: urban dance music and city spaces

As noted earlier, although urban dance music in Britain initially centred
around illegal mass gatherings in post-industrial urban locations and
remote rural areas, the implementation of the Criminal Justice and
Public Order Act 1994, combined with changes in the nature of urban
dance music itself as different styles have emerged in different regions
and cities, has resulted in the fragmentation of the wider urban dance
music scene into a number of smaller club and party-based scenes. This
in turn has introduced a new element of 'micro-social' politics into the
culture of urban dance music as clubbers articulate their commitment
to a particular dance music style, club or event in a language designed
to construct a sense of place within a particular set of 'local' circumstances; a particular 'version' of everyday life. This point is supported by
Straw's observation that 'the composition of audiences at dance clubs is
likely to reflect and actualize a particular state of relations between
various populations and social groups, as these coalesce around specific
coalitions of musical style' (1991, p. 379).

In the case of Newcastle upon Tyne, where much of the research for this study was conducted, the local urban dance music scene is characterised by what can best be described as a distinctive form of 'underground' sensibility. Again, while the term 'underground' may generally be taken, in its socio-musical context, to imply 'a grey area between music and social protest', it could be argued that the precise meaning of 'underground' will depend very much upon the nature of the particular social context in which it is articulated (Fountain: 1988, p. 52). On the basis of my research, it seems to me that the ideological touchstone for the underground sensibility that informs the urban dance music scene in Newcastle is the continual struggle in which enthusiasts in the city must engage in order to win space for the staging of urban dance music events and the various local interests that would appear to oppose, both directly and indirectly, the staging of such events.

The immediate problem facing those groups who wish to promote the growth of urban dance music in Newcastle is the distinct lack of an established network of *alternative* clubs in the city. One attempted solution to this problem has been the utilisation of existing clubs as a means of establishing a local urban dance music scene. This has generally involved urban dance music DJs or groups of enthusiasts approaching particular clubs and seeking permission to stage events, which, if they prove to be moderately successful in commercial terms, have been allowed to continue. Consequently, a number of venues on the mainstream club circuit in Newcastle now offer 'specialist' nights on which particular urban dance music styles such as *house* and *techno* are featured. However, these tend to be once-weekly or even once-monthly events and are generally held on a Monday, Tuesday or Wednesday evening as a means of generating extra income for the clubs. With the notable exception of one local venue, which, as I will demonstrate shortly has become something of a focus for urban dance music devotees, on Friday and Saturday evenings the majority of nightclubs in Newcastle revert to a more traditional nightclub atmosphere combining late-night drinking with a staple repertoire of contemporary chart music.

Clearly then, the physical nature of Newcastle nightlife, its spaces and resources, together with the ways in which these spaces and resources are characteristically used by the majority of local youth, is such that the scope that currently exists for the realisation of an urban dance music club scene in the city is, on the whole, fairly minimal. Thus, as a local techno fan explained to me:

It's a very limited scene here. You get people from the outlying areas coming into the town on a Friday and Saturday as you always have... I mean that's exactly what the Bigg Market's[9] all about really isn't it? But away from the Bigg Market and the disco nightclubs, I'll call them 'cause that's what they are really, there's not much of a youth-led movement really and certainly there's not much of an alternative scene... it's difficult to get that kind of space. If you want a good techno night out, they're few and far between in Newcastle... The dance scene is such a massive church, it's got so many different elements to it and many of those elements just don't seem to get much of an airing in Newcastle.

Such sentiments were in turn echoed by a number of other interviewees. In each case, the dominant influence of the traditional pub and club culture in Newcastle was identified as the most singularly apparent reason for the failure of an alternative club scene to thrive in the city. This view was summed up neatly by one young male interviewee who offered the following observation: 'In this town any place that sells beer will be full. Newcastle has never felt the need to embrace the underground club culture.' Hollands has suggested that the prevalence of such a drinking culture in Newcastle has gained added significance in recent times as a means of articulating a notion of local identity associated with Newcastle's industrial past. According to Hollands, in the context of Newcastle, the culture of drinking and its resonance with the notion a working man's weekend 'symbolises or stands in for a particular way of life that is no longer possible' (1995, p. 56). In turn, however, acceptance of such behaviour as the 'norm' in and around the centre of Newcastle informs a decidedly negative attitude to any type of club activity that attempts to break with this 'traditional' pattern of weekend leisure. During the course of my research in Newcastle, I interviewed the manager of a club that had been raided by the police on the pretence that the *house* music event taking place in the club on that particular evening was a 'rave' and therefore a potential site for drug abuse. The raid served to strengthen in the minds of regulars at the club the idea that their scene was the subject of unfair victimisation on the part of the Newcastle police.

Smith's research on youth culture in Leipzig, a city in the former eastern sector of Germany often referred to as 'the dance capital of the East', illustrates similar opposition to local dance music clubs. Thus explains Smith, following staunch opposition and stigmatisation on the part of the police and local authorities during the years of communist rule, post-1989 youth in Leipzig found that their cultural space was similarly threatened by capitalist property agencies who wished to redevelop many of those areas in which clubs and venues were situated. The local authorities put increasing pressure on young people to vacate such areas and looked for reasons to close down clubs and venues. This move, however, prompted collective resistance on the part of young dance music enthusiasts in the city. Thus, when on one particular occasion the local council closed down a much frequented dance music club 'because of fire regulations and licensing problems [the club's clientele] took their party to the square outside the town hall until the council helped to find an alternative site' (1998, p. 301).

While the dance music scene in Newcastle cannot lay claim to such direct forms of protest, the continual pressure to which the scene is subjected has led to an equally distinctive local sensibility among the city's dance music followers that centres around the collective belief that the Newcastle urban dance music scene is 'at the edge', that it occupies a precarious and threatened space bordered by an archaic, machoistic drinking culture on the one side and a coercive local policing strategy on the other. This in turn has served to create a particularly strong and distinctive form of neo-tribal bond between individuals who participate in urban dance music events in the city. Thus, although they may in some cases be only vaguely familiar to each other, as these individuals move between the various sites that comprise the Newcastle dance music scene, they share an intimate understanding of these sites as spaces of defiance against what they commonly perceive to be negative or oppressive aspects of the local social environment. A parallel example of such localised neo-tribalism is identified by Rietveld in her study of the Chicago house scene. Thus she argues, within the space of the weekend club event:

> new identities could be forged that were not necessarily there to be sustained throughout the rest of the week. The dance, the music, even the club itself were built for that moment in the weekend, to disappear once it had occurred. However, the sense of community and of a shared 'conspiracy' it created, as well as the force of the experience, could give you a greater confidence in a private identity constructed outside a mainstream (1997, pp. 127–8).

Such processes of neo-tribal identification in urban dance music culture are also central to a study by Malbon. According to Malbon, such forms of identification are articulated, and thus reinforced, through shared 'practices of performance [that]... constitute the glue which acts to bind the disparate personae together encapsulating the customs, traditions and norms that go to make clubbing a distinctive form of social interaction' (1998, p. 276). It follows that such in-club practices may also form links with other practices, knowledges and discourses which clubbers bring with them into the club environment and whose point of origin is distinctively local. Thus, in addition to informing patterns of conduct within club settings, the in-club practices of dance music enthusiasts may, as Rietveld implies, form very real connections with the kinds of circumstance and experience that they encounter in their everyday lives and may be used as a way of negotiating such circumstances and experiences. This dialectical relationship between club cultural sensibilities and sensibilities acquired in the wider local environment is clearly apparent within the Newcastle dance music scene, particularly in relation to the scene's rhetoric of 'otherness'.

'Pigbag': dancing in the 'divided' city

'Pigbag', like many other urban dance music features in Newcastle, is a once-weekly event. This said, however, there are several factors which set 'Pigbag' apart from other urban dance music club events in the city. To begin with, 'Pigbag' takes place on a Saturday evening, a time when, as I have previously noted, club space in Newcastle is given over primarily to the city's traditional weekend club clientele. Furthermore, as this scenario would suggest, the venue in which Pigbag is staged, The Waterfront, although a well-known and established club, is at the same time both musically and stylistically distinct from other clubs in Newcastle. Thus, while the majority of clubs in the city tend to view alternative forms of music merely as a means of generating extra profit on mid-week evenings, The Waterfront has traditionally had a strong commitment to the promotion of alternative music. Indeed, it is in this spirit that the club made the decision to feature urban dance music events. Thus, as the manager of The Waterfront explained to me:

> Our traditional market is indie music and live indie bands... but the music scene's changing... I mean there's the dance culture now, people of 18 have grown up with dance culture... they haven't grown up with live music culture... So we're looking more at clubnights now... because that's what young people want. Our house night on Saturday [Pigbag] is a good quality dance music night.

That last observation, regarding the 'quality' of the Pigbag event, was strongly endorsed by those who attended it. In particular, there was a firm belief among the young people whom I interviewed that the efforts of The Waterfront to hire in good quality DJs are 'what the dance music scene is all about really'. If a major aspect of urban dance music's appeal is its deeply eclectic nature, then equally important is the skill of the DJ in taking dance music tracks and blending them together in such a way that the music produced resonates with the mood of the audience. The need for the DJ to be able to connect with the audience in this way is also central to the dancer's desire for 'absolute absorption in the music' (Pini: 1997, p. 159). If dance music is regarded as an avenue for heightened sensations of pleasure and excitement, then dance itself is considered to be a form of expression for such sensations. Clearly then, if the DJ fails to read his audience correctly, the point of the whole event is essentially lost. Thus, as one young female dance music enthusiast put it: 'You can really tell the difference between the DJ who's checking how they're affecting the crowd and the DJ who's not really bothered and is just going through the motions... Even when you just walk into a club, you can sometimes just tell whether a DJ's in touch with the crowd or not.' Langlois has noted how some of the more well-known dance music DJs 'command their own following who will go to hear them rather than to any particular club' (1992, p. 234). Indeed, the status enjoyed by the most successful dance music DJs is similar to that of established rock performers. In dance music, the role of the DJ is not simply to provide a continuous sequence of dance tracks, but to be actively involved in the creation of the music and the mood of the club event. According to Dave Haslam, an experienced club DJ: 'DJ-ing is evangelism; a desire to share songs... you work the records, mix them, drop them, cut them, scratch them, melt them, beat them all together until they unite' (1997, p. 169).

For many Pigbag regulars, it was the quality of the DJs that, more than anything else, guaranteed Pigbag's stamp of exclusivity, thus setting it, and those who frequented it, apart from the urban dance music events that took place in the more mainstream clubs in Newcastle. This is clearly illustrated in the following account from another young female urban dance music devotee whose evaluation of Pigbag rests on her experience of attending mid-week urban dance music events in the city centre:

> There are similar events [to Pigbag] but there's nothing that gives you the sort of selection of musical styles within dance music. Kiss does a sort of copy type of event, but they don't get the sort of DJs that you would expect if you were somebody who really liked house music and you were

concerned about who was playing what records... So it wouldn't be classed as the same 'cause they're the sort of DJs that nobody's really heard of. Then you've got places like 'Venus' where they do have better DJs but only a certain group of them... they haven't got the sort of turnover in DJs and the things that you would expect from a proper house club that's bringing you the new changes in house music.

There is a clear correspondence between these comments and Thornton's concept of club cultural 'capital'. According to Thornton, 'name' DJs and their particular music styles are one of the ways in which dance club cultures mark themselves out from what they consider to be more 'mainstream' scenes. Thornton further suggests that 'the rightness and naturalness' of club crowds also act as important markers of collective exclusivity; as ways in which clubbers differentiate their scene from others that are deemed to blur into the homogenous mass of a bland and undiscriminating mainstream (1995, p. 111). Again, such a sensibility was clearly in evidence among the Pigbag regulars whom I interviewed. Thus, the Pigbag atmosphere was seen to act as a form of barrier which was not easily penetrated by those who were not part of the dance music scene. The specialist nature of the music and the relationship between the DJ and the crowd, it was argued, was such that genuine appreciation of the Pigbag event demanded a form of total absorption on the part of the individual. Such absorption, Pigbag regulars suggested, did not apply to more conventional types of club setting where the music, although danced to, also invariably acted as a backdrop for other forms of social behaviour, notably, talking and drinking. The type of music featured at Pigbag and the special way in which this connected with the crowd was deemed to ensure, therefore, that the event remained a protected space.

To some extent this was also guaranteed by the physical location of The Waterfront club itself. Set some considerable distance away from the centre of Newcastle, the club's spatial isolation served to prevent intrusion from city-centre clubbers or 'townies'[10] as they were often referred to. Rietveld provides a similar explanation for the success of Chicago dance club The Warehouse, from which the term *house* allegedly derives. Thus, argues Rietveld, the setting of The Warehouse 'away from any mainstream leisure area of Chicago, and its management policies and audience showed an attitude which enhanced its special and underground character' (1997, p. 126). A comparable 'underground' sensibility was apparent among those who frequented Pigbag. Moreover, given that a small number of clubbers from

Newcastle's city centre club scene did on occasion come into The Waterfront on a Saturday evening, the specialist nature of the music that they encountered there, combined with the Pigbag crowd's failure to observe the more conventional traits of club behaviour associated with the club scene in the centre of Newcastle, was deemed to exclude such individuals from participating in the event. Thus, as Joe, another Pigbag 'regular', explained to me:

> The people who come here do so because they specifically like the kind of music... and the kind of atmosphere that comes with this kind of music. You don't get people going 'where shall we go tonight? Oh I know, let's go there [to Pigbag] and get pissed!' It's not that kind of a thing. It's a specialist night for people who are into this sort of thing. So you don't get many pissheads in. You see them occasionally, but they don't understand what it's all about so they don't generally come back again.

Such *integral* processes of exclusion were also considered important because of the potential threat of violent and sexist behaviour which *outsiders* from the city centre club scene were deemed to present. Unwritten traditions of non-violent and non-sexist behaviour appear to be a central aspect of urban dance music culture with the effect that dance music events are, on the whole, 'typified by behaviour which is less aggressive, machoistic and violent than more conventional nightclubs' (Merchant and MacDonald: 1994, p. 22). This is a particularly appealing aspect of urban dance music events from the point of view of female clubbers in that they enjoy a freedom from the forms of male harassment often experienced by women in more conventional nightclub settings. Indeed, Russell has suggested that central to the ethos of urban dance music is a total rejection of 'the dated 70s notion of the disco as a meat market' (1993, p. 98). Again, such unwritten traditions are argued by many urban dance music enthusiasts to relate closely to the music itself or rather to result from the type of mindset that one who is 'truly into the music' acquires when dancing to it. Speaking about the non-sexist and non-violent atmosphere at Pigbag and other urban dance music events, a number of the young people I spoke to suggested that the 'happy' sound of the music unequivocally communicates a similar feeling to its devotees. Thus, as one young male interviewee explained: 'You just can't imagine getting angry. The music really makes you happy... you just want to dance about and jump up and down like a loony.'

Other interviewees, while maintaining the notion that such feelings bespeak a quality intrinsic to the music itself, at the same time suggested a more immediate link between the value placed by individuals upon this aspect of the urban dance music event and the opportunity that it presents to temporarily escape the oppressive atmosphere that they associate with Newcastle. According to these young people, however much urban dance music imparts its own form of 'feel good' sensibility upon those present at the Pigbag event, the individual's endorsement of this sensibility is accompanied by the deeper feeling that it in some way cuts against the grain of the aggressive *townie* sensibility deemed to hold sway in Newcastle and to dominate the leisure spaces made available to young people in the city, particularly on a Friday and Saturday night. This sentiment is clearly illustrated in the following discussion group extract:

Jason: The point is right, you put up with this hassle all the time. You never know when you might be threatened with 'aggro' right. By the time the weekend comes around you've had enough of all that, you're ready for something else, you're ready to party.

Pete: Yeah, that's right. You wanna party in as silly a way as possible like.

Jason: So you just get down to Pigbag and that's it. Whoosh!... and off you go. Everyone down there's the same, all giving it loads 'cause it's just a top laugh and that's what you need at the end of the week, a top laugh. It's pointless coming down unless you're up for that.

For these young people then, the dance music sensibility that they describe serves to consolidate the distance they perceive to exist between themselves and city centre clubbers and also offers a further form of barrier against intrusions by the latter. This collective belief is further enhanced by the notion that the type of dance engaged in at Pigbag is 'pure' dance and a form of total engagement with the music as opposed to the types of exhibitionist dancing which are deemed to characterise clubs in the city centre. DiMaggio has suggested that social dancing signifies 'a means of constructing social relations (and knowing what relationships need to be constructed). It helps to establish networks of trusting relations that facilitate group mobilization' (1987, p. 443). Similarly, Hanna argues that: 'Dance may function like swearing – as a form of release. The non-verbal mode... is more powerful than the verbal for expressing such fundamental feelings in social relationships as liking, disliking, superiority, timidity, fear and so on' (1992, p. 179). A more developed interpretation of dance, particularly in the context of this study, is offered by Novack who suggests that: 'A dance performance... is always a cultural performance as well. Dance is a form of meaning and action, and like all culture is multivoiced and flexible' (1990, p. 14).

Novack's observations imply that, as with other forms of cultural expression, the cultural meaning of dance is partly inscribed by social actors themselves. This view is substantiated by my own observations of Pigbag and other urban dance music events in Newcastle where the type of dancing engaged in appears to form part of a closed communication system in which the dancers articulate non-verbal statements to each other concerning their collective sense of ideological distance from the kinds of patriarchal and machoistic sensibility around which the act of dancing in city centre clubs is believed to orientate. Moreover, in further comparing urban dance music events with more mainstream types of clubnight, it is interesting to note how the normal spatial divisions between dance floor and non-dancing areas merge together. Individuals routinely make use of any given space, including areas normally designated as seating areas, and thoroughfares such as flights of stairs connecting different floor levels or leading from the dance floor to the bar. Furthermore, given the fact that dancers appropriate spaces that other individuals may need to use, the latter, in crossing this space, will make every effort to ensure that the dancer remains undisturbed and accidental bodily contact is normally followed by a brief, generally non-verbal, expression of apology. That such modes of collective practice underpin a deeper political sensibility, via which participants in Newcastle's urban dance music scene demonstrate to each other their sense of 'otherness' from the types of sensibility that hold sway in the city centre clubs, is further illustrated in the following account given to me by a group of female Pigbag regulars. Similarly, this account also re-emphasises the point raised earlier concerning the non-sexist atmosphere that prevails at urban dance music events and their consequent special appeal for female enthusiasts:

Sandra: I remember when I first came out to Pigbag and sat there and just went 'ahh I've never seen anything like this before in mi' life'. The way people interact together... it's so friendly and so open. I'd never been anywhere like that before, I'd only ever been to a normal nightclub where you're...

Jane: Where you're worried about some guy coming up and saying 'all right luv!' [all laugh].

Sandra: And people are dancing exactly how they want to dance and not self-consciously, you know. I really like that about it... you don't feel as if you're being watched by other people.

Julie: People aren't going there just to watch a person of the opposite sex and to go over and try and chat them up and stuff... it's not for that sort of reason that people come to Pigbag.

Sandra: And it's really lovely at the end of the night when the lights go on and people don't scuffle off into the corners and go and hide and try to fix their make up or whatever... people are still dancing to the very last second that the music's on you know.

Pini's London-based study of women and dance music culture makes similar observations in relation to the progressive sexual politics that many women appear to associate with dance music events. Thus, according to Pini: 'The absence of heterosexual "pick-up" ("copping off", being "chatted-up" and so on) [is] central to many women's accounts of [dance music's] appeal to them' (1997, p. 160). In the same way that the interviewees in my own research compare their enjoyable experience of dance music events with negative experiences of more 'traditional' nightclub settings, Pini's interviewees also use their knowledge of the machoistic and aggressive male sensibilities encountered in such settings as a key point of reference when attempting to account for their preference for the non-sexualised nature of the dance floor relations that characterise urban dance music events.

In the social context of Newcastle then, Pigbag serves a number of important functions. Most obviously, it offers a regular weekend space for groups of individuals to gather and collectively celebrate their enthusiasm for urban dance music. At a deeper level, I would argue, Pigbag allows local consumers of urban dance music to articulate a collective show of neo-tribal defiance against the types of *townie* clubber sensibilities that they associate with Newcastle city centre and against which they are collectively opposed. From the point of view of those who attend Pigbag, the event offers a social space in which an alternative club culture to that which holds sway in the city centre can be temporally constructed. Moreover, because of the threat that local urban dance music devotees believe exists to their scene, the isolated location of the host venue for Pigbag, The Waterfront, together with the latter's own alternative roots, serves to emphasise the underground sensibility and locally articulated rhetoric of 'otherness' around which this scene has come to be organised.

At the same time, however, the local circumstances governing the frequency of urban dance music club events in Newcastle have also led many enthusiasts to look beyond the limited opportunities offered by the local club scene and to establish a form of DIY urban dance music scene organised around house parties and other 'occasional', informal venues. In some respects these two scenes overlap. Certainly, many of those who attend Pigbag and other local club-based urban dance music events are also familiar with the informal scene. By the same token, however, the informal dance music scene in Newcastle has a number of features that set it apart from the club-based scene. Moreover, this scene has its own particular story to tell concerning the local character of Newcastle and the ways in which urban dance music is being used to challenge what many dance music enthusiasts perceive as the more negative and oppressive features of the city.

'Fighting for the right to party': DIY urban dance music events

> The global party adapts to local environments – in Blackburn (in the industrial north of England) acid house parties happened in warehouses; in Berlin techno took over East German bunkers; in Wisconsin it's ski-slopes and... *cow sheds?* (Champion: 1997, p. 115).

In many ways, the informal urban dance music scene in Newcastle plays a more important role than that of the club-based scene. Certainly were it not for the occurrence of informal events, then the opportunities to consume urban dance music in the city would be markedly reduced. Moreover, whereas the club-based scene is restricted both spatially and temporally, informal urban dance music events operate without such restrictions, making use of a range of different sites and occurring in a relatively spontaneous fashion at times that extend beyond the opening hours of local clubs. During the course of my research, I attended around twelve informal urban dance music events in Newcastle and was informed of many other such events that were 'happening' around the city. The events that I attended took place in locations as diverse as a nurses' halls of residence building, a 'student house' in the district of Fenham (in west Newcastle) and a flat in Elswick (another district in west Newcastle) which was described to me as 'nobody's place in particular, just a "giro-drop"'.[11] The importance of informal venues is documented in several accounts of urban dance music scenes. Indeed, there is a clear link between Newcastle's informal venue network and Rietveld's description of the house party scene in Chicago, which, according to Rietveld, offered an alternative space for those 'who wanted to transcend the oppressing boundaries of a racist, homophobic and sexist world' (1997, p. 129). In the same way that the Chicago house parties responded to the more negative features of their given social context, so Newcastle's informal dance music scene could be said to perform a similar form of cultural work in relation to the felt oppressions of the local urban environment.

As noted above, in many respects informal urban dance music events in Newcastle act as a means of compensating for the lack of an established alternative club scene in the city. However, embedded within the DIY sensibility of those groups that organise such events exists the basis for a wider form of protest against the policy-making institutions that effectively govern Newcastle's night-time economy and wider network of leisure industries. Castells has suggested that individuals 'tend to consider cities, space, and urban functions as the mainspring for their feelings' and will often articulate such feelings by defining 'an alternative social organisation, an alternative space, an alternative city' (1983, pp. 326–7). A pertinent example of such symbolic urban transformation realised through urban dance music is the LOVEPARADE, a one-day dance music event which takes place in the streets of Berlin each summer. Richard and Kruger suggest that the LOVEPARADE represents a form of 'everyday politics [through which] ravers take control of Berlin's most culturally and geographically important thoroughfares' (1998, p. 171). While the essential motive of the LOVEPARADE, a campaign for world peace, differs substantially from that of the informal urban dance music scene in Newcastle, both movements are at the same time tied by a thread of commonality, that is, the reflexivity of their respective discourses with the local circumstances in which these scenes are situated. In the case of the LOVEPARADE, the urban spaces in which the festival is staged belong to the former East Berlin. Thus, the LOVEPARADE represents both a physical reclaiming of urban spaces in which such forms of collective cultural participation were once systematically prohibited and a symbolic form of protest against the continuation of such forms of oppression in other parts of the world.

In a similar, if less dramatic way, Newcastle's informal urban dance music scene could also be said to engage in both physical and symbolic forms of protest with the more oppressive features of the local social environment. Thus, it could be argued that the informal dance music scene in Newcastle, rather than simply offering a range of musical choices, which are not readily available in the city centre, symbolises a form of social critique in which the nature of local policy-making regarding club entertainment, particularly as this relates to licensing laws, is not only brought sharply into question but also actively challenged. Indeed, speaking to individuals who participate in informal urban dance music events in Newcastle, they were often deeply critical of what they considered to be the conservative and dated policies under which nightclubs in the city were operated. Consequently, the informal dance music scene was deemed to open up a space, or rather a series of spaces for the articulation of an *all-nighter* or *weekender* clubbing sensibility recognised by these individuals as centrally significant to the urban dance music ethos but felt by them to be systematically denied in Newcastle city centre. Thus, as one young man explained:

> Clubs should have the same entertainment licensing as in Europe. It's starting to happen here a bit more now, in places like London, Leeds and Manchester. Clubs like Back To Basics [in Leeds] go through till six in the morning... but the clubs in Newcastle end at two thirty. That's an insult on your civil liberties, if I'm down in London I won't even go out until around twelve or twelve thirty. That's why the party scene up here is so important. A lot of people view the house parties and stuff as sort of 'the club part two'... they come out of the clubs still pent up and want to carry on so they go to a party. But then again there are a lot of people who aren't interested in the clubs up here, because of the way they operate... so they just go to the parties.

As the above account begins to illustrate, there exists among those individuals who facilitate and participate in the informal urban dance music scene in Newcastle a clear commitment to constructing a version of dance music culture that corresponds more closely with their perception of how this culture *should* be. This is based partly upon a reading of other dance music scenes, both in Britain and abroad, but also draws upon an intimate knowledge of the Newcastle club scene and the forms of local authority that dictate the nature of this scene. Indeed, viewed from this perspective informal urban dance music events are particularly significant because of the sense of empowerment that they give to those who participate in them. Thus, if part of the appeal of the informal scene is that it acts to challenge the status quo of Newcastle's city centre club scene, then equally important are the 'hands on' opportunities which the facilitation of this informal scene offers to individuals. Those who help to organise events do so in the knowledge that they are at the same time contributing to the physical realisation of the alternative underground sensibility to which they subscribe.

Such 'hands on' experience can take a number of forms. Most importantly, perhaps, the physical realisation of the informal dance music scene relies upon the fast and efficient transformation of chosen locations for events into credible venues. The centrality of this task to the viability of the informal scene cannot be overlooked. If informal events are to successfully operate in a counter-cultural fashion to the entertainment policies of official nightclubs in Newcastle, they must be in a position to offer the 'informal' clubber a number of facilities that approximate those that one would normally find in an alternative nightclub. Such facilities include, for example, suitable decor, suitable lighting and other visual effects, an adequate sound system and a good range and quality of music. Additionally, many informal events will attempt to provide some form of facility for the provision of refreshments. Thus, as several interviewees pointed out to me, when 'done properly' such informal events can generate the feel and excitement of a club atmosphere but without the restrictions imposed by local licensing regulations. Indeed, the commitment of those who organise informal events to providing an atmosphere comparable with that which one might find in an alternative nightclub was obvious to me at many events that I attended. For example, at one particular event, held in a small three-roomed flat, the sound system and a team of Afro-Caribbean DJs had been specially hired in for the occasion from Manchester. When I later asked one of the organisers why they had gone to such trouble, he replied:

> Well, we wanted to put something very special on. Now, the type of stuff that was featured the other night is a new form of music that's coming through... that's making it in Manchester, Birmingham, Bradford and the like, which is called 'jungle'. There isn't anyone up here in the North East that actually plays that type of music. So it was really with a view to the music that was on offer that we set this thing up. We wanted the type of music which that system provided. And if you ask me, I think that it was very well appreciated. Just a change, something a bit different. You couldn't have got that kind of a sound system from Newcastle and that's part of the appeal really.

A second event that I attended boasted a similarly elaborate sound system, or rather a series of systems. Because of the location of the event, a three-storey house, a number of different dance events were being staged simultaneously, each floor of the house featuring a different style of music from the next, with individuals moving freely between different floors and engaging with different crowds and musical moods (this characteristic corresponding with the point made earlier regarding the fragmented, neo-tribal nature of such events). Moreover, all the windows of the house had been blacked out and large drapes hung from the walls of each room in order to create a more intimate atmosphere. Similarly, in keeping with what my interviewees had reported, all of these events could be classed as *all-nighters*. None of the informal dance music events which I attended ended before 6.00 a.m. and several carried on until around 10.00 a.m. Still more elaborate examples of informal 'dos' were described to me by enthusiasts whom I met at or through attending such events. As one young man explained:

> I've been to one in, now where was it... ah yeah in Jesmond [in west Newcastle]. It was a three-storey house and the first two floors were empty... every room was covered in bin liners and black plastic... they had TVs mounted on the walls all round the house showing nature videos and stuff... and then they had other things such as flashing lights... and they'd obviously hired in the sound system. Yeah, they really go to some effort... so when it's a decent sized house, if it's a good event you'll end up with six hundred people or so crammed in there.

As the above accounts begin to reveal, in much the same way that Pigbag was deemed to be an exclusive event by its devotees, so the informal dance music scene was also argued to be characterised by a form of exclusivity by those who facilitated the scene and participated in it. Again, the musical aspect of such events was felt by many to confirm their exclusive nature, hence the great effort invested in hiring in sound systems featuring forms of music not normally heard in Newcastle clubs. Indeed, my research revealed a further way in which such DIY urban dance music scenes may facilitate notions of otherness via the musicalised marking out of urban spaces. Earlier in this chapter I noted how the catalyst for contemporary urban dance music was the digital revolution in music recording techniques which took place during the mid-1980s. The availability of cheap but high quality digital recording equipment has led to a situation where music production, particularly in the case of urban dance music, is becoming increasingly decentralised from the mainstream recording industry. Thus, while urban dance music continues to be a commercial concern, there are in addition a growing number of *home* or *bedroom* recording enthusiasts producing music of a quality comparable with that which is created in professional studios. Such instances of grassroots music production form part of a growing network of informal entrepreneurial activities engaged in by the youth of post-industrial societies in the west. Smith and Maughan expand this point by suggesting that such low-key examples of dance music production form part of an alternative, post-Fordist music industry organised by young dance music enthusiasts themselves via a growing number of non-mainstream initiatives which, in addition to music-making, include 'setting up record labels, distribution companies, specialist record shops, agencies, artwork etc.' (1997, p. 21).

Such informal channels have the capacity to distribute the work of amateur producers over a wide area. Thus, for example, specialist dance music shops in Britain invariably have links with similar shops in other European countries and in the United States. However, as an employee from one of these shops explained to me, the amount of product that can be distributed via this network is relatively small. On average, he informed me, a record distributed in this way 'will probably sell globally around 2000 copies'. Consequently, for many amateur urban dance music producers, the remunerative incentive is often much less pronounced than a desire simply to have their music heard. As one amateur producer pointed out to me: 'This music will never be popular, it will never be mainstream but that's not the mission. The important thing is that people should have access to it.' As such, a more viable outlet for the product of amateur producers is found in local urban dance music scenes and, in particular, low-key informal events such as house parties where DJs may be more prepared to feature local product.

Indeed, it could be argued that in the context of such informal, local dance music events such home-grown music can also become an important symbol of exclusivity. When a style of urban dance music becomes strongly associated with a particular informal scene then it in turn becomes an indelible aspect of that scene's character, informing a sensibility that also permeates the collective identity of those who participate in it. Thus, for example, in speaking about the *jungle* scene in Manchester an interviewee who was familiar with this scene explained: 'There's a real link between some of that music and the local people... some of the jungle sound is just about the people in that area... 'cause it's a different style of music compared to even just the next estate or whatever.' The dialectical relationship between local identity and locally produced *jungle* is extensively addressed by Noys, who argues that jungle is grounded in the same forms of local urban experience or 'urban topographies' that inform the production, performance and consumption of hip hop (1995, p. 326). According to Noys, the spread of jungle across the UK from its point of origin in London has been facilitated by the establishment of local jungle record labels in the provinces each of which have 'their own distinctive sound' (ibid.). The result of this, according to Noys, is a complex mapping between music, identity and place which results in a 'cultural energy as well as that energy which results from a rootedness in space' (ibid., pp. 326–7). Clearly then, locally produced urban dance music and the often unique association of this music with those house parties and other informal events at which it is featured provides a further resource via which members of informal dance music scenes are able to define an alternative space and construct a collective sense of 'otherness'.

During the course of this chapter I have begun to consider the relationship that exists between locality, identity and music via an examination of contemporary urban dance music. Using examples drawn both from my own ethnographic study of the local urban dance music scene in Newcastle upon Tyne and from a range of similar studies, I have endeavoured to show how local contexts frame a series of sensibilities among urban dance music enthusiasts which have, in their turn, resulted in the construction of highly localised urban dance music scenes. In the case of Newcastle, I have been concerned to examine how such sensibilities serve to inform the negotiation and symbolic *marking out* of local spaces in which to stage urban dance music events in the face of a local power structure that remains unequivocally oppressive in its policies regarding the staging of such events and a dominant local drinking culture that effectively blocks the establishment of an alternative club scene in the city. Clearly it follows that if local knowledges are seen to play such a formative role in the collective uses of urban dance music, then they must also influence collective responses towards other genres. In Chapter 5, I want to examine the way in which local knowledges influence the responses of young people of South Asian origin towards bhangra and the other forms of South Asian dance music which are rapidly gaining popularity among Britain's South Asian population.

NOTES

1. The rave events of 1987 were collectively termed the 'Second Summer of Love' due to their occurrence precisely twenty years after the original hippie Summer of Love in 1967.
2. For informed studies of the drug Ecstasy see Merchant and MacDonald (1994) and Saunders (1995).

3. For an in-depth account of the making of *Sergeant Pepper* see Martin and Hornsby (1979, pp. 199–219).

4. PA is the abbreviated term for Public Address, an elaborate system of amplifiers, loudspeakers and sound processing equipment used in a concert situation to convey the sound of a group or performer's music to the audience as accurately as possible.

5. 'White noise' refers to the extraneous sounds, typically hissing and humming noises, accumulated on multitrack tape from sources such as electronic instruments, microphones and sound processing effects.

6. A sample is a digitally stored sound, musical or otherwise. Popular 'samples' include orchestral and piano sounds, drum sounds, industrial noise and everyday sounds such as traffic, birdsong and breaking glass.

7. Quoted from an advertisement in the *Guardian*, 17 February, 1995.

8. A *riff* is the term given to a short sequence of repeated notes, generally played on an electric guitar or bass, which can be said to characterise the song or piece of music in which it is featured. Notable examples of riff-based songs include the Rolling Stones' '(I Can't Get No) Satisfaction' and, more recently, Michael Jackson's 1983 hit 'Beat It'.

9. The Bigg Market, an area in the centre of Newcastle with a large number of pubs and clubs, is a very popular nightspot for young people (see Chapter 5).

10. The term *townie* would appear to be commonly used in Britain by followers of alternative styles of music as a way of setting themselves apart from those whose musical tastes/fashion sensibilities are more mainstream and who consequently frequent the more conventional bars and clubs – the latter generally being situated in city centres and thus making up the central or 'town' scene. For a further account of the townie – alternative division, see Beattie (1990, pp. 44–8).

11. 'Giro', which is short for giro-cheque, is a British slang term for fortnightly payments of unemployment benefit.

Chapter 5

Bhangra and Asian Identity: the Role of Local Knowledge

In the previous chapter I began to consider the complex relationship between youth, popular music and locality via an examination of contemporary urban dance music and its cultural significance in different local settings. In doing so I drew attention to the role played by local knowledges in determining the way in which particular styles of popular music are appropriated and collectively used by young people. The mapping of such local instances of musicalised activity has been further complicated by patterns of migration. In attempting to settle into new cities and towns migrant groups begin a process of cultural relocation (Stokes: 1994). This leads to the formulation of what Back (1996a) refers to as 'new ethnicities' in which aspects of traditional cultural identity and 'invented' tradition (Hobsbawm: 1983) merge with sensibilities acquired from the new local environments within which migrant groups relocate. Music plays a crucial role in this process of cultural relocation. Indeed, the British popular music scene of the past four decades owes much to the musical and stylistic experimentation of Britain's immigrant populations. Since the early 1960s, new or recently arrived immigrant groups have used music as a way of establishing themselves and their respective cultural identities in Britain (see, for example, Hebdige: 1979, 1987).

During the course of this chapter I want to look at one of the more recent forms of music to emerge from this process of cultural relocation, a style known as bhangra. Originally a Punjabi folk music, during the early 1980s bhangra was fused with elements of western pop music by Asian musicians in Britain. The result was a distinctive bhangra–pop fusion which quickly found a wide appeal among Asian-diaspora populations in many different parts of the globe. Indeed, the apparent resonance of bhangra with the cultural politics of Asian ethnic minority groups, especially the younger members of such groups, has lead to claims that bhangra provides a sonic underpinning for a new 'Asian culture' (Baumann: 1997). Certainly, bhangra's continuing independence from mainstream pop would seem to support such a view. Thus, while the global music industry's appropriation of other 'diaspora musics', such as rap and reggae, has acted to loosen them from their immediate socio-political contexts and transformed them into broader platforms for collective expression (an issue that will be explored more extensively in Chapter 6's study of rap and hip hop), bhangra's global audience remains essentially Asian. This said, however, even as bhangra is seen to remain essentially 'Asian', the responses of young Asians to this musical form are so highly differentiated that it becomes inherently very difficult to speak in terms of a coherent cultural or 'subcultural' sensibility in connection with bhangra. Indeed, as I will presently demonstrate, even at the level of the local a variety of conflicting and overlapping meanings become inscribed within the bhangra text.

My study of bhangra begins with an examination of the music's origins and subsequent appropriation and development into a popular style by Asian musicians living in Britain. I will then begin to consider the cultural significance of bhangra as a local resource. As with Chapter 4, the basis for the empirical account that I present here is ethnographic research conducted in Newcastle upon Tyne. However, in charting the influence of bhangra on Asian identity in Britain, I will also refer to examples drawn from similar studies carried out in other British cities such as Birmingham and London.

The origins and development of bhangra

Bhangra originates from the Punjab provinces of India and Pakistan where it continues to retain its traditional significance as a form of folk music performed during the annual festival held to mark the completion of the sugar cane harvest. Bhangra is also used to celebrate the arrival of the new year in the Punjab (Banerji and Baumann: 1990, p. 140). During the mid-1970s, young Asians living in Britain began experimenting with bhangra music, retaining traditional bhangra instruments, most notably the *dholak*[1] and the *dholki*,[2] but also adding modern western instruments such as the electric guitar and bass, the keyboard synthesiser and the drum kit, thus infusing the rhythms and timbres of bhangra with the characteristic sounds and stylistic influences of western pop music (Baumann: 1990). Interestingly, early examples of this bhangra–pop fusion – known as bhangra-beat – emphasised local origins and identities, such as 'Southall Beat', Southall being a district in west London from which many of the early bhangra bands emerged, and 'northern rock bhangra', a variation of the bhangra style performed by bands based in the Midlands region of Britain (Back: 1996b, p. 130). Similarly, Glasgow-based bhangra band Bombay Talkie appeared on stage in clothes that incorporated Scottish tartan designs and performed Scottish folk songs such as 'Bonnie, Bonnie Banks of Loch Lomond' in a bhangra style.

Initially, bhangra-beat was embraced most readily by young Asians. Indeed, Banerji and Baumann suggest that this new style of bhangra 'was exactly what [Asian youth] wanted. Young, fresh, lively and modern, it was as genuinely Indian as it was recognisably disco' (1990, p. 142). However, because of its traditional roots and the elements of traditional music that characterised its sound, the appeal of bhangra-beat did not remain restricted to young Asians but extended to a much wider age range. This is evidenced by the fact that bhangra-beat quickly became popular at Asian weddings and other social functions such as Melas – Asian festivals featuring music, dance and a range of side stalls at which food, literature and Asian clothes are sold.[3]

A more exclusively youthful variation of bhangra emerged during the late 1980s and early 1990s as a new generation of Asian musicians influenced by contemporary dance music further modified the bhangra sound producing new forms such as *fusion*, which incorporates elements of *house* and *techno*, and *ragga*, a combination of bhangra, rap and reggae influences (Gilroy: 1993, p. 82). In doing so, they introduced bhangra into the mainstream British music scene with artists such as ragga performer, Apache Indian and fusion acts Bally Sagoo, Fundamental and Detrimental achieving considerable commercial success during the early 1990s. The widespread appeal of such artists among young Asians in Britain has lead to claims that bhangra-beat, and its various excursions into dance music, is giving rise to a new unified Asian youth culture in Britain. Lipsitz, for example, has argued that: 'Bhangra brings together Punjabis of many religions (Hindu, Sikh, Muslim, Jain, and Christian) and from many countries (India, Pakistan, and Bangladesh)' while Smith claims that 'in Britain Bhangra has, in the course of the past 10 years, become the property of the whole Asian nation' (1994, p. 129; 1994, p. 12). Similarly, Sanjay Sharma contends that: 'The cultural space created by Bhangra suggests a means for Asian youth to assert their "Asianness" and locate themselves firmly in their contemporary urban surroundings' (1996, pp. 35–6).

Arguably, however, such interpretations of bhangra's cultural significance for young Asians in Britain gloss over the true complexity of the
relationship that exists between the music and its audience. Thus, if
bhangra may in certain instances facilitate cross-cultural responses to
urban issues such as racism, racial discrimination and forms of racial
exclusion, on other occasions it may also serve to highlight the socio-
cultural and religious divisions that continue to exist between Asians in
Britain. Similarly, the various forms of identity that can be articulated
through bhangra will in each instance be underscored by issues of
locality, that is to say, they will address issues of ethnicity as these are
experienced locally. Again, this acutely problematises the argument that
bhangra speaks a common language to those who consume it. Using
my own research on bhangra in Newcastle as an empirical point of
reference, I want now to make a more detailed study of such locally
situated uses of bhangra, and their implications for the sociological
interpretation of the genre.

Bhangra in Newcastle: setting the scene

In comparison with a number of other British cities, notably Bradford,
Birmingham and London, the Asian population in Newcastle is
relatively small. According to the results of the 1991 census, 2.3 per cent
of the city's inhabitants are ethnic Pakistani or Indian while 0.5 per cent
are ethnic Bangladeshi (Hollands: 1995, p. 26). Newcastle's Asian
population is concentrated in the west of the city, largely, although not
exclusively, in the neighbouring districts of Fenham and Elswick. In
many respects this area represents a self-contained if not ghettoised
world for the Asian population of Newcastle. In addition to the
temples, mosque and community centre, there are Asian butchers'
shops, clothes shops, a general store and video rental shops that
specialise in Asian films. This socio-spatial segregation of Newcastle's
Asian population in turn has a strong influence upon the leisure
opportunities available to young Asians in the city. A study by Hollands
(op. cit.) has drawn attention to the issue of leisure provision for the
younger members of ethnic minority groups in Newcastle and begun to
question the extent of the city's accessibility for these groups, particularly in terms of nightlife opportunities (ibid., pp. 26–7). The results of
my own research indicate that very little evening leisure provision is
currently made for young ethnic minority groups in Newcastle.
Certainly, with respect to young Asians, there are no regular weekly
events or club nights designed to cater for their particular musical tastes.

It is, therefore, very difficult to speak in terms of a bhangra 'scene' in Newcastle as the opportunities that exist to consume bhangra are few and far between. Indeed, for reasons that will presently become clear, this situation has been exacerbated in recent times. Similarly, again because of the small concentration of Asians in Newcastle, there is very little production of bhangra music in the city. At the time of my research there were no bhangra bands in Newcastle and only two bhangra DJs. In addition to determining channels of access to the music itself, there is a clear sense in which the local arrangements governing the lives of young Asians in Newcastle serve to actively shape their individual and collective responses to bhangra and those events at which it is featured. Indeed, it is possible to identify a number of common responses among Asian youth in Newcastle regarding the consumption of bhangra music, which can in turn be linked with attitudes and values derived from the local discourses that inform their daily lives.

Bhangra as a celebration of 'tradition'

Much has been made of the potential that exists in bhangra for the forging of 'new' Asian identities and cross-cultural alliances between young Asians in opposition to the racism and racial exclusion encountered by the latter in Britain. A key text in this respect is Sharma *et al.*'s (1996) *Dis-Orienting Rhythms*. Using recent developments in Asian popular music and style as a basis for its analytical enquiry, *Dis-Orienting Rhythms* claims that the latter are facilitating a new proactive Asian youth culture made up of young people who are no longer willing to remain 'trapped' within the cultural world of their parents. Although it cannot be denied that bhangra and other forms of South Asian dance music effectively prise open popular stereotypes of Asians in Britain and the decidedly essentialist notions of race and ethnicity upon which such stereotypes are based, it could also be argued that two important factors are overlooked in *Dis-Orienting Rhythms*, these being regional variations in size of Asian populations throughout Britain and concomitant variations in access to bhangra and other forms of Asian dance music. On the basis of my own research, it seems to me that regional demographics and the local arrangements governing bhangra production and consumption can and do play a major role in shaping the cultural responses of young Asians towards bhangra music.

This is particularly noticeable in Newcastle which, as I have previously noted, has a relatively small Asian population in comparison with a number of other British cities. This factor, combined with the limited opportunities to collectively consume bhangra and the nature of bhangra events in Newcastle, has a marked influence on the way in which local Asian youth understand bhangra and its significance for issues of 'Asian' identity. Moreover, that such regional differences in response to bhangra exist is also clear to young Newcastle Asians themselves. A notable feature of many of my interviews and discussions with young Asians in Newcastle was the distinction that they tended to make between Newcastle and cities with larger Asian populations. In such cities, it was argued, bhangra was part of a 'daily life practice' for Asians. Nesrein, a 20-year-old Muslim woman, offered the following account: 'In Newcastle you get maybe half a dozen [bhangra events] a year if you're lucky and that's pushing it... but down south in Birmingham or London it's like every weekend you could go to one... and you're still like missing most of 'em.' Moreover, if bhangra was seen as a more central aspect of daily life for Asian populations in these cities then such centrality was in turn deemed to be consolidated by the responsiveness of local bhangra musicians and DJs to the various taste cultures that have positioned themselves around the differing styles now identified with the term 'bhangra'. Using the example of Birmingham, Khalid, a Pakistani Muslim, described the situation thus:

> There's a lot more Asians [in Birmingham] it's like a little India come Pakistan there... and there's a lot more variety in bhangra as well. There's like traditional bhangra music, so you get a lot of the older generation going for that kind of stuff and then you've got your mainstream which the young ones go for.

In contrast, bhangra events in Newcastle tend to be dominated by bhangra-beat which, as I have previously pointed out, has the widest ranging appeal among the modern bhangra-pop forms. The scarcity of bhangra events in Newcastle, combined with the style of music featured, has a profound influence on the nature of such events. Thus, as a local Asian radio presenter explained to me, a bhangra event in Newcastle is 'a cause for a family outing. You'll sometimes see whole family groups with the grandparents as well at bhangras'. Such descriptions were matched by my own experience of watching Achanak, one of the first bhangra-beat bands in Britain, perform at the Newcastle Mela in August 1995. This was the first time that a bhangra band had played in the city for many months and Achanak's performance served to confirm the celebratory quality that many Asians in Newcastle associate with bhangra. While much of the audience comprised Asian men and women in their early twenties, a large number of older people were present as well as family groups with babies and small children.

The relative novelty of bhangra events in Newcastle combined with the essential whiteness of the city results in particular forms of response to bhangra on the part of local Asians. In effect, bhangra events become sites for the celebration of 'tradition'. Such celebrations symbolise the efforts of the individuals involved 'to formulate a cultural identity in the midst of contradictions and uncertainty in the various spaces they occupy' (Shukla: 1997, p. 310). The form of tradition thus celebrated is an 'invented tradition' (Hobsbawm: 1983) in the sense that it draws upon a range of cultural images and sensibilities associated with 'Asian life' and reassembles these in ways intended to suggest unity and coherence both to Asians themselves and to others. Hobsbawm, from whom the concept of an invented tradition is taken, suggests that the latter is 'essentially a process of formalization and ritualization, characterized by reference to the past' (ibid., p. 4). Here, Hobsbawm is referring, for example, to the versions of tradition expressed in British folk music's play on notions of a rustic, communal life in a pre-industrial past (see MacKinnon: 1994) or the importance of tartan and clan imagery in the construction of the Scottish national identity (see Trevor-Roper: 1983). In the case of an invented 'Asian' tradition, however, inspiration is drawn not only from the past but also from idealised associations with the sub-Indian continent as a spiritual homeland and the 'ethnic stories and myths' that grow out of such associations (Shukla: 1997). Moreover, while in Hobsbawm's reading of invented tradition there is an implied consensus, of an almost clinical nature, concerning the necessary components of a 'tradition', the reality of such constructions may be rather less consensual. Indeed, a further issue arising from my research is the locally nuanced character of invented traditions. Thus, returning to the issue of Asian youth identities in Newcastle, while young Asians drew upon a stock of familiar but displaced images in discussing notions of tradition, at the same time this formed part of a highly reflexive discursive engagement with their local environment. This is clearly illustrated in the following extract from an interview with a mixed-sex group of young Asians all of whom were in their late teens and early twenties:

A.B.:   How do people dress to go to a bhangra event?

Sara: It depends really... something that's comfortable because you're dancing... just something smart I'd say.

Shaziya: I mean the girls wear Indian dresses don't they.

Sara: Yes that's true, you don't get many girls going in western outfits.

Hardeep: But then again, going down south [south of England] it's totally different.

A.B.:   So why do girls up here tend to dress more traditionally?

Shaziya: Because it's a night out, a social event really.

Sara: Personally, I wouldn't feel comfortable if I went to an Asian do and I was dressed in a western way. So I prefer to wear like Asian clothes... It's like, I'm going to an Asian do so I want to dress properly.

Shaziya: I do too because it's like the only chance I get to wear eastern clothes... Where I live there's like eleven people who are Asian... my mum will go into town with her Indian clothes on but I wouldn't dare... but then if you go to Birmingham or something people just dress how they want and it just doesn't matter.

From the point of view of the young Asians quoted above, bhangra is significant because of the way in which it connects with a locally experienced need to feel 'Asian' in the most 'traditional' sense, a need that in turn demands the use of bhangra as a means of promoting particular notions of what is considered to be traditional Asian life. Indeed, in the context of Newcastle, bhangra's significance in this respect is considerably enhanced in that the music provides an opportunity to temporarily articulate a form of ethnic identity that, it is felt, cannot be readily engaged in on a day to day basis. Local bhangra events permit such articulations of tradition by allowing young Asians to dress in the traditional clothes of their parent cultures, the wearing of such clothes being blocked at other times by the predominantly white nature of the local environment and the fear among young Asians of appearing to be *out of place*.

While an important marker in such celebrations, however, style of dress is by no means the only way in which young Asians in Newcastle signify this form of attachment to bhangra. Indeed, as the above interview extract implies, style of dress is on the whole very much a gendered issue among young Asians. Young men, I was informed, tend to wear traditional dress only at formal events such as weddings. Thus, for young Asian men, the significance of bhangra as a celebration of 'tradition' is expressed in other ways, most notably through style of dance. As one young man explained:

It's good to go to a bhangra event because... it brings back memories... it's like tradition. It's the same with the dancing like. There is a traditional dance... nowadays some people just move how they want to. But I think it [the traditional bhangra dance] does matter in some ways, 'cause it gives you a buzz to be doing something a bit traditional.

Baumann suggests that the nature of bhangra in Britain as a 'male and young people's dance' corresponds directly with music's role in 'the rural Punjab' (1990, p. 87). Arguably, however, there is a further dimension to this cultural 'borrowing', which again illustrates the innovation and invention informing the collective responses of young Asians in Britain to bhangra – aspects of Punjabi tradition and attendant forms of celebration being reinscribed with new, locally significant forms of meaning that move beyond straightforward associations with the Punjab. Thus in the context of Newcastle, as with the style of dress worn by young female Asians at bhangra events, from the point of view of young male Asians the bhangra dance can be seen to provide an important opportunity for the expression of an attachment to one's cultural and traditional roots in an environment where such expressions cannot be readily articulated in the course of everyday life.

Interestingly, for some of the young Newcastle Asians whom I interviewed the celebratory aspect of bhangra appeared to be more important than the music itself. Bhangra, it was suggested, was 'good music' for 'certain occasions'. This view was elaborated on by a young female interviewee who explained: '[Bhangra] is really suited to events where there's dancing... and celebratory events like the Mela. On occasions like that it's great. At other times I don't listen to it, I listen to chart music and stuff like Prince. I don't really like bhangra that much at other times.' Such accounts are consistent with the Maffesolian concept of *tribus* (tribes), examined in Chapter 4, which conceptualises individuals in late modern society as shifting personas moving between different sites of collective expression and reconstructing lifestyle orientations such as articulations of identity and musical taste accordingly (Maffesoli: 1996; Shields: 1992; Hetherington; 1992). Thus, in this particular instance, bhangra is acknowledged as an important aspect of the celebration of 'traditional' Asian identity along with other cultural images and resources such as traditional dancing and style of dress. As such, the music's appeal becomes fixed within the context of those occasions on which this identity is celebrated. At other times the musical preferences, style of dress and other indicators of these young people's identities orientate more closely around the western styles and influences with which they daily engage. Horak (1995) notes a similar pattern of shifting tastes in the musical preferences of young Croat and Turkish migrants in Vienna, whose musical preferences alternated between the traditional music of their parent cultures and western pop depending upon the particular context in which these musics were heard.

The rejection of bhangra: a celebration of 'otherness'

If certain groups of Asian youth in Newcastle considered bhangra as a valuable and necessary link with notions of tradition, other young Asians, through their rejection of bhangra, used it as a means of articulating their separateness from these same traditions. Again, there is a clear link between the sensibilities that inform this response to bhangra and the everyday experiences of Asian youth in Newcastle. Thus, while Newcastle's predominantly white-English environment imposes processes of exclusion upon Asians and other ethnic minority groups at the same time it communicates to them a series of lifestyle sensibilities beyond those encountered in the immediate environment of the family home. Clearly, such a situation is not specific to Newcastle as similar 'local' sensibilities can and do influence ethnic minority groups in all regions of Britain, including those with larger and more established ethnic minority populations. Thus, as Bhachu argues in a study of young Sikh women in Britain:

> Sikh women internalise styles, speech, and consumption patterns that are dominant in the localities in which they are situated... Thus, Sikh women in Birmingham are highly 'Brummie' in their expenditure choices and in the construction of their identities, just as London Asian women in Camden are Camdenian in their modes of operation, in their interpretation of their wealth, their clothes, the symbols important to the definition of their identities and styles (1991, p. 408).

It could, nevertheless, be argued that appropriations by young Asians of such regional traits are in themselves locally determined processes. Thus, in those cities with a larger concentration of ethnic minority groups, appropriations by the latter of local sensibilities, such as style of speech, mannerisms and even modes of dress, may not in every case be understood, nor justifiably interpreted, as the appropriation of local 'white' traits. Rather, such local sensibilities will themselves reflect the multiethnic character of the locality. Indeed, within such an environment, it may be possible to effect forms of alternative ethnic identity that are neither consistent with the traditional parent culture nor indeed with the local white population. This was clearly illustrated by the Bradford riots of June 1995 which followed the police's alleged victimisation of two Asian women suspected of prostitution. An article that appeared in the British newspaper the *Independent* shortly after the riots suggested that this collective action by young people from Bradford's predominantly Muslim Asian population served to expose a youth 'adrift from the values of their elders... attuned to the manners of contemporary Britain [but at the same time] immersed in... a DIY Islam... fed by the Islamophobia' encountered in Britain (Valley: 1995, p. 2). Similarly, Dwyer's study of young Muslim women in a suburb of northwest London notes how some women used different styles of dress, incorporating western designs, in an attempt to construct 'a more explicitly Islamic identity' thus challenging 'the ways in which culture and religion were often seen as synonymous by their parents' (1998, p. 57).

Sanghera suggests that the acquired notions of tradition that underpin such DIY forms of ethnic identity are themselves a product of particular forms of media representation. According to Sanghera, the 'Orientalism' constructed in western films, documentaries and news coverage of the Middle East, centring as it does around often conflicting notions of violence and exoticism, has had a twofold effect on young Asians in Britain; it has both glamorised the Orient and offered young Asians a sense of 'difference [and] uniqueness, and [a] feeling of power' (1994, p. 42). At the same time, however, I would argue that such experimentations with ethnic identity are by no means randomly placed, rather they are the product of particular local circumstances and resulting forms of local knowledge. Thus, it seems to me that the forms of constructed DIY ethnic identity described above are possible mainly because of the large concentrations of Asians located in Bradford and the northwest London area. Such experimentations are acted out against an established backdrop of cultural hybridity and cross-cultural fertilisation. A parallel process is evident in Sansone's study of Surinamese youth in Amsterdam, where the latter's exploration 'of new ways of being black in Dutch society' is caught up in the everyday life of a city where the intersection of a myriad of ethnicities and cultures facilitates a negotiation of the dominant white culture and the construction of a range of alternative, hybridised identities (1995, p. 115).

By contrast in Newcastle, where the concentration of ethnic minority groups is much smaller, there is little scope for such forms of experimentation with ethnic identity. Indeed, in rejecting aspects of Asian life it is interesting to note how many young Newcastle Asians achieve this not via a revision of the basic tenets of cultural or religious belief but rather through a wholesale appropriation of the 'image' constructed by local white youth, itself a derivation of the baggy style fashionable during the early 1990s, which involves the wearing of loose-fitting jeans or trousers, designer training shoes and baggy checked shirts. Indeed, given that sections of Asian youth in Newcastle did in fact wish to follow the example of young Asians elsewhere in Britain, for example by effecting a radicalised Islamic sensibility, this would prove extremely difficult in a city with such a small Asian population and where white hostility to such a movement would in all likelihood be heavily pronounced.

The role of music in the construction of ethnic identities is also crucially governed by the nature of the local environment. Yadwinder, a 19-year-old Sikh who moved to Newcastle several years ago from the Midlands, where he regularly returns to visit friends, gave the following account of the type of musically informed ethnic identity that he encounters in Birmingham:

> down there you get schools where it's all Asians and Afro-Caribbeans and they've grown up together and that's the way they've been brought up to feel. The Asians listen to reggae and rap and stuff, and they'll have black people singing on their bhangra tracks... the Afro-Caribbeans down there, they listen to bhangra music as well. It's a close knit sort of thing, they kind of like alienate themselves from the English music.

It is interesting to note the way in which the term 'English music' is being used in this context to describe types of music other than diaspora forms such as reggae, rap and bhangra, the latter being used, according to the interviewee, by Asian and Afro-Caribbean ethnic minorities in the Midlands region to demarcate a form of collective 'black' identity. This definition of 'English music' is in sharp contrast to that employed by Asian youth in Newcastle, particularly in the case of those who claim to have no interest in bhangra. The following extract is taken from a group discussion conducted at a comprehensive school in west Newcastle:

Sunil: None of us likes bhangra really.
A.B.:   What sort of music do you like?
Sunil: English music.
A.B.:   Such as?

Sunil: Rap.
Abdul Khan: I like rap and reggae.
Bobby: I like rap as well.
A.B.:   So what is it about bhangra that you don't like?
Bobby: It's too old fashioned.
Abdul Khan: Yeah, I think so too... It's like bhangra doesn't really fit in
                  with my other musical tastes.
A.B.:   Why is that, do you think?
Abdul Khan: Because of the lyrics really. I mean, I can understand
                  bhangra lyrics but it just doesn't sound as good for me.

Such differences in the definition and application of the term
'English music' relate back to and must be understood within the wider
context of the relationship that exists between locality, identity and the
politics of musical taste. Thus, in areas such as the Midlands the higher
concentration of Afro-Caribbean and Asian ethnic minority groups
means that musics such as rap, reggae and bhangra can be used more
readily to articulate alternative notions of ethnic identity into which
young people of Afro-Caribbean and Asian origin include themselves.
A useful model for understanding the locally situated nature of such
exprimentations with ethnic identity is Back's concept of the *cultural
intermezzo*. According to Back, a cultural intermezzo is a space in which
different cultural sensibilities merge and new identifications are
formed. Back further suggests that musical styles such as bhangra,
reggae and rap act as crucial points of reference in the formation of
cultural intermezzos and the new cultural identities that emerge from
them. Back illustrates this in relation to contemporary Asian dance
music artist Apache Indian. Born of Hindu parents from the Punjab
and raised in Handsworth, a multiracial district in Birmingham,
Britain's second largest city, Apache Indian pioneered a fusion style
known as *bhangramuffin* which combines the bhangra of his own home
background with the raggamuffin to which he was introduced by Afro-
Caribbean friends. According to Back, Apache Indian is in every respect
both a product and perpetuator of the local cultural intermezzo:

> He performs and expresses himself through snatches of Jamaican patois,
> Punjabi and a unique form of English which is being generated by groups
> of young people who are growing up alongside each other in
> Birmingham... [the music of Apache Indian] is a cultural crossroads, a
> meeting place where the languages and rhythms of four continents
> intermingle producing a culture which cannot be reduced to its
> component parts (1996b, p. 128).

As Back's description suggests, cultural intermezzos and the new sensibilities and identifications that emerge from the latter will vary from place to place depending upon local circumstances. Thus, while in Handsworth the multiracial character of the area results in the formulation of new 'local' sensibilities that draw simultaneously on cultural forms associated with Asia, Africa and the Caribbean, in Newcastle's primarily white working-class environment the cultural intermezzo is informed much more closely by the tastes and leisure preferences of the local white 'Geordie' youth. Indeed, from the point of view of the young Newcastle Asian, the appropriation of the styles and tastes associated with the local white youth can itself be a form of political statement in that it serves as a powerful indication to his or her family and peers of that individual's desire to rebel against or break away from the more traditional Asian way of life.

This begins to explain why the interviewees in the above extract refer to rap and reggae as 'English' rather than black music, the latter being widely listened to by white youth in the city (see Chapter 6). Bhangra, on the other hand, because of its failure to enter the mainstream, becomes consonant with the image of 'traditional' Asian life and is thus rejected by those young people who wish to set themselves apart from the latter. This view is supported by the following comments from a youth worker who had tried unsuccessfully to start up a bhangra workshop at a community music resource centre which had recently opened in the Scotswood district of west Newcastle. Thus, as the youth worker put it: 'Most of the young Asian kids that I talk to aren't into bhangra at all. They seem to view it as an old man's music and the kind of stuff that they're into seems to be fusion music like rap or dub reggae.' Indeed, the way in which many members of the older generation of Asians in Newcastle appear to embrace bhangra music as a channel through which aspects of Asian tradition can be preserved appears, in turn, to strengthen the resolution of certain groups of young Asians to adopt the musical tastes and attendant sensibilities of their white peers. As one young Asian man to whom I spoke at a youth club in Elswick pointed out:

> Because it [bhangra] was a traditional music, it had better acceptance among parents. When people started adapting bhangra that got acceptance too. Kids are encouraged to listen to bhangra... It's like when an Asian kid takes up cricket instead of football y'know. It's just seen as the right thing to do. The fear of parents is that their kids will slip away... they're either going to become a nice young polite boy or girl or a football

hooligan y'know. But when you ask kids yourself what kind of music they like bhangra never comes up... a lot of 'em will tell you that they like chart music.

This observation is in turn supported by the following account in which a young Sikh man explains how, in his opinion, his dislike of bhangra and preference for western popular music styles are rooted in the deep associations that bhangra holds for him with the traditions and customs of his home background:

> I was brought up listening to bhangra, because that's what my parents listened to... there was nothing else to listen to really. Then, as soon as I got to about thirteen or fourteen... I had different friends, white friends, and a different kind of atmosphere. I started listening to their tapes and I'd find out what I really liked which is dance music... Now I can't stand bhangra.

Significantly, however, such responses to bhangra music did not deter young Asians from attending bhangra events in Newcastle. On the contrary, despite their confessed dislike for the music itself, these young Asians still regarded bhangra events as an important site for sociality – as one of the few opportunities in Newcastle for Asian youth to be together in a space that was essentially their own. Thus, as one young Sikh man candidly reported: 'Bhangra! I can't listen to it... it doesn't appeal to me. It's the going out bit I like, the chance to see my Asian mates. Sometimes I just go for the girls like.' In effect, however, attitudes such as these contributed to a series of tensions that manifested themselves at bhangra events in Newcastle often resulting in violence between young Asians.

Violence at bhangra events in Newcastle: a discourse of conflicting identity politics

Violence between young Asian men has been a perennial problem at bhangra events in Newcastle. According to some observers, such violence, which in 1994 resulted in all of the major Newcastle nightclubs imposing an indefinite ban on bhangra events, is rarely if ever encountered at similar events in other cities. While I am unable to qualify such comments myself, I would, nevertheless, wish to argue that the incidence of violence at bhangra events in Newcastle can once again be attributed to issues of locality. First and perhaps most importantly, disputes arising at bhangra events appear to correspond very closely with the racial and religious conflicts of interest that characterise

Newcastle's wider Asian population. In addition, such violence is exacerbated through conflicts between those who maintain a more orthodox line of religious belief and those who have chosen to adopt westernised traits, but who, for reasons already noted, continue to attend bhangra events and other Asian functions. I will consider each of these issues in turn.

Solomos and Back have criticised the way in which the term 'community' is often applied to ethnic minority groups, suggesting that such 'identifications [do not relate to] "natural communities" [but rather] constitute moments where community and identity are defined: manifestations of racial and ethnic closure' (1994, p. 157). This argument was reiterated by an Asian community worker, who suggested that the term 'Asian community' and its common positioning as a form of ethnic 'subculture' existing within contemporary urban Britain is essentially a misnomer. The problem with this term, he suggested, is that it tends to gloss over the various conflicts of interest that arise between the differing religious and cultural interests that comprise the so-called 'Asian communities' in Britain. Nevertheless, during the course of my research in Newcastle, I found references to the 'Asian community' to be a common aspect of popular discourse, not only in the case of white observers but also when talking to Asians. In situating themselves in relation to Newcastle's white population, Asians routinely used the term 'Asian community' as a means of demarcating their own sense of collective identity. Clearly then, the notion of 'community' as this relates to the Asian population in Newcastle is both highly complex and contradictory. While it may function on the one hand as a means by which Asians are able to define their otherness from Newcastle's dominant white population, the obverse side of this form of identification is a rather strained notion of 'community' – a number of diffuse cultural and religious sensibilities each striving to maintain its own respective sense of identity.

Baumann's distinction between *dominant* and *demotic* discourse is a useful model in beginning to comprehend this seemingly contradictory use of the term community by Asians in Newcastle. Dominant discourse, that is a discourse applied by the dominant society to minority groups deemed to constitute a community, employs the term 'community' 'as a conceptual bridge that connects "culture" with ethnos' (1997, p. 213). Conversely, demotic discourse, that is, the discourse used by those individuals deemed to constitute a community, is based upon notions of difference; that is to say upon notions of '"communities" within communities, as well as "cultures" across "communities"' (ibid., p. 210). According to Baumann, individuals do not become trapped into one or the other of these discourses but rather develop a 'dual discursive competence', switching between discourses 'depending on their judgements of context and purpose' (ibid., p. 216). This begins to explain why Asians in Newcastle are able to employ the term 'Asian community' when speaking of themselves in relation to the city's wider population while simultaneously observing cultural differences and attendant divisions within this 'community'. Baumann's work, based on a study of ethnic minority groups in London's Southall district, also points to the considerable local differences that can characterise the nature of such discourse. Thus, according to Baumann, older Asians in Southall 'define their cultural distinctiveness with regard to far more particularist pre-emigration heritages' while for young Asians the fact of being born in Southall 'involves them in, and qualifies them for, the conscious creation of a comprehensively "Asian culture"' (ibid., pp. 219, 218). Significantly, Southall is one of the areas associated with the origins of bhangra-beat. Indeed, for Baumann, in the local context of Southall, bhangra provides one of the key cultural resources in the construction of a new unified Asian youth culture. Thus he argues:

> One can hardly overestimate the popularity of Bhangra among young Southallians... The adaptation of Bhangra that complements traditional lyrics and drum rhythms with electronic keyboards and guitars, synthesisers and new 'sampling' and 'scratching' techniques of recording is indeed largely a local invention... What is of greatest interest here is its expressive and symbolic contribution to young Southallians' conceptions of a new 'Asian *culture*'... the idea of Bhangra as an 'Asian music for Asians' replaces... internal divisions [with] a shared external distinctiveness (ibid., p. 219).

In Newcastle too, bhangra can be seen to inform a demotic discourse via which cultural alliances are established. There are, however, noticeable differences in the form of demotic discourse which feeds into and is sustained through the collective consumption of bhangra music in Newcastle as compared with that observed by Baumann in Southall. I have previously noted how one of the Asian community workers whom I interviewed in the course of my research rejected the term Asian 'community' because of its tendency to gloss over the cultural and religious conflicts that continue to exist between Asians in Britain. The same community worker also took issue with the view, central to Baumann's work, that such conflicts are by and large perpetuated only by older Asians in Britain. In certain areas, he argued, tension was also

common among the young. Speaking about the nature of such tensions
and resulting conflicts, and relating these to the particular problems
encountered in Newcastle, the community worker then made the
following observation:

> There are always divisions between different Asian communities. For
> example, within the Pakistani community, they tend to divide up again in
> terms of the parent language so the Punjabi speakers might have their own
> distinct group... Other language speakers have their own distinct groups as
> well and the way that this transforms itself is that people form little pockets
> of power... often management committees at mosques or community
> centres... Now, in Newcastle, the main black populations are Pakistani
> Muslim and Bengali Muslim. The Bengali community is divided again
> within itself because one set controls the community centre and the other
> set controls the Mosque... they don't speak to each other and nobody, even
> they themselves, can explain why it is that they don't get on. Now, this
> creates divisions and it's often because of these divisions that young people
> see divisions for themselves as well.

The above observation suggests that in the demotic discourse of
young Newcastle Asians notions of culture and identity as directed by
the parent culture are strongly pronounced. Paradoxically then, a
potential effect of cultural events, which are designed to bring groups of
Newcastle Asians together, could be in fact to highlight and perhaps
intensify the types of division referred to above. As I have previously
pointed out, owing to the lack of leisure facilities that exist for ethnic
minority groups in Newcastle bhangra events provide one of the few
occasions on which young Asians are able to gather in large numbers. I
have also suggested that, for many young Asians, such gatherings
provide an opportunity to engage in a collective celebration of tradition
which is not possible at other times. In staging such celebrations,
however, on the basis of the evidence presented above it follows that
young Asians will be, to a greater or lesser extent, directed by the beliefs
and practices that inform the respective religions, primarily Hindu,
Muslim and Sikh, to which they belong. By using bhangra music in this
way, young people will in effect highlight the religious and other
cultural differences that exist between them. Moreover, the ways in
which such differences are in turn negotiated by young people will
depend largely upon how these differences are seen to be negotiated by
significant others such as parents and local religious figures.

Indeed, much of the violence that occurs at bhangra events in
Newcastle appears to result from young people of different religions

acting out for themselves those same divisions and conflicts that characterise the social fabric of the city's wider Asian population. This is clearly illustrated in the following account by a young Sikh man: 'I was at this bhangra do one night with some mates and this Pakistani lad knocks into me and starts giving me hassle. So we starts arguing. All the Pakistani lads join in on his side and all the Sikh lads joined in with me and we had this big fight.' A Muslim man in his early twenties, who had attended many of the bhangra events in Newcastle, spoke to me at length about the violence he had witnessed and provided his own conceptualisation of the problem which, he surmised, resulted from the disjunctive quality of the event itself. Thus he argued:

> These bhangra occasions are basically to say 'well look, we know you guys like it so why don't yoos all come down and have a good time 'cause it's not very often that you're provided with what you want'... but they say 'well why should I be in the same room with X, Y and Z?' So all that happens is that it erupts into a massive fight between factions... so that the Pakistani lads say 'we're gonna sort the Sikhs out' and the Sikhs and Pakistanis say 'we're gonna sort the Hindus out'... it basically spoils the whole occasion... so the music, it just plays a small part really.

It is interesting to note how, in the above account, the sensibilities relating to religious belief are deemed to cancel out those governing musical taste with the effect that the music itself becomes a relatively insignificant part of a bhangra event. It seems to me, however, that incidences of violence such as those just described occur not because the sensibilities of musical taste are subverted by those of religious belief but rather because contemporary bhangra music addresses both of these discourses simultaneously. As noted at the beginning of this chapter, in much the same way that other forms of popular music and their attendant styles are often constructed via an ad hoc 'borrowing' of cultural resources from around the world, so the 're-invention of bhangra', to borrow Baumann's (1990) terminology, was also achieved via the merging of traditional Punjabi folk styles with elements of western pop thus erasing forever bhangra's exclusive association with the Punjab. Indeed, it is significant in this respect that for many consumers of bhangra the music is now associated as closely with 'Bollywood', the nickname for the main South Asian popular culture industry located in Bombay, as with it is with the Punjab (see Sharma, A.: 1996). At the same time, however, this shift in the significance of bhangra has also acted as a prime mover in the attachment of a more polysemic significance to the Punjab. Indeed, as Manuel points out, in addition to bhangra many other 'aspects of Punjabi culture... have had prodigious impact beyond the Punjabi's borders, and have been especially receptive to creative syncretism with Western Culture' (1993, p. 178).

It can be argued that this fragmentation and hybridisation of Punjabi culture has led to the symbol of the Punjab becoming a marker of both commonality and difference among peoples of the Asian-diaspora. Thus, returning to the issue of bhangra, there is a clear sense in which audiences at bhangra events become multiply situated in terms of their relationship to the music. Thus, on the one hand, bhangra and its attendant Punjabi images function as a cultural beacon for those in search of a medium around which to stage a celebration of tradition. On the other hand, such celebrations will in every instance be mediated by the meanings that bhangra gives to particular notions of ethnic identity and the ways in which such identities are understood in terms of the broader sets of relationships that characterise local Asian popula-tions. Thus, while it is not my intention to suggest that the music itself is directly responsible for the incidence of violence at bhangra events in Newcastle, at the same time it seems clear to me that the floating discourses inherent in the bhangra text resonate perfectly with the tension that builds as a disparate affiliation of cultural and religious practises struggles on the one hand to present an image of coherence and strength to the local white populace while at the same time engaging in a series of internal struggles concerning more particularised notions of ethnic identity.

If the incidence of violence at bhangra events in Newcastle can in many ways be linked to the inter-racial conflicts occurring within Newcastle's Asian population, conflicts that, as we have seen, are bound up with issues of religion and tradition, then the appropriation by some young Asians in the city of local 'white' traits has served to create further tension among audiences at these events. As I have already pointed out, even for those young Asian people who have adopted the attitudes and habits of the local white youth in Newcastle, bhangra events still provide an important means of socialising with their Asian friends. At the same time, bhangra events also act as a medium for those young people who have rejected religious practices and other aspects of Asian custom to articulate their own sense of ethnic identity. However, in a setting where many of the social actors are highly sensitised to the need to be seen endorsing fundamental aspects of their respective traditional identities, those who detract from such traditions are often singled out and stigmatised. Thus, for example, a young Muslim man, who has himself been the subject of such stigmatisation at bhangra events in Newcastle, made the following observation:

> There's a lot of Muslim people now who, like me, drink alcohol. A lot of the bhangra dos now take place in clubs and obviously there are bars there. Sometimes lads will come up to you and say 'why are you drinking, you're supposed to be a Muslim?' It can get really heated sometimes, I've seen fights and all sorts. They just can't seem to understand. There's all this narrow-minded codswallop that says 'well if you're a Muslim you're supposed to do this but you can't do that'. It's sickening sometimes.

In beginning to understand the nature of such conflict, Back's (1996b) concept of cultural intermezzos, which I discussed earlier, again provides a useful starting point. As previously noted, cultural intermezzos constitute points at which discourses of ethnic/cultural identity cross and produce new identities. As such, cultural intermezzos are the product of local circumstances. I have also suggested that, while in multicultural areas intermezzos draw upon a wide variety of cultural resources, in predominantly white areas such as Newcastle intermezzos will be much more closely informed by local white sensibilities. This aspect of the local cultural intermezzo in Newcastle is clearly illustrated by the references of a number of Asian youths whom I interviewed to their trips 'down the Bigg Market', a district in Newcastle city centre with a large number of pubs and clubs making it a popular nightspot for young people (see Lancaster: 1992, pp. 59–65). Hollands has suggested that 'the Bigg Market phenomenon... is an illustrative case study of post adolescence and the ritualization of local identity' (1995, p. 56). From the point of view of the young Asian this ritualisation of local identity becomes a double articulation as any expression of affinity with the Bigg Market is not only a powerful statement of association with western customs but also an indication of the individual's acceptance into the local white 'Geordie' culture.

Moreover, there is a clear sense in which such a ritualisation can also be seen to contribute to the violence that has been observed at bhangra events in Newcastle. For many of those young Asians who choose to articulate their association with the sensibilities of local white youth through an identification with the Bigg Market, it becomes necessary in turn to absorb and re-enact the local knowledges and urban myths that have grown up around this aspect of Newcastle nightlife. A particularly resilient stereotype in popular representations of the Bigg Market is that of 'Bigg Market brawling' (Armstrong: 1995, p. 5). Despite recent attempts to dispel this myth (see Lancaster: 1992, p. 63 and

Hollands: 1995, p. 56), for many the Bigg Market continues to be strongly associated with an atmosphere of aggression often erupting into acts of violence. Such representations in turn become a testing board for many young Asian men in their articulation of the Geordie identity. A Muslim man in his late twenties, who had himself previously visited the Bigg Market on a regular basis, gave me the following graphic account:

> When you go down the Bigg Market well it's all sort of image, public image. At one time black guys were afraid to go down the Bigg Market at any time of day... I mean I used to think 'well, I've heard such bad things about it' and I was expecting to just walk down there at ten o'clock in the morning and somebody'd drag you into the back lane and beat you up, which is of course not the case. When I started going down there sort of... eh well other [Asian] people would start going down and you'd get a bit more confidence... it's like, you'll get this image through going out down the Bigg Market with all the big, tough drug dealing white guys [laughs]... but really, that's how some of the Asian lads sees it... so then they says 'well we have to keep up our reputation' so they gets into fighting within themselves and it develops from there.

The problem of violence at bhangra events in Newcastle then, as with the other types of audience behaviour thus far examined, must be viewed in the context of the local knowledges and sensibilities that inform those individuals who converge on the dancefloor. Thus, while such violence may result from a common desire on the part of the differing collectivities present at bhangra events to articulate their respective, and in many cases competing, notions of ethnic identity to each other, such identities and the forms of tension that are seen to exist between them are, in their turn, framed within a locally defined discourse that supplies Asians living in Newcastle with a series of options as to how the notion of ethnicity is constructed and mediated to others.

If locality is to be understood as being primarily responsible for structuring those options that exist for ethnic minority groups to articulate notions of ethnicity, then it must also be seen as ultimately responsible for posing the limitations that ethnic minority groups see for themselves in attempting to stage such articulations. I have already discussed this issue to some extent in considering the significance of bhangra events for Asians in Newcastle as one of the few opportunities to collectively celebrate 'traditional' Asian life. In Newcastle, however, it is not simply the notion of traditional ethnic identity that is problematic. The incidence of racism, particularly in the west of the city, has problematised the whole issue of race and ethnicity. Indeed some observers believe that the added tensions and frustrations created among the youth of ethnic minority groups by the behaviour of white racists have also contributed in their own way to the violent outbursts witnessed at bhangra events. Thus, as a local bhangra DJ put it, 'part of the reason for this violence is that people are feeling so oppressed... they don't have the strength to fight against the attackers, so they begin to fight amongst themselves in a desperate bid to vent their anger'. The problem of racism in Newcastle has in part inspired the growth of another music-driven sensibility among young Asians in which bhangra is again being used as a pivotal discursive text.

The *Bhangra Hustlers*

> We're doing a show called the *Bhangra Hustlers*, which is basically a show which fuses bhangra with all other types of music, be it jazz, or reggae, hip hop, soul... anything. Just to prove that bhangra isn't something that should be isolated (Programme DJ).

The *Bhangra Hustlers* is broadcast weekly on Kool FM, a community radio station established several years ago by a group of enthusiasts keen to promote contemporary dance music forms, such as rap, jungle and bhangra, which currently receive little airplay on the major radio stations. In recent years the growth of community-based radio stations, particularly pirate radio, has opened up new possibilities for the interplay between the use of radio formats and the nuances of locality. As one pirate radio DJ has put it: 'All we talk about is the latest tune, who's playing it, where he's playing it, what the rave was like last night' (Spillius: 1995, p. 15). Similarly Gilmore, in a Leicester-based study of pirate radio, argues that the latter provides 'an alternative to more mainstream... radio [utilising] a format which gives certain excluded groups access to cultural resources and representation. Pirate radio also provides an outlet for non-mainstream music and local artists. Most importantly, it is a network of representation for ethnic communities' (1995, p. 1). Another characteristic trait of both pirate radio and many of the newer community-based legal radio stations is the emphasis that is often placed, in keeping with the sensibilities of contemporary urban dance music, upon the role of the DJ as a primary interlocutor of the musical text. In the context of community broadcasting then, music itself may function as a resource for addressing local issues such as the problem of racism or broader themes relating to the issue of race relations.

Kool FM's *Bhangra Hustlers* programme is one such example of an attempt, using the medium of music, to address the problem of race relations as this is experienced at a local level. Using bhangra as a central musical theme in the programme, young Asian men and women are given the opportunity to become community DJs, mixing bhangra tracks together with other forms of contemporary music such as rap and house. The aim of those involved with the *Bhangra Hustlers* is to effectively reinvent the bhangra sound and, in doing so, articulate their own localised interpretation of the syncretic quality that they identify with bhangra and other forms of popular music. Thus, as one of the programme's organisers explained to me:

> On this show we want to appeal to a wide audience. It's a dance music station and we know that in addition to Asians we're gonna have a lot of white people listening to the music too. We want to show that the basis of all music is that it is made up of beats and rhythms and that it can be combined well. So what we do is we mix bhangra with dance music, which is what I like, house music in particular, Afro-Caribbean ragga... which is mixing dance with reggae beats... and we'll use rap as well. Then within that we might also include something like Peter Gabriel.

In addressing the deeper political agenda of the *Bhangra Hustlers*, one of the DJs spoke of the need to get away from the archetypal image of the Asian as someone whose way of life is completely at odds with the rest of Britain. Indeed, that such stereotypes remain fixed in the British popular imagination is undoubtedly the primary motive for the continuing high incidence of racism directed against Asians in Britain. Gilroy and Lawrence have suggested that the perceived 'out-and-out alien characteristics' of Asians serve to make them 'the object of a purer hatred', which is not directed at other 'black' ethnic minority groups who, if not totally accepted by white Britain are, nevertheless, deemed to be *more* acceptable than ethnic minorities of Asian origin (1988, p. 143). This sentiment is well captured by Pearson in his semi-ethnographic study '"Paki-Bashing" in a North East Lancashire Cotton Town':

> The West Indian is 'more like us'. He speaks our language (or so we tell ourselves) and he is of our culture – or so we fool ourselves. 'Pakis' (that is, Indians and Pakistanis) on the other hand are not like us at all, or so the distinction says: they speak a different language, they eat peculiar

food which does not smell like our food, and they keep to themselves (1976, p. 50).

Similarly, it is also widely acknowledged by sociologists and cultural theorists that the white appropriation, for example in the case of the skinheads, of musical and stylistic innovations associated with Afro-Caribbean culture has resulted in a certain degree of tolerance and acceptance of this ethnic group on the part of white Britons (see, for example, Hebdige: 1976a, 1976b, 1979). Likewise, white-British appropriations of African-American music and style have worked to a broadly similar effect in facilitating a wider acceptance of blacks in Britain. Thus, as Back argues: 'Young white people may [now] have more in common with Bobby Brown than John Bull, with the result that it is impossible to speak of a black culture in Britain separately from the culture of Britain as a whole' (1993, p. 218). However, such shifts in the relations between black and white Britain have done little to change popular perceptions of Asians. Thus, despite the affinity of many young Asians with the lifestyle orientations and cultural practises of 1990s Britain, Asian communities are still considered by many to exist at the margins of British social life. Indeed, as Malik points out: 'The constant conflict between a sense of ease and familiarity with British culture and a sense of rejection and frustration created by racism is a problem for all Asian youth' (1995, p. 23). Similarly, Andrews and Fowler have noted how young Asians living in Scotland, despite feeling at home there, 'recognised the difficulties presented by a sense of cultural difference. As one young woman said, "I can not [sic] choose my friends without parental interference, nor do I feel free to go into many places where there are no Asians. Even if my parents allowed me to go to nightclubs I would be afraid because of being Asian"' (1996, p. 11).[4]

The problem of racism in Britain, while obviously a national issue, can also be usefully understood as a locally constructed social sensibility. Thus, as Smith argues, 'forms of racial antipathy [often] exhibit marked variations according to demographic, socio-economic and locational criteria' (1989, pp. 148–9). In west Newcastle, an inverted form of what Back terms 'neighbourhood nationalism' is exercised against all ethnic minority groups. According to Back, neighbourhood nationalism defines the attempt by residents in particular localities to 'shrink' the nation 'to a size which mirrors [the] immediate set of social relations within the neighbourhood' (1993, p. 220). Back's use of the term relates to the way in which nationally articulated racisms are subverted by a 'neighbourhood' discourse of inter-racial harmony based on familiarity and established networks of trust between white and non-white residents. It seems to me, however, that neighbourhood nationalism may also work in a broadly opposite fashion as racist groups address their interpretation of the 'race problem' at a local level by directing aggressive and exclusionary practices at the members of ethnic minority groups who share their neighbourhoods. This would certainly seem to be the case in west Newcastle where racist groups construct a neighbourhood discourse that excludes all non-white ethnic groups, who are then treated as outsiders. As one Afro-Caribbean resident put it: 'Racist behaviour is highly concentrated in the west end. Occasionally it does rear its head in the town and it usually results in a punch up or two, whereas when it's highly concentrated in an area such as Elswick then the effects are much worse.' Because Asians constitute the larger and thus more directly visible ethnic minority in west Newcastle, they are often targeted by racist groups and subject to racial abuse.

The situation just described is in marked contrast to Watt and Stenson's study of Asians in a small town in southeast England. According to Watt and Stenson, the young Asians involved in their study 'led a localist existence' centred around areas identified by the latter as 'safe spaces' because of the large concentrations of Asians living there (1998, p. 257). Watt and Stenson's work again serves to emphasise the substantial role played by local environments and their demographic characteristics in determining levels of racism. Thus, despite the essential whiteness of many parts of the South East region, the presence of recognised and established Asian and Afro-Caribbean districts serves as a form protection against the threat of violence from white racist groups who view such districts as no-go areas. In the case of Newcastle, however, no such form of protected localist existence is possible. The territorialistation of space identified by Watt and Stenson is problematised in Newcastle due to the smallness of the Asian population. Although most Asians in Newcastle live in particular areas of the west end, none of these areas could realistically be called 'Asian' districts as many of the residents are white. Thus, even in those areas of Newcastle with the highest concentrations of Asians and other ethnic minority groups day to day life is overshadowed by the constant threat of verbal abuse or physical attack from racist agitators. The following accounts are drawn from a discussion that took place between myself and a group of young Asians during a meeting of the Black Youth Collective. The latter was established to allow young Asians and Afro-

Caribbeans living in west Newcastle to meet with community workers and discuss issues such as racism and racial exclusion as it affects them on a day to day basis:

Mehli: When I came here [to Newcastle] I couldn't speak a word of English. The kids who I went to school with taught me English... and all the swear words too. Now those same kids swear at me.

Abdul: The young kids are the worst, they are really insulting... but you know you can't do anything otherwise you'd be in trouble yourself so you just leave them.

Mehli: Yes but it's the parents who start it. They'll say things like 'go over there and spit on that darkie' to their kids and that's how the kids learn it.

Significantly, when the organisers of the *Bhangra Hustlers* first launched the programme they recruited many of their young DJs from the Black Youth Collective. As such, there is a particularly keen awareness among those young people who feature in the programme of the need to begin to tackle the misconceptions that continue to dominate white perceptions of Asians in Newcastle. At the same time, however, it is also recognised that because of the absence of a strong Asian presence in the city, and the particular bearing that this has upon local levels of racial tolerance, the medium of community radio is the logical starting point for this type of project. Conversations with *Bhangra Hustlers* DJs inevitably led to comparisons between their role in the community and that of African-American community DJs who often operate literally at 'street level' using a turntable and portable speakers or, alternatively, a 'ghetto-blaster'. Thus, as one of the *Bhangra Hustlers'* DJs explained:

Avtar: I think most of the kids who work on the programme would love to have a go at that... I myself would love to take a ghetto-blaster out on my shoulder, but, eh it'll be taken off my shoulder very quickly.

A.B.: By whom?

Avtar: For want of better wording, it would basically be done by misguided white youths. But then again, getting to try your hand on a community radio station is better anyway because it's gonna be much better quality, and because of the way things are here [in Newcastle] you're gonna get a lot more respect for it. People are actually gonna pay attention and listen to it.

The collective sensibility that underpins the aims of the *Bhangra Hustlers* project works out of a local knowledge base in which the nuances and complexities of the race problematic in Newcastle are minutely understood. Rather than aggravating the problem by attempting to focus attention on the area of the city in which racism is most highly concentrated, the programme provides a vehicle for young Asians to address the issue of race relations at a city-wide level. Indeed, the medium of community radio allows for a much wider form of engagement with the issue of race relations in Newcastle. As those who work on the *Bhangra Hustlers* concede, thus acknowledging the wider processes of ethnic closure operating in the city, the problems of exclusion and racial discrimination facing Asians in Newcastle are not merely associated with the issue of racism. Rather, there is an overall ignorance and indeed indifference on the part of the city's predominately white populace regarding the nature of Asian life in Britain and the way in which this is steadily changing as new generations of Asians become increasingly westernised in terms of their social sensibilities and lifestyle orientations.

Some evidence that the *Bhangra Hustlers'* approach may yet serve to effect at least an element of change in the local white population's responses to bhangra music, and thus begin to draw their attention to Asian youth's increasing proximity to the lifestyle orientations of contemporary Britain, is provided in the following extract from a discussion group in which both white and Asian young people were invited to give their views on bhangra:

A.B.:   Where do you think bhangra's going?
Jim: It's going to be kept in the Asian community... I can't see it going any further really.
A.B.:   So you don't think bhangra will cross over into the mainstream?
Jim: No, not like reggae, I mean like that crossed over no problem.
A.B.:   Why do you think that white people go for reggae but they won't go for bhangra?
Steve: I think it's actually the way that the music sounds and the way the singer... I mean I can't... that's the thing that gets on my nerves like, the high-pitched women singing and the instruments aghh... Indian music, I really hate it. Like with

reggae, you can listen to that, it's more bass and the singing is really good... but Indian music, that high pitched singing they do...

Harpal: Yes but the thing with reggae is like, they're singing in English... patois is a form of English. Now of course you're not gonna understand Indian... and eh, how can you say it's a daft accent? Now if I was to play you an Indian reggae song or one of the new Bally Sagoo one's or something like, you'd be lying if you said you didn't like it at all.

Steve: Aye maybes your right, perhaps I'm not being fair like. The only stuff I've actually heard is that stuff they play on the films late at night[5]... so if I heard bhangra, I might like it.

During the course of this chapter I have argued that bhangra, despite various claims that the music functions as a vehicle for a common form of cultural expression among young Asians in Britain, must in each case be understood as forming part of a highly particularised local discourse. Drawing upon the results of empirical research conducted in Newcastle and relating these to the findings of similar studies done in other British cities and regions, I have demonstrated how the collective *uses* of bhangra music by young Asians living in Britain, together with the various statements and expressions of ethnic identity that such uses are intended to articulate, are in each instance underscored by local knowledges, that is to say, by forms of knowledge and attendant sensibilities acquired as a direct result of living in particular urban locations. In Chapter 6, I will consider how hip hop, another cultural form whose origins could be broadly described as diasporic, is also being crossed with local knowledges and sensibilities with the result that it is becoming, in effect, a *glocal* culture.

NOTES

1. The *dholak* is a large double-headed drum beaten with sticks. During bhangra performances, the *dholak* player carries the instrument on a shoulder strap which enables him to move around on the stage. The *dholak* is considered to be the central instrument in a bhangra band, and *dholak* player the leader of the traditional dance which often accompanies the performance of bhangra music (see Banerji and Baumann: 1990).

2. The *dholki* resembles the *dholak* but is smaller and is played with the hands. Unlike the *dholak* player, the *dholki* player performs seated (see Banerji and Baumann: 1990).

3. In Britain, Melas are held annually each summer in many major cities and are usually free 'open air' events.
4. For a comprehensive account of Asians in Scotland, see Maan (1992).
5. The interviewee is referring to Indian films shown late in the evening on the British public TV channel, Channel 4. Such films often feature soundtracks that incorporate adapted Indian classical music pieces (see Sharma, A: 1996).

Chapter 6

Hip Hop am Main, Rappin' on the Tyne: Hip Hop Culture as a Local Construct in Two European Cities

> Aa dee it coz aa can green eggs and ham,
> People always tell iz that am just like me mam,
> Aa wuz born aa was bred in smelling distance
> o the tyne,
> An a couldn't give a toss that the fogs not mine,
> Aa like me blaa an a like a pint,
> But ave never needed speed for an alreet neet,
> Aa divvent drive a car 'coz they just get twoced,
> Me ken's kanny safe it's on top of a shop...
> (Ferank, Newcastle poet and rapper: 1994)

Among contemporary youth cultural forms, hip hop has attracted a great deal of interest from academic theorists and researchers. It is also fair to say that hip hop is one of the most contested cultural forms from the point of view of its representation in academic texts. Much of the debate surrounding hip hop relates to the issue of authenticity. Thus, while some theorists maintain that the authenticity of hip hop remains firmly rooted in its origins and continuing significance as an African-American street culture, others suggest that the themes and issues expressed in hip hop contribute to the musicalised dialogue that is held to exist between those displaced peoples of African origin who collectively make up the African-diaspora. More recently, a new school of hip hop theorists, in considering the existence of hip hop culture outside the African-American and wider African-diasporic world, have contested earlier interpretations of hip hop, suggesting instead that hip hop is culturally mobile; that the definition of hip hop culture and its attendant notions of authenticity are constantly being 're-made' as hip hop is appropriated by different groups of young people in cities and regions around the world.

In this chapter I want to consider some of the different sociological arguments that have been used to explain the cultural significance of hip hop. I will then offer my own interpretation of the cultural work performed by hip hop in the form of an ethnographic study that examines the local hip hop scenes in two European cities, Frankfurt am Main, Germany, and Newcastle upon Tyne, England. Through a consideration of hip hop's significance in these two cities, I will suggest that arguments and discussions among young people concerning the merits of hip hop as an authentic form of cultural expression correspond closely with the differing local contexts in which hip hop culture is played out. In exploring the relationship between hip hop and the local, I will also refer to comparable studies of 'local' hip hop cultures in Italy, France, Southern Ireland, Sweden, Australia, New Zealand and Japan.

The origins and sociological representation of hip hop

There is a general consensus among both academic and non-academic accounts of hip hop that the style originated in the South Bronx area of New York during the early 1970s. A key figure in the creation of hip hop was an ex-street gang member known as Afrika Bambaataa. Aware of the inner-city tensions that were being created as a consequence of urban renewal programmes and economic recession, Bambaataa formed 'The Zulu Nation' in an attempt to 'channel the anger of young people in the South Bronx away from gang fighting and into music, dance, and graffiti'[1] (Lipsitz: 1994, p. 26). Hip hop has since become more widely known because of rap, the aspect of its style that has been most successfully commercialised. Rap is a narrative form of vocal delivery in which rhyming lyrics are spoken or 'rapped' in a rhythmic patois over a continuous backbeat. According to Keyes, the distinctive vocal technique employed in rapping 'can be traced from African bardic traditions to rural southern-based expressions of African Americans – toast, tales, sermons, blues, game songs, and allied forms – all of which are recited in a chanted rhyme or poetic fashion' (1991, p. 40). The backbeat or 'breakbeat' in rap is provided by a DJ who uses a twin-turntable record deck to 'mix' sections of vinyl recordings together in a way that seamlessly recombines aspects of existing songs and instrumental passages into a new musical piece (Back: 1996a, p. 192). A further technique employed by rap DJs is 'scratching', where the records themselves are used to a rhythmic, percussive effect by rapidly running their grooves to and forth against the record player's stylus to produce a scratching sound (Rose: 1994b).

If there is agreement among theorists as to hip hop's point of origin and the socio-economic conditions from which it emerged, there is much less agreement concerning the ethnic dimensions of hip hop and its significance as a form of cultural expression. Thus, according to one school of thought, the significance of hip hop as a cultural form orientates exclusively around its dialogue with the experience of African-American youth. Beadle, for example, has suggested that rap is 'to the black American urban youth more or less what punk was to its British white counterpart' (1993, p. 77). Thus, argues Beadle, relying only upon the ability to 'talk in rhythm', rapping has become the perfect 'vehicle for pride and for anger, for asserting the self-worth of the community' (ibid., p. 85). Similarly, Light defends the essential 'blackness' of hip hop in the face of its commercialisation and 'white' imitations by groups such as the Beastie Boys. According to Light, hip hop 'is about giving a voice to a black community otherwise underrepresented... It has always been and remains (despite the curse of pop potential) directly connected with the streets from which it came' (1992, p. 232). The notion of hip hop as a purely African-American cultural form has been further fuelled by its reception among sections of white US society. Rap music, and in particular '*gangsta rap*' with the often violent and misogynistic overtones of its lyrics, has instilled a form of moral panic among the US white middle classes. According to Sexton, attempts by white institutions, notably the Parents Music Resource Center (see Epstein *et al.*: 1990), to censor rap lyrics has led in turn to a form of 'clinical paranoia' among black hip hop circles in the US (1995, p. 2). Similarly, African-American writer Dyson argues that: 'While gangsta rap takes the heat for a range of social maladies from urban violence to sexual misconduct, the roots of our racial misery remain buried beneath moralizing discourse that is confused and sometimes dishonest' (1996, p. 178). While debates concerning the legitimacy of such claims continue, the point remains that rap and hip hop are being discussed exclusively in African-American terms, a trope that also conveniently excludes the involvement of Puerto-Rican and white youth in the development of hip hop (Flores: 1994; Mitchell: 1998). Indeed, one could go as far as to say that such readings of hip hop historicise and sociologise the latter in a way that closes off any consideration of its significance in non-African-American contexts. This aspect of African-American centred writing on hip hop is exemplified by Potter, who, in response to the growth of interest in hip hop outside the US, suggests that 'there is always a *danger* that it will be appropriated in such a way that its histories are obscured and its message replaced by others' (1995, p. 146; my emphasis).

The implied notion in the work of Potter that hip hop's only authentic cultural resonance is with the experience of inner-city African-Americans is challenged by a number of theorists who argue that hip hop, while it may indeed have emerged from the ghettos of US-America, is, like other aspects of African-American culture, historically rooted in the removal by force of native Africans from their homelands during the western slave trade of the sixteenth to nineteenth centuries (Lipsitz: 1994). Despite the gradual abolition of slavery in Europe and America during the nineteenth century, the African-diaspora created by the slave trade has continued to grow as people have left Africa and former slave colonies such as the West Indies in order escape political and religious persecution or in an attempt to secure a better standard of living and better opportunities for themselves and their children (see, for example, Foner: 1978; Hebdige: 1987). Against this African-diasporic backdrop, it is suggested, cultural forms such as music function as 'privileged site[s] for transnational communication, organization and mobilization' (Lipsitz: 1994, p. 34). This argument is central to a study by Cobley and Osgerby of Afro-Caribbean hip hoppers, in the Peckham district of London, whose attachment to hip hop, it is argued, is 'engendered by diasporic identification' with African-Americans (1995, p. 11). The centrality of the African-diaspora to the cultural dialogue of hip hop is similarly emphasised in the work of Decker, who points to what he identifies as the Afro-centric sensibilities expressed in the work of US-based rap groups such as Arrested Development. According to Decker, such Afro-centricism attempts 'to reverse a history of Western economic dependency and cultural imperialism by placing a distinctly African value system... at the centre of the worldview' (1994, p. 111).

Such work is arguably more useful in assessing hip hop's increasingly global significance than are studies that centre exclusively around the latter's African-American properties. At the same time, however, there remains a danger of essentialising hip hop as a 'black' cultural form. Indeed, it is increasingly evident that the appeal of hip hop is not merely limited to young people connected with the African-diaspora. On the contrary, hip hop and its various cultural activities appear to attract young people from very diverse socio-cultural backgrounds. Significant in this respect is the work of Gilroy, who challenges the contested blackness of hip hop through his positioning of the African-diaspora as a dynamic cultural force whose rootedness in the development of western capitalism has transformed it into a primary influence on global popular culture. Thus states Gilroy, 'the transnational structures which brought the black Atlantic world into being have themselves developed and now articulate its myriad forms into a system of global communications constituted by flows' (1993, p. 80). In this way, argues Gilroy, 'black' culture becomes a global culture, its styles, musics and images crossing with a range of different national and regional sensibilities throughout the world and initiating a plurality of responses.

Gilroy's views and their implications for the interpretation of hip hop's cultural significance are developed in a new body of work that collectively examines the role of hip hop in a range of globally and culturally diffuse settings. Mitchell's research on hip hop in Europe and Oceania illustrates wide-ranging uses of rap and other aspects of the hip hop style in these areas of the world. Thus, in France and Italy hip hop has become a vehicle for the discussion of subjects such as 'racism [and] police harassment' while in New Zealand Maori rap groups campaign for the rights of indigenous peoples around the world (1996, pp. 40, 244–50). Fillipa (1986) provides a further insight into the localisation of rap and hip hop in the context of Europe with an account of rap's incorporation into the suburban and rural cultures of southern Italy. Bjurström considers the significance of hip hop among the youth of ethnic minority groups in Sweden as a form of collective resistance to the white skinhead style, suggesting that hip hop and skinhead represent 'the most conspicuous opposite poles in the ethnic-stylistic warfare of Swedish youth culture' (1997, p. 49). The diversity of hip hop culture at a global level is further illustrated by Harpin in a review of Southern Irish rap group Scary Eire, who, according to Harpin, 'turn local problems, like high unemployment and the cost of everyday living, into sharp rhymes' (1993: p. 58). Finally, Condry's (1999) research into the significance of hip hop among Japanese youth illustrates how local hip hoppers use their musical and stylistic preferences as a means of marking themselves out from what they consider to be the 'mainstream' youth of Japan. As such work begins to reveal, the commercial packaging of hip hop as a global commodity has facilitated its easy access by young people in many different parts of the world. Moreover, such appropriations have in each case involved a reworking of hip hop in ways that engage with local circumstances. In every respect then, hip hop is both a global and a local form.

Global, local and 'glocal' cultures

As noted in Chapter 3, there has been considerable debate among cultural theorists as to the effects of globalisation on local cultures. One school of thought has maintained that globalisation can have only a pathological effect on local differences, which are gradually eroded away by a one-directional flow of cultural commodities from the west, thus producing, according to Ritzer (1993), a gradual 'McDonaldization' of the world. Such views have been challenged by theorists such as Lull (1995), whose concept of *cultural reterritorialisation* provides a framework for an understanding of cultural products as malleable resources that can be *reworked*, that is, inscribed with new meanings that relate to the particular local context within which such products are appropriated (see Chapter 3). Lull's approach is developed by Robertson who illustrates more graphically the interplay between the global and the local. Thus, argues Robertson:

> It is not a question of *either* homogenization or heterogenization, but rather the ways in which both of these tendencies have become features of life across much of the late-twentieth-century world. In this perspective the problem becomes that of spelling out the ways in which homogenizing and heterogenizing tendencies are mutually implicative (1995, p. 27).

Robertson suggests that the crossing of such tendencies is best considered in terms of a process of *glocalisation*. While it could be argued that each of the musical forms and stylistic sensibilities considered in this study is in one way or another illustrative of such a process of glocalisation, it seems to me that hip hop, particularly in view of the often fractious 'in-scene' debates that accompany its appropriation in local contexts, provides an especially animated example of a 'glocal' culture. Beginning with a study of the local hip hop scene in Frankfurt am Main, Germany, I will now consider how the localisation of hip hop, rather than being a smooth and consensual transition, is fraught with tensions and contradictions as young people attempt to reconcile issues of musical and stylistic authenticity with those of locality, identity and everyday life.

Hip Hop am Main

Frankfurt am Main is an international centre. The city's population currently stands at around six hundred thousand people of whom approximately 25 per cent are foreign in origin. Many of Frankfurt's foreign residents, particularly the large Turkish and Moroccan populations, live in the city as 'Gastarbeiter' (guest workers)[2] while many more have fled religious or political persecution in their home countries. Additionally, Frankfurt is the banking centre of Germany and a central European base for a range of multinational companies. Consequently, the city's shopping areas, business quarters and suburbs are filled with the sights and sounds of a variety of different national cultures. Indeed, the Frankfurter Flohmarkt (flea market), held each Saturday on the south bank of the River Main, illustrates perfectly the mix of cultures that exist side by side in the city. To walk through the Flohmarkt is to experience at first hand the multicultural atmosphere of Frankfurt. Hip hop in Frankfurt also owes much to the international flavour of the city, albeit an internationalism borne out of somewhat different historical circumstances. As with other German cities, early experimentations with hip hop in Frankfurt were largely influenced by the African-American rap groups featured on American Forces Network (AFN), the radio station and TV channel established to serve personnel of the US Army, which maintained a presence in central Germany between 1945 and 1996. Similarly, the presence of several large US Army bases in and around Frankfurt meant that the local citizens were kept constantly in touch with many aspects of US culture – particularly US films, shown both in German and in their original English versions, US-style diners and, most importantly, US music and fashion. Thus, as one interviewee explained:

> Frankfurt was introduced very early to soul, funk and so on. There were so many GIs here and they had such a great influence. So many new clubs opened while they were over here.

Similarly, a second interviewee gave the following account:

> When I was about seven years old my family moved to Ginnheim [a town just outside of Frankfurt]. On both sides of the apartment block where I lived were American Army quarters. The guys on one side used to listen to heavy metal music and the guys on the other played soul, funk and rap and stuff all the time.

It was due to this abundant supply of US American cultural resources and information that the first Frankfurt hip hop 'posses' and rap 'crews' were formed. Sachsenhausen, a district in the south of Frankfurt and a principle location for live music venues in the city, is generally acknowledged as the place where the live hip hop scene in Frankfurt began. A local rapper of Spanish-German origin who worked in one of the district's bars remembers it thus:

> During the mid-1980s Sachsenhausen was a traditional meeting point for American GIs, many of whom were into hip hop. As a consequence, it was also the crystallisation point for the local hip hop scene. And that set a precedent y'know. In the beginning the Frankfurt hip hop scene modelled itself very much on the example set by the GIs.

As a general trend, however, this stage in the development of Frankfurt hip hop was rather short lived. A large percentage of Frankfurt's hip hop following comprises young people from the city's numerous North African, South East Asian and southern European ethnic minority groups. In due course, a number of these young people, particularly those who came from Gastarbeiter families and whose social status in Germany remained decidedly unclear, began to make the realisation that, as with African-Americans, theirs was a 'distinct mode of lived [ethnicity]' which demanded its own localised and particularised mode of expression (Gilroy: 1993, p. 82). As a result of this, such groups began to seek ways in which to rework hip hop into a form that could be used as a vehicle for the expression of more locally relevant themes and issues.

The localisation of hip hop in Frankfurt

> We've found our way of communicating... and now the German rappers have got to do that too [African-American rapper commenting upon rap in Germany].[3]

In Frankfurt, as with other German cities, an early attempt to rework hip hop into a medium for the expression of local themes and issues came as a number of local rap groups began incorporating German lyrics into their music. If much has been written about the cultural significance of popular music lyrics (see, for example, Denzin: 1969; Laing: 1971), rather less attention has been focused upon the cultural significance of the language in which they are sung. Arguably, however, language in popular music cannot be assessed merely in terms of the themes and issues that it conveys or in relation to the sound or 'grain' of the voice (Barthes: 1977). Rather, the simple fact of language itself can also play a crucial role in informing the cultural sensibilities that become inscribed within conventions of musical taste. One might think, for example, of the nationalist sentiment encapsulated in the

Welsh 'Celtic rock' movement of the 1970s when the fact of performing and listening to lyrics written in Welsh became a form of political statement in itself (Wallis and Malm: 1984, pp. 139–43). Similarly, in many former Eastern bloc countries, English-language popular music became highly fashionable among young people, not primarily because the lyrical content of the songs was understood but because of the counter-cultural stance that could be implied through listening to such music (Easton: 1989; Pilkington: 1994).

Parallel notions of language as a signifier of particular cultural sensibilities can be identified with the turn towards German-language rap within the Frankfurt hip hop scene. In switching over from English to German-language rapping, it could be argued, a new measure of accuracy was made possible between localised social experience and linguistic representation. For many young Frankfurt hip hoppers, German, if not their mother tongue, had become their adopted tongue following many years of living in the country. Thus, at a fundamental level it was much easier for these young people to rap in German than in English, their knowledge of English being for the most part very limited. At the same time, however, a more ideological motive can also be seen to underpin the move towards German-language rap. Thus, among many Frankfurt rappers and rap fans whom I interviewed, it was argued that only when local rappers started to write and perform texts in the German language did their songs begin to work as an authentic form of communication with the audience. Frankfurt rap group United Energy gave me the following account of their own move towards rapping in German:

> In the beginning people didn't think that rapping would sound like it should if we tried to do it in German. But then people began to realise that it was too limiting rapping in English, because their knowledge of the language wasn't good enough. So now a lot of rappers have begun to rap in German and it's just better, more effective. Anyway, we're living in Germany, so we should rap in German.

Mitchell (1996) identifies similar motives underpinning the popularity of Italian-language rap. In particular, argues Mitchell, the use of regional dialect in Italian rap has become a dominant marker of hip hop's significance in the articulation of local identity. Mitchell also illustrates how the turn towards rapping in Italian has facilitated rap's use as a means of engaging with more nationally felt issues such as neo-Fascism and racism. Comparable examples of such nationally felt issues, and their manifestation at local level, inform the move towards German language rap in Frankfurt and other German cities.

'Ich habe einen grünen Paß'

Two thematic issues that appear regularly in German-language rap songs concentrate respectively upon the fear and anger instilled in ethnic minority groups by racism and the insecurity experienced by many young members of such groups over issues of nationality. The first theme has in recent years become one of national concern in Germany. Since the German reunification in October 1990, there has been a steady rise in neo-Fascist attacks against Gastarbeiter and refugees in Germany[4] (Fekete: 1993, p. 162). This in turn has led to growing support in Germany for anti-Fascist movements such as 'Rock gegen Rechts' (Rock Against Racism).[5] A point often made by German rappers, however, is that despite the well-meant intentions of anti-racism concerns, neo-Fascists and other racist groups will not single out people on ideological grounds but will go for the easy targets, those who can be identified by the colour of their skin. This was the theme of amatuer Frankfurt rap band Extra Nervig's song 'Gib die Glatzen keine Chance!'[6] (Stop the skinheads!).

> You tell me you're on my side,
> Well your fancy words are fine,
> But you're not kicked to the ground,
> Just because of the way you look...

While there are fewer incidents of racial violence in Frankfurt than in other German cities, although this is on the increase, racism is often experienced in other ways. As I have already pointed out, much of Frankfurt's non-German population is made up of Gastarbeiter (guestworkers) who, as with the Asians and Afro-Caribbeans who emigrated to Britain from the 1950s onwards, were called upon to meet the increasing demand for manual labourers in post-war western Europe. Because many Gastarbeiter have a relatively poor command of the German language and occupy minor positions in the labour market, they are often regarded as second-rate citizens, a label that is also ascribed to their children despite the fact that they have been born and educated in Germany, speak the language fluently and often have a skilled trade and, increasingly, a college or university qualification. This problem is, in turn, compounded by the issue of citizenship, which, in contrast to many other countries, is not given automatically to any child who is born in Germany. As a consequence, those people who have acquired German citizenship often find that they are subject to the same sort of stigmatisation as those who have not. The term 'Asylant' or 'Asylbewerber' (a person seeking political asylum) is often carelessly used in youth clubs, cafes and other public places and can be very offensive, especially to those in possession of German citizenship.

Rap group Advanced Chemistry's song 'Fremd im eigenen Land' (A Foreigner in my own Country), along with its simple yet effective promotional video, was one of the first German rap songs to underline the severity of this type of misunderstanding and the hurt that it can cause. Performed by three rappers, each holding German citizenship, but with respective origins in Haiti, Ghana and Italy, the song chronicles the struggle of each to be accepted as German and orientates around the phrase *'Ich habe einen grünen Paß, mit einem Goldenen Adler drauf'* – 'I have a green passport, with a golden eagle on it' (this being the design of the old German passport). In the video, each member of the group is questioned about his nationality. On one occasion group member Frederick Hahn is approached by a white German youth who asks, 'where do you come from, are you African or American?' When Hahn replies that he is German the youth begins to ridicule him and accuses him of lying, only retreating when Hahn produces his passport and sarcastically retorts, 'is this the proof you're looking for?' In a further scene, another member of Advanced Chemistry is asked by a white girl if he is 'going home later?', as in back to his 'home' country, to which Hahn replies 'always the same stupid questions... I've been living in this country for twenty years'. In an interview with journalist Lee Harpin, Advanced Chemistry spoke of their concern to expose the racial exclusion suffered by Germany's ethnic minority groups. Thus, as one of the group explained: 'We rap in German in order to reach our own public, in order that they understand our problem... it's a fact of life that if you're not recognised as a full German citizen you face constant harassment and identity checks' (1993: pp. 59–60).

Since the release of 'Fremd im eigenen Land', a number of German-language rappers in Frankfurt have endeavoured to develop its theme and have also used the rap medium to explore a range of similar issues. The resulting work by groups such as United Energy and Extra Nervig has consolidated in the minds of many of those who attend their performances the link between rap as a politicised discourse and the various insecurities experienced by members of ethnic minority groups in Frankfurt. Indeed, the centrality of rap and hip hop within local strategies of resistance to issues such as racism and racial exclusion is not limited to Germany but can also be seen in a range of other European contexts. Mitchell, for example, has noted how French rap artists such as MC Solar focus on issues of racism in their country while in Italy hip hop provides a powerful critique against the growing support for Fascist ideology and far right political groups (1996, pp. 40, 149–50). Similarly, Bjurström's work on ethnicity and identity in Sweden illustrates how local hip hop fans have embraced Swedish rapper Papa Dee's tongue-in-cheek claim to be an 'Original Black Viking' as a means of negotiating the hostility exhibited by white racist agitators who 'celebrate the mythical Viking as an ancestor to German Nazists [sic] and their modern counterparts' (1997, p. 54).

By the same token, however, to claim that hip hop's role in opposition to locally manifested instances of racism and Fascism must in each case involve such forms of dialogic engagement with issues of nation and national identity is oversimplistic. Thus, to return to the context of Germany, while the lyrical themes of groups such as Advanced Chemistry may find appeal among some sections of Germany's ethnic minority youth, for others the mutuality of German-language rap with the desire to be seen as 'German' is viewed negatively and has resulted in alternative forms of local hip hop culture which actively seek to rediscover and, in many cases, reconstruct notions of identity tied to traditional ethnic roots.[7] This, is particularly so in the case of Frankfurt where the percentage of ethnic minority inhabitants is higher than in most other German cities. During a conversation with a group of hip hoppers from Nordweststadt, a particularly multiethnic area of Frankfurt with a large number of Gastarbeiter families, I noted how German-language rap groups such as Advanced Chemistry were continually criticised for their failure to acknowledge any form of ethnic identification other than that symbolised by their German passports, a failure that was perceived to amount to a symbolic betrayal of the right of ethnic minorities to 'roots' or to any expression of cultural heritage. Thus, as a young Turkish woman put it: 'I think that they [Advanced Chemistry] should be proud of their roots. When people say to me "are you German?", I say "no I'm not" and I'm not ashamed to say that.'

Such sentiments are encapsulated in the Turkish rap styles that are also an integral part of the Frankfurt hip hop scene. In the same way that Asian musicians in Britain have experimented with western popular music and traditional bhangra styles learned from cassette tapes acquired in Asian shops (see Banerji and Baumann: 1990, p. 144), so young Turkish people living in German cities are able to obtain cassette recordings of traditional songs and music very cheaply from local shops established to cater for their cultural needs. Using rhythms and melodies learned or sampled from such cassettes, traditional Turkish musical styles have been fused with African-American rap styles to produce a distinctive variation of the rap sound. If German-language rap has come to signify the voice of the second-generation immigrant attempting to integrate into German society, then Turkish rap works to a broadly opposite effect, the whole Turkish rap movement translating into a singly defiant message aimed at the Turk's white German hosts.

While employed as a youth worker in Frankfurt, I was invited to sit on the judging panel of a talent competition for local bands in the neighbouring town of Schwalbach. As well as those bands taking part in the competition, a number of other local groups had been booked to provide entertainment between the various heats, including a Turkish rap group. Prior to the group's performance, an incident occurred in which some of the young Turkish people who had come specially to see the group began hurling eggs at a white group performing 'Deutsch-rock' (rock music with German lyrics). The Deutsch-rock group's performance had to be temporarily interrupted while those responsible for the disruption were removed from the building. When the group returned to the stage their singer attempted to quell the situation by assuring the audience that, although the songs performed were in German, their lyrics were not racist and should not be regarded as such. Nevertheless, the young Turkish people remaining in the hall continued to act in a hostile fashion and accused the group of being Nazis. Later, as the Turkish rap group took to the stage, a large cheer went up and those who had come to see them moved onto the dance floor in a symbolic show of defiance regarding the incident that had occurred previously. Although many white Germans in the hall appeared to appreciate the music, few of them ventured onto the dance floor, wary of the nationalistic fervour that was manifesting itself there.

Scenes within scenes

The two versions of hip hop examined above importantly illustrate how, even within the same city or region, hip hop scenes can be crossed by competing knowledges and sensibilities which, although working out of the same nexus of local experience, generate a multiplicity of musicalised and stylised solutions to the often problematic issue of place and identity. Interestingly, while researching in Frankfurt, I identified a third hip hop sensibility which, while also acting as a resource via which the youth of ethnic minorities are able to mark themselves out from the city's white population, relies upon an altogether different strategy to that of actively reworking hip hop. Rather, this realisation of the hip hop identity relates to the possibility that it presents for the formulation of a romanticised association with the African-American experience. It is significant that in much of the work that focuses on non-US examples of hip hop, there is an implication that 'localisation' necessarily involves some element of stylistic and musical transformation in hip hop. Thus, for example, Mitchell argues that the development of an Australian hip hop scene has been 'given some degree of "official recognition"' by the release in 1995 of a compilation of rap tracks by Australian artists whose musical and stylistic direction indicates that the local hip hop scene 'no longer needs "supporting"' (1998, pp. 9–10). It seems to me, however, that there is a danger here of essentialising the process of localisation so that it becomes synonymous with obvious innovation. In this way such an interpretation of 'localisation' overlooks some of the more subtly nuanced properties of appropriation and transformation for which Robertson (1995), as previously noted, coins the term *glocality*. Arguably then, the process of localisation, as this relates to rap and hip hop, or indeed other forms of music and style, need not involve any obvious physical transformations of musical and stylistic resources but may, alternatively, rely on localised affinities, which are experienced more at the level of the experiential and which, in turn, demand a more abstract form of analytical engagement with the situating properties of local environments.

Thus, returning to the context of Frankfurt, I would argue that the African-American-based hip hop sensibility described above could also be seen as the expression of a 'local' hip hop culture in that its origins are similarly rooted in the recent socio-historical context of Frankfurt. I have previously noted above how the Frankfurt hip hop scene developed in part because of the influence of African-American GIs whose impromptu rap performances in the city's clubs, bars and other public spaces encouraged imitation among local hip hop enthusiasts. Thus, in this sense, African-American representations of hip hop could be said to have been a 'part' of the local scene from the outset. Furthermore, now that the US army's occupation of central Germany has officially ended, there are clear indications that African-American hip hop will not only continue to be highly influential in Frankfurt but is also set to remain an integral part of the local hip hop scene. Thus, as a journalist working for a local hip hop magazine explained to me:

> Infrared [a small independent hip hop label in Frankfurt] have recently signed a US rap group called Poverty. They were all stationed over here in the army and now they want to stay here and try and develop their career as a rap group. You get that quite a lot. Or American soldiers stationed over here invite relatives over who are into rap and hip hop and they like it here so they decide to stay. In the US there's a lot of competition, very hard competition, between rappers... on every street corner there are ten rappers trying to get a recording deal. It's a lot easier for them over here, particularly if they come from the ghetto, the way of life is much less aggressive here... and the labels are often attracted to them, not least of all because they know that with any luck they can sell their records in the US which means a lot of money for them.

The continuation of African-American hip hop's acutely physical presence within the local Frankfurt scene in turn ensures that it also continues to play a role in the formulation of local hip hop sensibilities. Thus, even today, for many enthusiasts hip hop continues to make 'authentic' sense only in its African-American context. As one young hip hopper argued:

> How can you talk about German hip hop, what meaning does it have? What are you gonna do, sing about the ghetto? I'm into hip hop because of where it's at now y'know. It's a good style, you shouldn't mess with it. Some of those black guys are so cool. I look up to them and respect them... When I go out on the street, they're the ones I'm thinking about, that's who I wanna be like y'know.

At the same time, however, it seems to me that this form of aesthetic attachment to the genre also derives from other distinctive forms of physical and visual experience acquired in Frankfurt's local environment. To put this another way, it could be argued that there is a direct correspondence between the significance of African-American-style hip hop as an authentic cultural practise in Frankfurt and the various terrains, both physical and symbolic, of the city itself. In many of the conversations I had with devotees of German-language rap, strong opinions were voiced against those who continue to listen to African-American rap artists. On one occasion, in speaking about the popularity of US-style 'gangsta rap' in Frankfurt, a German-language rapper explained to me:

There are people who don't understand a word of English, but they like the music so they pretend that they understand what they're listening to and I personally have a problem with that. For a lot of people, the commercial side of it, the image and the clothes are more important than the music and I find that ridiculous. They pretend to be 'gangsta' rappers from the USA and yet we've got enough social problems here which need to be addressed.

It is interesting to note the way in which the word 'pretend' is used in the above account to denote a form of 'playing' or 'acting' out a role, which, according to the interviewee, is how those who favour the African-American style of hip hop must inevitably come to understand their aesthetic attachment to the hip hop genre. An interesting analogy between public life and the conventions of theatrical performance is offered by Chaney. It seems to me that Chaney's conceptualisation of the modern city centre as 'a stage for public drama', together with its underlying implication that the modern urban experience, rather than complying with a commonly acknowledged and 'objective' social narrative, comprises a series of competing fictive interpretations, provides a fitting theoretical starting point for a further exploration of the deeply ingrained visions of America that continue to inform much of the hip hop culture acted out in the streets of Frankfurt (1993, p. 68). If, on the one hand, Frankfurt's multiple fictions of collective life are sustained by the multicultural composition of the city, since 1945 the changing face of the city itself has increasingly enhanced the flow of public drama. In particular, US-directed post-war redevelopment has brought with it a variety of structures, surfaces and images which have met head on with the increasing flow of popular culture resources from the US to produce an enduring visage of America in Frankfurt.

The view from 'Mainhatten'

During the Second World War, Frankfurt was heavily bombed by enemy aircraft and much of the city centre completely destroyed. After the war, reconstruction work was facilitated in Frankfurt and other German cities with considerable financial assistance from the US government in the form of an ambitious loan package known as the Marshall Plan (Mayer: 1969). While care was taken in certain parts of the city to restore buildings as they had appeared in the pre-war years, in other areas modern high rise constructions (Hochhäuse) replaced bomb damaged eighteenth- and nineteenth-century German architecture. In the city centre, such redevelopment programmes completely revised the appearance of the old business quarters and shopping districts. Indeed with its futuristic skyline, notably the Bundesbank, a high rise, glass fronted building with a twin tower design, and the more recently erected Messeturm (trade centre), Frankfurt city centre has taken on the look and feel of a modern North American city. It is perhaps of little surprise then that this part of Frankfurt has become known locally as 'Mainhatten'. Indeed, when such elements of local urban folklore are read in conjunction with a prolonged absorption in Frankfurt's impressive infrastructure of consumer, leisure and public transport facilities, the city centre increasingly comes to resemble the physical realisation of Baudrillard's (1988) 'cinematographised' US, which, Baudrillard argues, has become the primary way in which non-Americans experience the US and thus construct images and ideas concerning the nation, its people and culture (see also Smart: 1993b and Gane: 1993).

Such a visage is perhaps most evident in the pedestrianised shopping precinct known as the 'Zeil' and two adjacent open areas, the 'Konstablerwache' and the 'Hauptwache', which are each built over main intersections of the Frankfurt underground system. Over the years, these locations have become central meeting places for young people, accommodating skateboarders, breakdancers, buskers, street artists and the like. On either side of the 'Zeil' familiar US icons, such as the Disney Store and MacDonald's, as well as a number of imitation US-style fast food outlets, amplify the illusion that this is indeed a scene from a US city. Similarly, the main entrance to Hertie, a large department store, is bedecked on either side and above with multiple TV screens which provide visitors to the Zeil with a twenty-four hour transmission of American MTV.

In the context of this scenario it is easy to see how a version of hip hop culture grounded in notions of African-American style and a form of romanticised association with African-American street culture has become as much a part of Frankfurt's convoluted urban narrative as the politicised German-language variation of hip hop considered above. Offering as they do, a sonic and visual backdrop of Americana, public spaces such as the Zeil provide a perfect stage for the acting out of a hip hop sensibility that imagines itself to be a part of the African-American experience. In this sense, the Zeil becomes simultaneously 'both a real and an imaginary place' (Chambers: 1992, p. 188). Speaking about the popularity of US rap in Frankfurt and attempting to account for this, the manager of a local independent record label specialising in rap made a number of points that add weight to the above observation. Thus, he argued:

The thing about hip hop that people keep forgetting, is that it's not just one definite thing. It's a lot of things, different sounds, different styles, different feelings. You can basically do with it what you want... A lot of kids here go for the groove and the image. They see the videos, they see the clothes and the 'cool image' and the kids enjoy that, they want to be like that. They're just play acting the whole thing. And you know, Frankfurt is this big international city... there's lots going on here, movies, gigs. It's got really Americanised y'know. There's lots of places to go where you can hang out with your friends on the street, listen to your music real loud... just like in the States. English is used a lot here too and even if a lot of the kids don't know it so well they're used to the sound of it and they can pick out key phrases. And that influences tastes in rap music. English [that is, African-American] rap is simply cool, it's in, and you can relate it to what's going on in the street here.

In the social context of Frankfurt am Main then, collective notions of hip hop and its significance as a mode of cultural expression are governed by a range of differing local factors which have, in their turn, given rise to a number of distinctive localised variations in the formulation of hip hop authenticity. It follows, therefore, that if notions of hip hop authenticity are intimately bound up with forms of local knowledge and experience then, in the context of other urban and regional locations with differing social circumstances and conditions, versions of hip hop culture and debates concerning its authentic usage will be based around a rather different range of social and aesthetic criteria. In order to illustrate this point more conclusively, I want now to conduct a further examination of hip hop culture and its attendant notions of authenticity as these are realised in the context of a different local urban setting, Newcastle upon Tyne in northeast England.

Rappin' on the Tyne

In terms of both its socio-economic history and ethnic composition, the cultural context of Newcastle upon Tyne is markedly different to that of Frankfurt am Main. As should by now be clear from Chapters 4 and 5, Newcastle is a predominantly white, working-class post-industrial city. Thus, as was illustrated in Chapter 5, although small Asian and Afro-Caribbean minorities do exist in Newcastle, their influence upon its cultural environment, including the local music and club scene, has been nominal as compared with other British cities with larger Asian and Afro-Caribbean populations. This is also true of the small hip hop scene that has grown up around Newcastle, the neighbouring city of Gateshead and a number of outlying towns and villages, such as Blythe and Cramlington, this scene being dominated by white male enthusiasts. Indeed, the male-centred nature of the Newcastle hip hop scene is another factor that sets it apart from the Frankfurt scene which, although also largely male, is characterised by a growing number of female hip hop enthusiasts and rap groups. This is indicative of both the wider acceptance in Germany of women and girls taking part in music-making activities and the emphasis upon music as a learning resource, which has in turn led to the establishment of numerous community-based music-making projects, many of which offer courses and workshops exclusively for women and girls (see Meinig: 1993; Pohl: 1993; Bennett: 1998). In Britain, by contrast, it could be argued that women and girls wishing to become involved in music-making activities continue to be confronted by indifference and hostility from their male peers. Cohen, for example, notes that girls were discouraged from taking part in community music projects in Liverpool for fear of being 'criticized for wanting to do something that was mainly a boy's activity' (1991, p. 204; see also Bayton: 1988). Similar sensibilities appear to prevent the participation of women in the Newcastle hip hop scene. Thus, although none of my male interviewees claimed to object to female hip hoppers, their code of speech contained a number of male-centred terms such as 'new jack' and 'homeboy', which suggested that they considered hip hop culture to be an essentially male-orientated pursuit.

Hip hop and 'whiteness'

The issue of white British working-class youth appropriating African-American and other black musical forms is one that has long been addressed by theorists of youth culture and popular music. Significantly, however, there has been little attempt to study white appropriations of hip hop in the context of the UK. The essential 'whiteness' of hip hop culture in Newcastle, in addition to providing an ideal setting for beginning such an enquiry, also casts further light on the micro-social issues that inform the 'localisation' of hip hop. In many parts of the UK, the localisation of hip hop has involved its appropriation by Afro-Caribbean and Asian youth, whose collective use of the style has turned partly on its deemed failure to translate into white terms. Such a belief is manifest among Afro-Caribbean hip hoppers in Cobley and Osgerby's (1995) research on the hip hop scene in London's Peckham district. According to Cobley and Osgerby, while Afro-Caribbean hip hopper's acknowledged white appropriations of the hip hop style they refused to take such appropriations seriously, much less view them as authentic expressions of hip hop culture. Similarly, Ashwani Sharma's account of London and Midlands-based Asian rap groups, such as Asian Dub Foundation, Fun Da Mental, Hustlers HC and ADF, argues that these groups' bhangra–rap fusions perform an instrumental function in the marking out of a '*strategic* Asian identity' through their articulation of 'significant dimensions of Asian cultural and political life in Britain' (1996, pp. 44–5). Finally, Back, in considering hip hop's translation in the context of south London suggests that it has moved beyond its initial focus 'on particular British circumstances' and now appropriates 'the language of black New York... to document and mythologize happenings in South London' (1996a, pp. 207–9). As will shortly become evident, such discourses and sensibilities of African-American hip hop also feature in the Newcastle hip hop scene but are translated into white terms. That such a translation is possible in Newcastle, while remaining problematic in other British cities, has much to do with the ethnic composition of the local urban population which, as previously noted, is predominantly white. Indeed it could be argued that the essential 'whiteness' of Newcastle and, by definition, the local hip hop scene, facilitates a highly particularised series of responses to the 'black' characteristics of the hip hop style which, among certain sections of the local hip hop community, amounts to a celebration of blackness in the absence of blackness.

A general supposition of those who have attempted to account for the appropriation of African-American musics by white British working-class youth is that the structural position of white working-class Britons and African-Americans is sufficiently similar to allow for African-American musics to perform a binary role in which the oppressions experienced by each group are simultaneously addressed. Thus, for example, Chambers has suggested that the 'oppositional values' contained in African-American music also 'symbolise and symptomatise the contradictions and tensions played out in [white] British working class youth' (1976, p. 166).[8] Certainly one could argue that sections of white working-class youth may appropriate black music and aspects of black style in symbolic recognition of their felt affinity with African-American and other black ethnic minority groups. At the same time, however, it is also important to acknowledge the actively constructed nature of such a cultural association rather than viewing it simply as a product of structural circumstances. In this sense then, the use of black music and style on the part of the white working-class youth becomes a particular form of lived sensibility; a reflexive lifestyle 'strategy' (Chaney: 1996, pp. 112–25). Moreover, if this line of argument is followed to its logical conclusion, it follows that a number of other actively constructed ideological positions may also be articulated by white working-class youth via their appropriation of black musical forms in which symbolic associations with the fact of 'blackness' itself are considered to be less important. To this must be added the significance of place. It is often taken for granted that white British appropriations of black music and style routinely take place in settings where a prominent black population serves as a continual point of reference for such appropriations. This is the case with Jones's (1988) research on white appropriations of reggae, which was carried out in a mixed-race area of Birmingham, and is also evident in Hebdige's work on the origins of mod and skinhead culture (1976a, 1976b, 1979). In reality, however, white working-class youth's experimentation with black music and style occurs in a range of differing local contexts and thus against a variety of referential socio-cultural backdrops which may or may not include an established black population.

Black music in the North East

The North East region of England has a long established tradition of appropriation from African-American music. During the 1960s, Newcastle group the Animals achieved international success with a style of music based closely on the urban blues of African-American artists such as Robert Johnson (Gillett: 1983, pp. 269–72). Rhythm and blues continues to be immensely popular in the area with a significant number of local 'R&B' groups performing in local pubs and clubs, while each August the County Durham town of Stanley plays host to an internationally renowned blues festival. Similarly, during the 1970s, a number of dance venues in small towns in the neighbouring region of East Yorkshire featured 'Northern Soul', an all-white 'underground' soul scene that centres around rare black soul imports primarily from the US (see Milestone: 1997). Significantly, in the case of northeast England, such white appropriations of black music and style have largely taken place without physical reference to a local black population. As such, the point raised above positing the issue of black 'association' as something that is actively constructed by white youth in their appropriation of black music and style, rather than as a structurally determined 'given' of such appropriation, is perhaps more clearly illustrated. Indeed, the consciously articulated nature of black association in the North East region is particularly evident when one considers the competing sensibilities that characterise the local hip hop scene in Newcastle. At the centre of this scene, a hardcore of hip hop enthusiasts share the belief that their intimate understanding of hip hop's essential 'blackness' as the key to its relevance for the white working-class experience guarantees them a form of aesthetic supremacy over other local white hip hop fans who, according to this group, have no such understanding of the genre and thus no authentic claim to the title 'hip hopper'. Conversely, a number of other local hip hop enthusiasts firmly reject the notion that hip hop can be understood only in terms of its African-American context and attempt to rework it as a platform for the expression of issues that relate more directly to their own day to day experiences. I want now to consider each of these responses to hip hop in turn. In doing so, I hope to illustrate how, as with the various hip hop sensibilities examined in the case of Frankfurt, these responses, despite their obvious stylistic differences, are each intimately bound up with the particularities of local experience.

'You into that "nigger music" then?'

In his study of the music scene in Austin, Texas, Shank (1994) draws attention to the important role played by local independent record shops in authenticating particular scenes by providing a space for like-minded individuals to meet, discuss their tastes in music and argue over the merits of particular tracks and artists, thus positioning themselves in relation to other music scenes located in the same city or town. In the context of the Newcastle hip hop scene, a comparable role is performed by Groove. Groove is a tiny independent record shop in the centre of Newcastle dealing exclusively in US rap which is specially imported and, consequently, not readily available in the high street chain stores. The proprietor of Groove, a white Newcastle man named Jim, is a devotee of African-American rap music and hip hop culture. Having listened to soul music during his teens, he then turned to rap as it became more widely available in Britain during the 1980s. Groove has become something of a meeting point for those who believe, like Jim, that rap and hip hop can only be understood in terms of their African-American cultural context. On the surface, the group of local hip hop enthusiasts who frequent Groove appear to correspond unproblematically with the commonly expounded sociological thesis that African-American dance music is somehow able to connect with the experiential world of white working-class youth in Britain. Below is an extract from a discussion I conducted with Jim and several of the regular visitors to Groove during which I asked them to comment on the issue of *white* hip hop:

A.B.:   There are a lot of white rap fans in Newcastle who are using hip hop to talk about their own experiences.

Jim: There's no such thing as white hip hop.

A.B.:   Why is that?

Jim: Because hip hop is a black music. As white people we should still respect it as black music.

Jeff: All the time before, white people were into black music, hip hop's just the same. There's a message in black music which translates for white working-class people.

A.B.:   What is that?

Dave: It's about being proud of where you come from...

Jeff: Yeah and because it [black music] offers a strength and intelligence which no British culture does.

Jim: The trend at the moment is to be real... to rap in your own accent and talk about things close to you... don't try to be American like. But that's why British hip hop will always be shite... I went to New York, well actually to Cleveland near New York, and stayed with a black family. It was brilliant, it changed my life. You can't talk about white hip hop, it doesn't exist.

Clearly then, among the Groove regulars there is a shared sense of belief that the essential blackness of hip hop is also the key to its use by white working-class youth as an authentic mode of cultural expression. Interestingly, however, when the wider cultural context of Groove and those who frequent it is studied in more detail, it becomes evident that such a belief in the nature of hip hop carries a level of symbolic importance that goes beyond a shared sense of affinity with the African-American experience. Within the local Newcastle music scene, Groove has a reputation for being one of the few 'specialist' record shops in the city. As such the shop enjoys something of an 'outsider' status. Indeed, as a local hairdresser and popular music enthusiast who is familiar with Groove suggested to me one day as I sat in his chair: 'I can't see how he [Jim] makes any money from that business. It's more a labour of love for him really.'

In many ways, the above observation constitutes a highly sensitive reading of Groove and the type of cultural work that it performs. In the context of Newcastle, Groove, although ostensibly a business venture, at the same time plays host to a type of self-styled local hip hop elite in which an intimate understanding of hip hop's black roots is combined with a comprehensive knowledge of rap music and what, on the basis of the group's understanding of the music's cultural significance, counts as good or bad rap. This form of local 'cultural capital', into which the local reputation of Groove is included, is then used as a way of articulating the group's difference from the 'new jacks', a term given to those who are considered to be hip hop 'tourists', that is, those who listen indiscriminately to rap music before moving on to a new trend. Thus, as Jim pointed out:

> These new jacks, you can spot them a mile off. They're just into hip hop 'cause it's trendy like. They come in here and they don't know what the fuck they're talking about. They'll buy about one record a month for a year or something and then get into something else, house or something.

Marks has suggested that white appropriations of black musical forms are often symbolically transformed into 'badge[s] of exclusivity', particularly if such conspicuous displays of black taste on the part of young whites enable them to 'manifest their difference from the cultural mainstream' (1990, p. 105). Clearly, this observation goes some way towards explaining the shared sensibility of those local hip hop enthusiasts who frequent Groove and their collective response towards the perceived fickleness of the new jacks' attachment to the genre.

Arguably, however, there is a further reason why these and other likeminded local hip hop enthusiasts are so passionate in their symbolic association with African-American culture. In a Birmingham-based study Jones has noted how young whites' 'displays of affiliation to black culture' result on occasion in them becoming 'the objects of a "deflected" form of racism' (1988, p. 199). In the social context of Newcastle, perhaps because of the city's predominately white populace, such physical challenges to forms of black association occur more frequently. On one particular evening, I accompanied a group of local hip hop enthusiasts, several of whom were regular customers at Groove, to a bar in the centre of Newcastle where a weekly 'hip hop' night was being held. On the way to the bar the group, who were dressed in typical African-American hip hop style clothes such as loose fitting shorts, basketball caps, designer training shoes and sunglasses, attracted comments such as 'are you going to a fancy dress party?' and were also subject to several shouts of *'wigger'* (white nigger) from other young club and pub-goers. The use of 'wigger' in this context is particularly significant in that it involves a localised reworking of the term. Cobley and Osgerby note how in London, Afro-Caribbean hip hop enthusiasts use 'wigger' as a way of marking out the deemed inauthenticity of 'white youth [who] appropriate "black" styles' (1995, p. 6). In the context of Newcastle, however, 'wigger's' white on white application suggests that it is being used as a way of stigmatising those who are seen as 'wanting to be black' and thus deviating from the locally established norm. Clearly, such 'deflected' racism cannot be equated with the systematic abuse and physical violence that continues to be directed at ethnic minorities in Britain by white racist groups. It does, however, suggest the need for a broader consideration of the factors contributing to racist behaviour and the ways in which the symbolic alliance of whites with African-American and other ethnic minority groups, through mediums such as music and style, might be viewed as a form of cultural betrayal by other sections of white youth.

Such a view is substantiated via other accounts I received of the deflected racism encountered by hip hop enthusiasts in Newcastle. Thus, for example, as another Groove regular explained: 'I used to work in a record shop and I'd always be getting loads of shit from the customers... they'd say "what do you like this nigger music for?" Or, "you only like this music 'cause it's black!" The particular hostility of deflected racism in 'white' settings is graphically portrayed in the following account by a white hip hop enthusiast from Glasgow, another British city with a predominantly white population, whose expertise in breakdancing had led him to move down to Newcastle where he worked part-time in a local dance school. This hip hopper's account of his experiences in Glasgow is comparable with those of the Newcastle hip hoppers noted above. Thus, he explained:

> We were always different like... 'cause we always used to go in the park and that and you'd get these idiots comin' up and saying 'what yoos doin' there, that breakdancin'?'... and they'd do us in... And we used to go to nightclubs and that and the DJ was one of our mates. He'd clear the floor and say 'right we're havin' some breakdancers up now, some really hardcore hip hoppers', and they'd all start spittin' on us.

If the essential whiteness of given local settings can lead to such expressions of prejudice and hostility regarding white associations with 'blackness', at the same time those who are stigmatised for their 'deviant' identity politics often use the fact of such negative responses as a key resource when marking out a cultural territory for themselves. Thus, in the case of the Newcastle hip hoppers, the displays of hostility that they encountered resulted in them becoming even more forthright

in terms of their 'black association', this symbol of 'exclusivity' being
turned around and worn with an air of defiance in the face of a crowd
whose racism, it was argued, went hand in hand with its small-minded-
ness and conservative tastes in music and fashion. Thus, as one of the
group exclaimed: 'I fucking hate the town scene, all that crap commercial music and fashion stuff. As far as I'm concerned it has nothing to
do with my life whatsoever!' Within the group then, there was a
carefully fashioned sensibility which dictated that in being frank about
their dedication not only to African-American hip hop but also to the
stylistic and ideological forms of address they deemed to be a part of it,
they were in turn revealing an honesty and integrity within themselves,
thus setting the group apart from the small town mentality that was
deemed to prevail in Newcastle. Indeed, one could go as far as to argue
that for this particular group of hip hoppers, their staunchly adhered-
to hip hop identity had become a form of external faith, the latter
being reconfirmed each time the group was subject to abuse by 'non-
believers'. As such, incidents of abuse had become not so much
insulting experiences or tests of patience, but rather provided the group
with a platform for displays of collective martyrdom to their cause.
This 'localised' response on the part of white youth to African-
American hip hop style further emphasises the point made in relation
to the continuing significance of African-American hip hop in
Frankfurt. Thus, in relation to Groove and those hip hop enthusiasts
whose shared discourse of authenticity and integrity revolves around
being a part of the Groove 'scene', the local significance of rap and hip
hop derives not from any obvious physical reworking of the latter but
more from a locally forged sense of affinity with hip hop based upon a
sense of its *strength and intelligence* in comparison to what is seen as a
fickle and undiscerning local mainstream youth culture.

A 'street thing!'

A somewhat different if equally constructed hip hop sensibility can be
seen in relation to those individuals who make up what could be
termed Newcastle's *white* hip hop culture. For these local enthusiasts,
hip hop's use as an authentic mode of expression does not centre
around the form of felt association with the African-American experience shared by those individuals who frequent Groove. Rather, there is
a commonly held view among *white* hip hoppers that the essence of hip
hop culture relates to its ready translation into a medium that directly

bespeaks the white British working-class experience. Thus as one self-styled 'Geordie' rapper explained to me:

> Hip hop isn't a black thing, it's a street thing y'know, where people get so pissed off with their environment that they have to do something about it. And the way to do it and get the word to the people is to do it creatively, be it writing on a wall or expressing it in a rap... or wearing baggy clothes y'know. It's all part of this one thing of going 'oh look man, we've had enough of this and we're gonna change it in our way'.

An interesting comparison here is a study by Maxwell of the hip hop scene in Sydney, Australia. According to Maxwell, although the Sydney hip hoppers' realisation of their scene involved taking 'the simulacrum of a culture which they had accessed through the electronic media' the physical realisation of this simulacrum brought it into contact with a new reality, one located in the streets and neighbourhoods of Sydney (1994, p. 15). In a similar fashion *white* hip hop enthusiasts in Newcastle are attempting to rework the hip hop style so that it becomes a form of address that resonates intimately with the nature of their own particular local circumstances. I want now to consider two specific examples of the way in which hip hop has been taken up by white working-class youth in Newcastle as a way of addressing issues encountered on a day to day basis in the city.

'Am that dreadlock hippy bastard that comes from the toon'

This chapter begins with an extract from 'Aa dee it coz aa can' (I do it because I can) by Ferank, a Newcastle poet and rapper. Originally written as a poem, 'Aa dee it coz aa can' was later recorded as rap. As with much of Ferank's work, this rap deals directly with his own experiences of living in Newcastle and is performed in a local Geordie accent, a feature that Ferank feels adds an important element of authenticity to his style. Thus, he argues: 'I'm not American, so it's pointless for me to do a rap in an American accent... Anyway, the Geordie accent that myself and other rappers up here are using is a dialect, just like patois, and so it should be used.' 'Aa dee it coz aa can', which is a essentially a commentary on aspects of Newcastle life and the local Geordie culture, works at a number of different levels. Thus, in one sense the rap is intended to deliver a firm message to those living in other places, both in Britain and abroad, whose impressions of Newcastle are dominated by the notion of the typical Geordie stereotype. Using his own starkly profiled local identity as a springboard, Ferank attempts to demonstrate, through the medium of his informed reading and poetical summary of the local situation, that the stereotypical image of the Geordie character is erroneous. As Ferank explained to me:

> I was tryin' to change people's perceptions of what they think o' Geordies. Flat caps and this Geordie pride thing which I don't feel. Eh, I'm proud o' where I come from and of the people that I care for and who care for me. But eh, there's a lot of malice in this town and a lotta people who need an education. And I'd like to think that I've had one of sorts, and I've always been from here. So it was kinda sayin' 'oh look man for fuck's sake, I might be from here but I'm not your typical Geordie!'. While I am... while I should be accepted as the most typical Geordie.

At the same time, however, 'Aa dee it coz aa can' also criticises the cultural conservatism that Ferank identifies with sections of Newcastle's population, especially when confronted with someone who fails to conform with accepted conventions of appearance such as dress and hairstyle. It is Ferank's opinion that such conservatism is destined to remain a part of the city's character for a long time to come as, from a very early age, children are indoctrinated by their parents into believing that those who are in some way 'individual' or 'eccentric' in their appearance or manner are misfits and should therefore be subject to a form of systematic stigmatisation. Again, as Ferank himself explained to me:

> When I'm out in the street I'll get someone pass a comment on how I look, within earshot of myself and they don't mind if I hear. Y'know... and that's their attitude to everything here... Like I'll walk past kids in the street and they'll be with their parents and that and even the parents'll join in wi' like 'look at the state o' him, they look like bloody rats' tails in 'is hair'. Y'know, they're really blatant about it... These people need an education. You can't get away with that, you gotta expect a reaction. And they normally get one from me... They get it in a rhyme, they're there y'know. And maybe they'll see themselves and go 'oh hang on a sec... I need to think a little differently about what I'm sayin'.

Ferank's visual image combines a dreadlock hairstyle with a broadly eclectic if eccentric dress sense in which brightly coloured garments are often combined to dazzling effect. Thus, as he explains: 'I love to dress up myself, I always have. So amongst my mates it's like, "whoa fuckin' hell, look what Ferank's got on!"' In his rap, Ferank contrasts the playfulness implied in his own chosen image with the harsh reactions which this image often elicits and makes it pointedly clear that, whatever others may think of him, he is determined to stand by his right to be an individual.

> It shouldn't really matter that me skeets are aal tatty,
> An a wear funny clothes wi' me dreads aal natty,
> 'Coz underneath am just like yeez,
> Or have aa just managed to outrun the disease...
> An me eyes just sing the sad, sad song,
> Of the hatred the parents install in tha young...
> ...aal never shaddap an aal never siddoon,
> 'Am that dreadlock hippy bastard that comes
> from the toon.

While Ferank describes his work as a form of protest against the conservatism he encounters on the streets of Newcastle, there is a clear sense in which, at a deeper level, he is also exposing the contradictions inherent in the sensibilities of a local white youth culture that collectively appropriates black cultural resources while simultaneously stigmatising certain individual experimentations with black style as in some way going 'too far'. In many respects, Ferank's personal battle for self-expression serves to re-confirm the fact that many young whites, especially those who live in predominantly white areas, maintain a double standard in which an acceptance of black music and style goes hand in hand with an intolerance of black minority groups. While Ferank, who is regarded as a white 'imitator', remains untouched by the more brutal and disturbing aspects of such intolerance, the reactions of local white youth to his experiments with aspects of black style serve as telling reminders of considerable local variations which characterise racial tolerance and multiculturalism in Britain.

At the same time, Ferank's work illustrates another of the ways in which hip hop is being modified or reworked by white working-class youth in Newcastle so that it becomes a more localised and, in Ferank's case, highly personalised mode of expression. Indeed, it is clear from Ferank's own account of the meanings underlying his work that his personal attachment to hip hop results directly from the artistic licence it grants him. Through the medium of hip hop Ferank is able to publicly voice feelings and opinions that would otherwise find little scope for expression. In this sense, a further similarity can be seen between the *white* hip hop culture of Newcastle and the German-language rappers of Frankfurt in that both of them consider hip hop's value as an authentic mode of expression to be primarily rooted in the power it gives them as individuals to comment upon the nature of their own day to day experiences. This form of attachment to hip hop is further illustrated below where a second 'Geordie' adaptation of the hip hop sensibility is considered.

The 'Broon Ale' ward

Ferank is often to be heard performing his raps at Mac's Bar, one of the few venues in Newcastle that provides an opportunity for local rappers to air their skill in a live situation. While much of Ferank's work is composed beforehand, many of the rappers who frequent Mac's Bar engage in a form of rapping known as 'freestyle'. Basically, this involves taking a particular theme and verbally improvising a series of ideas and points of view around the chosen theme. This form of rapping has also become a primary way in which local *white* rappers address issues that are particular to Newcastle and its people. Indeed, in many ways, 'freestyling' provides a more effective form of local address than written rap as it enables the rapper to engage in a relatively spontaneous form of discourse. Thus, snippets of local 'street' gossip and more widely acknowledged local themes and issues can be verbally woven together with pieces of local urban folklore to produce particularly pointed, hard-hitting and, on occasion, humorous cameos of local social life. The following account is drawn from a conversation with a member of one particular group of freestyle rappers who regularly perform at Mac's Bar:

> We used to use a lot of 'Americanisms' in our raps, but then when we started comin' down here we heard pure Geordie rap. Like with Ferank... it was just like 'oh yeah check out Ferank's flow'. And then people'd be sayin' to us 'why don't you do a rap theme about like eh, like an American rap crew would do a song about Crack and about how it's affecting their city an' that?' An' we started thinkin' 'well aye why not, lets 'ave a go at doin' something about Newcastle Brown Ale' because there's lots of 'isms' for Newcastle Brown Ale. 'The Dog', 'Geordie into space', all these different names and it's... y'know all these different reputations it's got. They used to have a ward up at the General [hospital] which was the 'Broon Ale' ward [owing to the number of people admitted with injuries caused through fighting when drunk]. So we thought, 'yeah, that's the stuff we should be rappin' about'. It's like our version of 'Crack on the streets' with a bit a' humour in there an' all y'know.

While the notion of a white Newcastle rap group rapping about the local drinking culture may initially seem rather comical, it is important to understand the local circumstances to which the group is responding. As with many of those young people involved in the Newcastle dance music scene (documented in detail in Chapter 4), there is growing cynicism among local hip hoppers concerning the city centre pub and club scene and the aggressive, machoistic atmosphere that often manifests itself there. Thus, in a very real sense, by rapping about the problems of excessive drinking and alcohol-related violence, the white rap group quoted above are addressing an aspect of their local environment which, they feel, needs to be acknowledged and changed. Additionally, it is also widely held among members of Newcastle's hip hop scene that the possibility of staging hip hop nights in the city is being continually reduced because of the more commercially successful mainstream club nights that increasingly dominate Newcastle's night-time economy. Consequently, the freestyle raps heard in Mac's Bar assume a dual resonance in that they not only attack the senseless violence that characterises the local mainstream club scene but also deal with the latter's steady encroachment on the hard-won club space of Newcastle's more underground and alternative youth cultures.

The obvious connection of such 'home grown' rap with the shared sensibilities of local hip hoppers is clearly evidenced by the particular type of listening sensibility that it appears to invoke in Mac's Bar. When the 'freestylers' take to the floor, usually towards the end of the evening, the audience, who have up to that point been lazily dancing to a mix of mainly US rap sounds, stop dancing and gather around the performers to listen to their raps. In doing so they are acknowledging the fact that the improvised stories these local rappers are relating work out of a shared stock of local knowledges and experiences that are in many ways uniquely relevant to Newcastle and the surrounding area. In listening to the 'freestylers', regulars at Mac's Bar are receiving accounts of their own lives depicted via a form of quickfire verbal reference to locations and events, names and faces with which they are all intimately familiar. Again, this instance of local hip hop activity is indicative of the close links that prefigure collective notions of authenticity, identity and local experience in hip hop. When the Geordie rappers take to the floor, there is an obvious shift in the audience's response. From the point of view of the audience, the music ceases to provide purely a rhythm for dancing or a background noise over which to talk and becomes something to be listened to, something that actively involves them. In drawing around the stage to listen to the Geordie rappers, the audience collectively endorse the more locally relevant focus of the rappers' messages, thus celebrating its particularised 'authenticity'.

The purpose of this chapter has been to demonstrate how hip hop cultures and attendant notions of authenticity are in each case a product of locality, that is to say, the particular local circumstances under which hip hop is appropriated and subsequently used as a collective form of expression. Using examples of different local hip hop scenes, I have attempted to illustrate how, in each instance, the particular version, or versions, of hip hop culture created, together with attendant debates as to which individuals are *authentically* portraying the hip hop sensibility, is underpinned by a stock of distinctive local knowledges. In each of the local hip hop cultures examined here, the particular characteristics of the wider social context have been shown to greatly influence the manner in which enthusiasts frame their association with the hip hop genre. In addition to looking at localised receptions of recorded rap music, during the course of this chapter I have also made some consideration of how live performances by local rappers can similarly serve to articulate notions of local identity. If 'recorded' musical texts can be reworked by audiences to act as powerful statements of regional place and identity, then local 'live' music scenes and the musicians who participate in them can also play a crucial role in the communicating such themes and issues to local audiences. In Chapter 7, I want to consider more fully the part played by the performance and consumption of live music in local settings in informing notions of locality and local identity.

NOTES

1. Aside from rap music, 'graffiti' is perhaps the most characteristic aspect of hip hop culture. However, because of the nature of this chapter's enquiry, which focuses primarily upon the local significance of rap, it will not be possible to engage in any in-depth discussion of hip hop graffiti. For a more informed analysis of the latter, see Lachmann (1988), Brewer and Miller (1990) and Deppe (1997).
2. 'Gastarbeiter' is the term applied to those individuals, typically from Turkey and Morocco, who have been granted special permission to enter Germany in order to meet the country's demand for unskilled manual labour.
3. Excerpt from the documentary *Lost in Music* broadcast on ZDF, March 1993.
4. This is particularly so in the former East Germany where the influx of capitalism from the west has not, as was expected, led to a better quality of life but has rather resulted in high levels of unemployment and related social problems such as homelessness.

5. For an account of the Rock gegen Rechts movement see de Cologne (1980).
6. The term '*Glatzen*' (plural of *Glatze*) derives from the German adjective *glatt* which means 'smooth'. '*Glatze*' is a slang term often applied to a bald person. In the wake of the neo-Fascist movement in Germany the term has been appropriated by opposers of the movement and used in relation to all German skinheads as a way of linking them with neo-Nazi ideology. This automatic association of 'skinhead' culture with the neo-Fascist movement is, however, largely inaccurate. In Germany, as in Britain, many skinheads are themselves anti-Facists. For a fuller account of this general misunderstanding and the special problems it has caused for skinheads in Germany, see Farin and Seidel-Pielen (1994).
7. It should be pointed out that German-language rap is almost exclusively performed by groups who originate in whole or in part from Germany's ethnic minorities. 'All white' German-language rap groups, the most famous example of which is Die Fantastichen Vier, remain conspicuously apolitical in their music. This has lead to criticism from more politicised German-language rap groups such as Advanced Chemistry, who have suggested in a TV interview that Die Fantastichen Vier are a 'hit pop' group whose style is little more than a fashionable pastiche of hip hop culture.
8. For historical accounts of white appropriations of black music in Britain, see Oliver (1990) and Fryer (1998).

Chapter 7

The Benwell Floyd: Local Live Music, Sociality and the Politics of Musical Taste

In addressing the cultural relationship between youth, popular music and locality, I have up to this point made only a limited attempt to examine the ways in which local audiences appropriate and rework 'live' music, that is, music produced and consumed in the context of a live performance. Although some reference to live music has been made, this has been secondary to a discussion of music as an electronically reproduced medium. The point remains, however, that live music, as performed by local amateur and semi-professional musicians, can also play a significant role in determining the ways in which audiences appropriate and subsequently relate to given musical texts. Indeed, it follows that if, as this study attempts to illustrate, individuals' responses to specific musical styles constitute in part a form of dialogue with the particularities of locality, then local musicians, as members of particular communities, also engage in such dialogues. As such, live performances by local groups and solo artists add a further dimension to our understanding of the way in which musical meanings are produced via an intermeshing of musical texts and genres with particular local knowledges and sensibilities.

The focus of this chapter is the Benwell Floyd, a Pink Floyd 'tribute band' from the district of Benwell in west Newcastle. The Benwell Floyd are one of several hundred bands in the Newcastle area who regularly perform on the North East region's pub and club circuit to audiences ranging in size from 60 to 200 people. In many of these venues basic facilities, such as a stage, lighting and some form of public address system, are provided for the bands. By and large, the atmosphere at such performances is quite informal, bands establishing a rapport with the audience especially when the audience is made up in part by friends or relatives of band members. As such, this type of live performance situation offers an opportunity to study the significance of pub and club venues as sites for forms of what I refer to in this chapter as 'musical' and 'extra-musical' sociality. Much of the analysis that I present during the course of this chapter is based upon interviews conducted with the Benwell Floyd and members of the group's audience, together with other observations and insights gleaned while attending Benwell Floyd performances. Before going on to discuss the results of this research, however, it is useful to consider in more detail how the production and consumption of live music in a local context feeds into and helps to sustain particular notions of place and identity.

Music-making in a local context

In recent years a small body of work has emerged that focuses on the relationship between local music-making activities and the micro-social spaces in which such activities take place. A particularly comprehensive investigation into the local knowledges that underpin music-making at the micro-social level is conducted by Cohen in her study *Rock Culture in Liverpool*. Situating music-making in Liverpool in the context of the city's socio-economic climate, Cohen demonstrates the particular closeness of the relationship between musical and local discourses in the Liverpool area. Thus she writes, 'in a city where the attitude of many young people was that you might as well pick up a guitar as take exams, since your chances of finding full-time occupation from either were just the same, being in a band was an accepted way of life and could provide a means of justifying one's existence' (1991, p. 3).

A further insight into the relationship between music-making practices and local settings is offered by Finnegan in her study of music-making in the southern English town of Milton Keynes. Finnegan makes the valuable point that in considering the local as a source of musical activity, it is important to understand the local as a polymusical environment, that is, an amalgam of differing and overlapping 'musical worlds' (1989, p. 6). According to Finnegan, by studying the polymusical character of a given locality, instead of focusing exclusively upon a 'single tradition', one can begin to understand more fully the social dynamics that inform both the acquisition of musical taste and the local meanings and significance attached to particular musical genres (ibid., p. 7). Thus, argues Finnegan:

> what is heard as 'music' is characterised not by its formal properties but by people's view of it, by the special frame drawn round particular forms of sound and their overt social enactment. Music is thus defined in different ways among different groups, each of whom have their own conventions

supported by existing practises and ideas about the right way in which music should be realised (ibid.).

The notion of the local as a polymusical environment also informs Shank's study of the local music scene in Austin, Texas. Shank begins by mapping out what he refers to as 'the musical construction of community' (1994, p. 9). This involves an imaginary tour of Austin's various live music venues accompanied by a narrative overview of the role played by each venue in contributing to the overall character of the local music scene. In employing such an approach, Shank effectively illustrates the heterogeneous and dynamic quality of the music scene in Austin, established local musics such as Cowboy Song existing side by side with more recently appropriated musical styles such as punk rock. Shank suggests that each of these genres, despite their different historical connections to Austin, have gained equal standing as *authentic* local musics owing to the common forms of vernacular knowledge that underpin their performance and reception. According to Shank, Cowboy Song has become a 'musicalized performance of Texan identity', the 'image of the authentic cowboy [as] autonomous, strong, independent' depicted in such music continuing to inform the 'cultural practice' of the Texan male (ibid., pp. 20, 31). Such issues of Texan masculinity also feature in music by local punk rock groups such as the Huns and the Re*Cords. Here, however, the stress is upon self-mockery and satirical reflection as seen, for example, in the Re*Cords song 'Big Penis Envy' where the local emphasis upon masculinity and male superiority becomes a subject of laughter and ridicule for local punk groups and their audiences (ibid., pp. 112–13).

If the relationship between local music-making practices and notions of locality and local identity is now becoming a focus for sociological attention, so too are those spaces in which local live music is produced and consumed, a growing number of studies examining the cultural significance of local music venues. Fonarow, for example, offers a valuable account of the way in which local venues for 'indie' gigs are spatially organised in terms of the different ages of the audience. Thus, according to Fonarow: 'The young fan in the front is ardently expressive. Moving further from the stage, age and distance increase to the perhaps equally ardent but less expressive older fan in the back' (1995, p. 369). Similarly, Street's study of the establishment of Norwich's indie rock venue The Waterfront illustrates how, in addition to responding 'to an evident need [that is] a suitable size venue for rock music' in Norwich, The Waterfront also represented a cultural space for an articulation of 'otherness' by local musicians and consumers 'who saw their musical careers or their musical tastes as existing outside the national network or the mainstream' (1993, pp. 47, 50). Such studies add considerably to our knowledge concerning the significance of local venues as sites for the articulation of particular forms of collective identity in a local context. At the same time, however, it is important to acknowledge the plurality of local identities which may position themselves around the performances of local bands and the band–audience relationships that play a part in the construction of the latter. Indeed, on the basis of my own research, it would appear that when band and audience already share a common sense of local identity, which may be reinforced through kinship or friendship ties, special forms of band–audience relationship can result in which issues of musical taste, while not insignificant, may be seen as less important than other links between band and audience. Owing to their established function as spaces for informal sociality, pub venues, the typical site for performances by local bands, are in many ways pre-disposed to such forms of band–audience relationship.

Pub venues and 'local cultures'

In his study of British folk music, MacKinnon suggests that the latter 'has moved on from being a conscious attempt to re-create, preserve and rearticulate Britain's vernacular musical heritage, towards being a genre whose central function is to celebrate live, accessible, small-scale music making' (1994, p. 66). If MacKinnon's observation denotes a relatively new development within British folk music then it simultane-ously chimes with a sensibility that has been a feature of local pub venues for many years.[1] Pub venues have long provided outlets for accessible small-scale local music-making and the opportunities for sociality that such occasions facilitate. Indeed, as a primary locus for forms of local social exchange, the pub, perhaps more than any other venue in which music is featured, acts to particularise processes of musical production and consumption, particularly in cases where band and audience are already linked by common local roots. In the context of the pub venue, local musicians and their audiences become highly attuned to the commonality of social experience, which bonds them together, this in turn playing a decisive role in framing the politics of performance and reception. A similar observation is made by Björnberg and Stockfelt in their study of pub music in the northern Danish town of Skagen. Thus, in their description of the relationship between performers and audience in the pub Skansen, where the research was conducted, Björnberg and Stockfelt note how the performers

> mingle [with the pub regulars] when they come to prepare for the evening. They obviously have a very special position, but except for the rather unconventional clothing, you would not know it by observing the interaction in and around the bar. Everybody is a known individual with his or her special characteristics, everybody has known each other for quite some time, everybody is definitely at home (1996, p. 133).

This aspect of live music in pub venues is further enhanced by the attitude of pub musicians themselves. Thus, if many musicians are initially drawn to the pub circuit because of the financial incentive (groups and solo artists often receiving a fee of between one and two hundred pounds for a night's work), in discussing their reasons for remaining on the pub circuit, musicians typically focus on the actual experience of working this circuit and the personal satisfaction that it gives them. This became evident to me as a result of my own experience as a pub musician performing in pub venues around East Yorkshire (see Bennett: 1997). Thus, I would often converse with other musicians who frequently expressed a deep enjoyment of playing in pubs. Such enjoyment, I was informed, stemmed not only from the relatively easy money that could be made but also from the rapport that these musicians enjoyed with the audience, the familiar faces that they encountered at the various pub venues where they performed and the fact that a night's work, which generally involved performing three half-hour 'spots',[2] also allowed time for drinking and socialising with members of the audience. Moreover, such a view was not only expressed by older musicians. I spoke to a number of pub musicians in their late teens and early twenties who also claimed to enjoy the opportunities for socialising, both with other members of the band and with the audience, which playing in pubs afforded them.

Pub audiences become similarly attached to the informal atmosphere of the pub venue, formulating their own particularised patterns of consumption. Again, on the basis of my experience as a pub musician, it seems to me that audiences' attachment to local pub venues also revolves heavily around the 'social' aspects of pub performances – the way in which the music, combined with the consumption of alcohol, generates a relaxed atmosphere in which stories about the day's events and particular situations and experiences can be related. Indeed, such informal sharings of information and aspects of local knowledge often resonate with the music being performed in the pub. Cover versions of songs such as Carly Simon's 'You're So Vain'[3] or Rod Stewart's 'Do Ya Think I'm Sexy?',[4] in addition to frequently providing fitting musical backdrops for discussions between friends and partners, can also be transformed into 'tongue in cheek' renditions by altering parts of the lyric to fit in with certain local characters or events. Such renditions and the characters, points of gossip and other aspects of day to day life, which give rise to them, subsequently become inscribed in the meanings of these songs with the effect that each time they are performed in that particular pub venue the same localised associations are elicited. A similar observation is made by Finnegan, who argues that:

> Pub audiences at musical performances usually [contain] a core of people who [know] each other or at least [have] the common experience of shared participation in specific forms of music, aware of the unwritten traditions of that pub and usually with the *same* conventions for listening to musical performance (1989, p. 232; my emphasis).

Pub audiences then, like the musicians who play for them, are attracted to the pub venue not merely because of the musical performance itself but because of the occasions for sociality which such performances facilitate. Thus, while it would be incorrect to say that the music performed in pub venues is of secondary importance, neither is it accurate to suggest that the discourse that underpins such performances is a purely musical one. It is rather the case that the appeal of certain styles of music or certain songs, and even in some cases the issue of musical taste itself, becomes bound up with forms of vernacular knowledge shared by musicians and their audiences (Bennett: 1997). It is upon the basis of this interpretation of music-making and consumption in the context of local pub venues that·I now turn to the main theme of this chapter, a detailed study of the Benwell Floyd and the socio-musical factors that, on the basis of my research, would appear to contribute to the band's local success.

The Benwell Floyd

As noted previously, the Benwell Floyd are a Pink Floyd 'tribute' band from west Newcastle. A relatively new phenomenon, tribute bands differ from the more commonly found 'cover'[5] bands in that, while the latter perform a variety of songs by other groups and artists, tribute bands generally concentrate purely upon performing the work of one particular group or artist (Jourard: 1998, p. 60). Indeed, tribute bands will often go to great lengths in order to emulate as many aspects of the chosen band or artist's sound, and in some cases image, as possible (Oakes: 1995). In the case of the Benwell Floyd, however, the band's performances are restricted to a musical tribute to Pink Floyd. Indeed, as I will presently illustrate, such a decision has in many ways considerably enhanced the Benwell Floyd's appeal as a 'local' North East band, allowing them to develop an onstage discourse that draws upon distinctively local frames of reference. Formed in 1994 and publicising themselves as 'The Benwell Floyd: A celebration of Floyd's classics 1970–1995', the group have achieved considerable local success, playing an average of ten live shows a month in pub venues around the North East, more often than not to capacity audiences. Without a doubt, a major aspect of the band's local appeal rests upon the unquestionable musical skill of its individual members, illustrated by their ability to reproduce with considerable accuracy the progressive rock style of Pink Floyd. 'Progressive rock' is the term given to a style of music that emerged during the late 1960s and early 1970s in which the volume and dramatic stage presentation of rock were combined with the type of 'musical virtuosity and technical wizardry' more commonly associated with jazz and classical music (Lull: 1992, p. 10). In its formative years progressive rock was an essentially British genre, leading exponents being groups such as Pink Floyd, Yes, Genesis and Emerson, Lake and Palmer (see Macan: 1997), although there were also several European progressive rock bands, notably Can and Faust from Germany and Dutch group Focus (Martin: 1998). While British progressive rock groups have also enjoyed considerable commercial success in the US, their appeal has been eclipsed somewhat by US bands such as Styx, Boston and Kansas who have successfully tailored the progressive rock sound into shorter, more radio-orientated songs (Straw: 1983).

Early accounts of progressive rock by subcultural theorists suggested that its complex musical style and often cryptic lyrics made it almost exclusively the preserve of middle-class students and hippies whose 'educated' listening ability and skill in the use of hallucinogenic drugs, it was argued, enabled them to fully appreciate the meaning and significance of progressive rock songs (see, for example, Murdock and McCron: 1976; Willis: 1978). Certainly, middle-class associations are more easily observed in the case of progressive rock than in the genres of popular music that preceded it. The original line-up of British progressive rock group Genesis met and begun recording while at Charterhouse Public School in the south of England (see Macan: 1997, pp. 147, 150).

Similarly, the artwork of progressive rock album cover designers, such as Roger Dean, drew upon themes and images inspired by the literary works of writers such as J.R.R. Tolkien (Martin: 1998). Nevertheless, more recent academic work has challenged the contention of earlier studies that progressive rock was an exclusively middle-class phenomenon. Thus, for example, Whiteley has argued that:

> there is little to suggest that progressive rock was the exclusive property of the counter-culture. Rather, it seems that there were correspondences between musical practices and social relationships... Progressive rock, like all music, relied on communication and positive identification. As such, it had an intrinsically collective character which suggested that it was capable of transmitting the affective identities, attitudes and behavioural patterns of the group identifying with it (1992, pp. 4–5).

Whiteley's view is supported to some extent by the accounts I received from working-class Newcastle people, now in their late forties and early fifties, of their attendance at major rock festivals, such as the 1970 Isle of Wight Festival, and of adventures on the 1960s 'hippie trail' to Morocco and further east to India. Clearly, however, there is limited value in attempting to determine the class composition of progressive rock audiences so long after the fact. Thus, as Macan points out, 'it is nearly twenty years too late to do a statistically accurate demographic study of progressive rock fans' (1997, p. 151). Whatever the nature of progressive rock audiences in the past, however, it is clear that such audiences are today much more heterogeneous. Indeed, progressive rock now draws its following from a range of socio-economic backgrounds, including some of Britain's most economically depressed areas. In January 1989, an article entitled 'The Dark Side of the Mersey' appeared in the popular youth magazine *The Face*. Its author, John McReady, drew attention to the growth of interest in the music of Pink Floyd and similar bands from the late 1960s and early 1970s among young working-class male adolescents in Merseyside. According to McReady, this phenomenon, which the writer believed to be restricted to the Merseyside area, was a backlash to the judged effeteness of post-punk music. Thus, he argued, as post-punk bands such as the Jam and the Clash 'fought and fizzled out [the youth of Liverpool] could make no sense of the grey overcoat uprising that was left behind. Groups like Joy Division, Magazine and the whole Zoo label axis based in Liverpool were ridiculed as "student crap"' (1989, p. 56). Other observers have suggested a somewhat different motivation for this interest in Pink Floyd among working-class youth. While conducting the preliminary fieldwork for this study, I interviewed a Durham youth worker who explained to me that on entering the youth work profession he had initially been surprised to discover how many young working-class people in the North East area listened to Pink Floyd music. When I told him about McReady's article and its treatment of the youthful interest in Pink Floyd music as a Merseyside phenomenon, the youth worker replied by saying 'yes, but it's a North East thing too... it's actually a drug thing'.

Certainly, changing patterns of drug use among young people in Britain during the 1990s (see Measham *et al.*: 1994), and especially the increasing use of the soft drug marijuana (see Blackman: 1996), may well be a contributing factor to the interest among working-class youth in Pink Floyd and other progressive rock music. Returning to the Benwell Floyd, however, it seems to me that the group's success hinges upon its own set of distinctively localised criteria. Certainly, interviews with individuals connected with the band did reveal a use of soft drugs, captured in comments such as 'I'll often go home, "light-up" and stick a [Pink] Floyd CD on'. However, such drug-speak rarely entered into conversations relating directly to the Benwell Floyd, these conversations being dominated by a rather different range of themes and issues. Significantly, Benwell Floyd audiences are composed largely of overlapping kinship and friendship networks into which members of the band are themselves included. From the point of view of these networks, Benwell Floyd performances provide an important opportunity for sociality. Moreover, those members of the audience who are not included into such networks can often identify with other 'social' aspects of the band's performances, most notably the ways in which these are apt to become occasions for the celebration of aspects of regional place and identity. In this respect, the cultural work performed by local North East bands such as the Benwell Floyd can be compared with that identified by Shank (1994) in relation to local bands in Austin, Texas, in that musical and cultural experience, for band and audience alike, become similarly intertwined and thus inseparable. All of this is not to suggest that the music itself plays no part in the appeal of the Benwell Floyd, many members of the group's audience being devotees of Pink Floyd music. This said, however, in the context of a Benwell Floyd performance, the politics of musical taste become framed within a series of locally grounded discourses sustained by the various forms of association that exist between band and audience. Indeed, the Benwell Floyd's own acknowledgement of these links has, in many ways, become a 'built-in' characteristic of their approach to live performance.

'It's just a cardboard wall!'

The Benwell Floyd's show of affinity with their audience is perhaps most noticeable in the steps that the group take to involve the audience in performances. During the summer of 1995 the Benwell Floyd's live set opened with a Pink Floyd medley containing a number of songs from the deeply introspective 1979 Pink Floyd album *The Wall.* Accordingly, the group had constructed a cardboard mini-version of the 'wall' stage-set that featured in the original Pink Floyd tour to promote the album. In the course of the medley, the Benwell Floyd performed an excerpt from the song 'Another Brick in the Wall Part 1', which contains the line: 'All in all it's just another brick in the wall', signifying former Pink Floyd vocalist Roger Waters' increasing sense of alienation from, among other things, the audiences at Pink Floyd performances. When Steve, the Benwell Floyd's vocalist, sang this line he modified the original lyric, singing alternatively: 'All in all it's just a cardboard wall'. In doing so he introduced an element of humour into an otherwise deeply serious lyric by drawing attention to the makeshift quality of the stage prop behind the group. At the same time, however, Steve also used the connotations of artificiality associated with the word 'cardboard' to illustrate the Benwell Floyd's sense of distance from the original meaning implied in the song, simultaneously reaffirming the band's affinity with their audience.

In other instances the band rely upon their audience's own knowledge of the Pink Floyd back catalogue as a way of involving them in the show, which again serves to affirm the links between band and audience. During one particular performance at the White Swan, a pub in Newcastle, Steve approached the microphone after a rendition of the lengthy first half of the Pink Floyd song 'Shine On You Crazy Diamond', upon which the following exchange between him and the audience ensued:

Steve:	Thanks very much. That was 'Shine On', as I'm sure you know, and that's from the *Wish You Were Here* album which came out in eh... when did it come out?
Audience:	Nineteen seventy-five.
Steve:	Aye, seventy-five that's right, bloody hell that's a long time ago. It's a good job yoos lot can remember... Well we all know why we're here, it's 'cause we're all mad about Pink Floyd. Right, you

can help us again. This one's called 'Fearless'.
Which album's that from?

Audience member: It's from *Meddle.*
Steve: *Meddle* right. Seventy-two I think?
Audience member: No, it's seventy-one.
Steve: Aye so it is. Yoos caught us out again. You're
                      obviously on form tonight.

In the context of a Benwell Floyd performance, the correspondences
that Whiteley (1992) notes between musical practices and social
relationships (see above) are augmented by the mutual affinity of the
social actors involved and thus become doubly articulated. In effect, a
form of cultural synthesis occurs, intermeshing musical and extra-
musical sensibilities, with the effect that the quality of a Benwell Floyd
performance is judged not merely upon its musical merits but also by
what is known of the musicians up on the stage and the way in which
they constantly reaffirm their associations with those watching. During
one particular conversation with Steve, I asked him for his own opinion
as to why the Benwell Floyd had become so successful. His comments
serve to support the observations just made. Thus, he answered:

> Well if you're asking me why we've become so popular, I suppose the short
> answer to that is that we're liked, not only as a band but as people as well.
> Wherever we go there's always a core of people there who we know and vice
> versa. But I also think it's how we're doin' it... I mean, I like Pink Floyd a
> lot, but there's this thing you know, you're shelling out a load of money to
> watch four dots on a stage half a mile away. What we're doing is
> accessible... it's there like... for people to see.

A similar answer was forthcoming when, on a separate occasion, I put
the same question to one of the band's fans:

A.B.: Why do you think the Benwell Floyd are so popular?
Fan: Why? Ha that's easy man, a' can tell you in two sentences. They
         play Pink Floyd music well, you can't fault them. An' they're a
         good set o' people an' all.

As this brief overview begins to reveal, thus corresponding with my
earlier evaluation of local live music performed in the pub setting, the
nature of a Benwell Floyd concert is such that the performance and
consumption of Pink Floyd music, while this is certainly an important
aspect of the event, is conflated with a collective reading of the event's

significance as a 'social' occasion. Moreover, if at one level the band members themselves encourage a form of sociality through their efforts to involve the audience in their performances, then equally there exist other opportunities for sociality which are staged around the actual performance. During the course of my research on the Benwell Floyd and members of the group's audience, several such forms of what I will call 'extra-musical sociality' became apparent to me. Interestingly, each of these forms of extra-musical sociality appears to be grounded in its own particular politics of musical taste.

'My mum's favourite band!'

With the exception of Steve, the group's bassist/vocalist and frontman, who was a teenager when the best-selling 1973 Pink Floyd album *The Dark Side of the Moon* was released, all the members of the Benwell Floyd are in their late teens or early twenties. The band's line-up, although predominantly male, also includes a female member, Jackie, who plays keyboards.[6] According to other members of the Benwell Floyd, Jackie had never played keyboards prior to joining the band and mastered the instrument during intensive hours of practise at home and during the band's early rehearsals. Similarly, Julie, the girlfriend of Robbie, the Benwell Floyd's lead guitarist, has become a proficient lighting engineer through her involvement with the band, while several other friends of the group now act as 'roadies'[7] and instrument technicians. The relatively young age of the band and their entourage, combined with the sense of pride experienced by those who are close to them, ensures that whenever the Benwell Floyd perform live a section of their audience is always there to cheer on sons, daughters, siblings or friends. Thus, as one member of the band explained to me: 'As far as mates and family goes, most of them support us... there's always somebody from the band has someone there... friend, lover, mother, brother, sister.' This was echoed by another member of the band who added: 'My mum's the Benwell Floyd's biggest fan. She's been to about five gigs I think.' And again by Julie who told me: 'My sister's too young but she'd love to come to a gig... But she's got a poster of the band on her bedroom wall.'

In the case of those audience members drawn from the group's own kinship and peer group networks, a preference for the music of Pink Floyd is sometimes secondary to the novelty of seeing a relative or friend on the stage. This is not to say that such audience members have no interest in the music itself, but rather that their musical appreciation is acquired according to different criteria than, to adopt a description once used by Steve, the type of 'dyed in the wool Pink Floyd fan who's been to see 'em umpteen times and probably has all their albums at home'. As I discovered while researching the Benwell Floyd and members of their audience, for those with familial or peer group attachments to the band, it was sometimes the case that Pink Floyd was first heard as 'Benwell Floyd' music and thereafter appreciated primarily in relation to the young group's skill in recreating the Pink Floyd sound and the 'local' reputation that they had consequently earned. Thus, as the girlfriend of one of the band members put it: 'I heard that they were doing this Pink Floyd tribute thing. I'd never heard Pink Floyd before so I went down and listened one day and really liked it. Then I started going to Benwell Floyd gigs.' In other cases, this sense of pride in the group's achievements had motivated some acquaintances to revise their previous feelings towards Pink Floyd music. Thus, as a friend of the Benwell Floyd explained to me: 'I used to hate Pink Floyd music. Y'know, it was like when it came on I'd leave the room. But when they [the Benwell Floyd] started doin' it, well I mean they do it so well don't they. I really like it now, in fact I've got nine of Pink Floyd's albums.'

At the same time, however, such an 'acquired' liking for the music of Pink Floyd on the part of friends and relatives was also underpinned by the opportunities for 'extra-musical' sociality which Benwell Floyd performances offered. More often than not, for these individuals such performances became social 'gatherings' taking on something of a party atmosphere. As such, Pink Floyd music became synonymous with the notion of a 'good night', musical appreciation becoming intertwined with the other conventions of sociality that often prefigure gatherings at which groups of friends or family members are present. Thus, for example, it was typical for friends and relatives to carry on conversations during performances in the course of which they would relate pieces of local news and gossip to each other, laugh and joke, discuss other members of their family and peer group, arrange future meetings and so on, seemingly oblivious to the music itself. Oblivious, however, they certainly were not as they would occasionally demonstrate by interrupting their conversations and turning to the stage in order to show support for the band, shouting out the name of the band member or members with whom they most strongly identified or, alternatively, making visual gestures such as waving their hands in the air and giving 'thumbs up' signs. Similarly, such groups were inclined on occasion to join in with the most apparently 'sing-along' parts of the group's repertoire, adding in collective shouts or chants of support, such as 'c'mon Robbie!' (the Benwell Floyd's lead guitarist) or 'bloody excellent!' Björnberg and Stockfelt note similar patterns of audience behaviour in their research on pub gigs in the northern Danish town of Skagen. Thus they observe:

> The music and the stage performance... do not interrupt any socialising or hinder any unfinished conversations – they add to the floor show without subtracting anything, making the mixture of social events and opportunities even richer (1996, p. 134).

For many relatives and friends of the Benwell Floyd then, the live performances of the band, although in themselves highly revered, were often understood in terms of the wider patterns of 'extra-musical' sociality, the collectively construed 'good times', to which such performances gave rise. The following conversation took place at a pub bar, during my first outing to see a Benwell Floyd performance. My conversation partner was a young man who, as I later learned, was a longstanding friend of the group:

Friend: What you doin' here like, do you know 'em?
A.B.: Know who?
Friend: The band like, the Benwell Floyd.
A.B.: I do know them, yes.
Friend: Bloody great eh! Were you at the Mile End gig, yeah you must a' been eh...?
A.B.: No, I haven't seen them before.
Friend: Ah right, it's yer first time is it! It won't be yer last mind, it's always a good night out, a bloody good do. I get down as much as I can like. 'Al see yers later.

At the same time, however, it became obvious to me that not all friends and relatives of the Benwell Floyd who attended the group's performances interpreted these events in such a way. For some, particularly parents and older siblings of band members, the Benwell Floyd represented the pinnacle of their attempts to musically educate the younger members of their families. During Benwell Floyd performances, many people, particularly those who were watching the band for the first time, expressed surprise at the fact that the group, despite their young age, were able to perform Pink Floyd music with such competence. As one female fan in her late twenties put it: 'Apart from the lead singer none of them look much over twenty-one. I mean when *Dark Side of the Moon* came out most of this lot weren't even born and yet they play it brilliantly. That's an achievement.' Sometime later I mentioned this comment to the members of the Benwell Floyd and asked them how they had initially become interested in performing Pink Floyd music. One of the band said that he had first 'got into Floyd' in the spring of 1994 following the release of *The Division Bell*, the first new Pink Floyd studio album in seven years. Another said that he had begun to listen to Pink Floyd music after seeing the film version of *The Wall* on video.[8] Several band members, however, gave an altogether different account of their introduction to the music of Pink Floyd. Thus, as Pat, the Benwell Floyd's drummer explained: 'Floyd have been up that long... they've been making records since 1967, they're still doing it now... so there's that wider audience... I've been brought up with 'em me... my brother's always loved 'em since being a young lad and I've always liked 'em from being a young lad.'

As Pink Floyd join the growing number of veteran popular music artists who can now celebrate over thirty years in the music business, the notion of children inheriting their parents' and older siblings' tastes in popular music is one that is quickly gaining credence among journalists and academics. In the wake of Pink Floyd's phenomenally successful Earl's Court appearances during the Autumn of 1994 an article in the *Guardian* observed: 'IT ISN'T JUST [sic] the 30-to-50-somethings who are flocking Floydwards. There's a new generation of listeners in their teens and twenties, who have been brought up to revere the Pink Floyd imprimatur by parents or older siblings' (Sweeting: 1994, p. 8). Similarly, Cohen's Liverpool-based ethnographic research revealed that many young people in the city 'listened to the same music as their parents' thus inheriting their parents' musical tastes (1991, p. 19). In a separate study, Cohen and McManus (1990) discovered a whole infrastructure of informal and semi-professional family music-making in Liverpool sustained by similar processes of musical 'inheritance'. Likewise, in her study of local music-making practices in Milton Keynes, Finnegan observes that: 'Several local rock players came from families in which one or both parents had performed in pubs or working men's clubs; in such cases playing in a rock band was a kind of continuity' (1989, p. 310).

It seems to me, however, that there is an altogether different sense in which this type of inter-generational musical inheritance can be understood. Rather than simply involving a straightforward appropriation of musical taste, such inheritance becomes a form of ongoing dialogue between family members. This can be clearly illustrated in the context of a Benwell Floyd performance. Thus, for those members of the Benwell Floyd whose interest in Pink Floyd music stems from such an informal musical education received in the family home, the memories of this education accompany them onto the stage. As such, the performance becomes in part a musicalised reminiscence which is also shared by family members in the audience. What follows is an affirmation of the felt links between the young musicians and their families in 'musical' terms. When the Benwell Floyd perform for their families they are, in part, engaging in a celebration, along with parents and older siblings in the audience, of the musicalised moments that have accumulated over the years and that have made the performance possible. When the band and their families sing the words to certain Pink Floyd songs, they are collectively reliving the memories that, for them, have become woven into the understanding of such songs. Similarly, the performance of certain musical phrases can also elicit collective meanings which, for particular family groups, have become embedded in such phrases. As Steve pointed out to me: 'It's really amazing the number of emotions that you go through on stage. And when you look at the audience, you see it mirrored in a way... the silence throughout "Wish You Were Here"... the singing throughout "Another Brick in the Wall"... the crying on "Us and Them".'

Significantly, the sight of family members singing along to popular music being performed live by their children or, alternatively, by brothers and sisters is becoming increasingly commonplace in local pubs and similar venues such as community centres and village halls. In addition to Benwell Floyd performances, I have attended a number of pub and other local performances in Britain, Germany and North America where the band–audience relationship was essentially similar to that of the Benwell Floyd and its audience and where similar forms of exchange occurred. Similarly, while working with the Rockmobil, a mobile music-making project based in Frankfurt, Germany (see Bennett: 1998), I was involved in the organisation and co-ordination of several 'showcase' concerts in local youth clubs. Such concerts were designed to allow the young groups, who had formed as a result of their participation in Rockmobil workshops, to gain experience of live performance. At each of these concerts, a considerable section of the audience was made up of family members of the musicians concerned, the former openly enthusing about the way in which their sons and daughters or brothers and sisters had mastered the art of playing blues, rock or punk records which they had first heard as a result of being 'introduced' to such records in the family home. On a separate occasion, during a guitar workshop which I gave at Howden[9] Secondary School in 1986, I was asked by two of the participants, who I later learned were brothers, if I was able to play 'Brighton Rock', the opening track from the Queen album *Sheer Heart Attack* released some twelve years before. Having played a short extract from the song, I asked the boys about their seemingly unusual request upon which I discovered that they regularly listened to and attempted to play music from their father's record collection. Such instances of musicalised familial interaction provide another indication of the ways in which instances of collective participation in musical life are in each case unique, localised instances of social expression informed by particularised knowledges and sensibilities. The same case can also be argued for the following example of 'extra-musical sociality' staged around the live performances of the Benwell Floyd.

'I'm a Dopeski man!'

Having seen the Benwell Floyd perform live on a number of occasions in the North East region, I asked the band members which pub venue they most enjoyed playing at. All agreed that by far the best one was located in Consett, a former steeltown in County Durham. 'It's the place to be [I was informed] you go to play a gig on a Saturday night and it's a weekend job... There's just some atmosphere there, you know it's going to be a good gig and you know it's going to be parties all night.' When I enquired as to who organised these parties I was somewhat surprised at the answer I received:

Robbie: The parties are all done by the old bikers... thirty year olds upwards. They really know how to party.
A.B.: By old bikers?
Steve: Aye, there's a lot of bike lads and ex-bike lads up there. A lot of guys who are reliving their teens I suppose it's fair to say.

I asked Steve if it would be possible to meet some of the Consett biker crowd and was subsequently introduced to a group of friends who referred to themselves as the 'Dopeskis'. During the weeks that followed I attended a number of Benwell Floyd performances with the Dopeskis. Several interesting features of this particular audience group quickly became apparent me. For many years, the only available sociological research on motorbike or 'biker' culture was that conducted by Willis (1972, 1978) in the early 1970s. Willis's depiction of biker culture at this time was of a male-dominated 'subculture' whose stylistic preference and musical taste continued to centre around 1950s rock 'n' roll. Thus observes Willis:

> The motor-cycle gear looked tough with its leather studs and denim, and by association with the motor-bike, took over some of the intimidating quality of the machine. Hair was worn long, in a greasy swept-back style, drawing on connotations of the early Elvis image (1978, p. 20).

In a recent study, McDonald-Walker suggests that such images of biker culture have little relevance in the context of the 1990s as 'stringent legislation has largely eroded the distinction made by Willis between the "motorbike boy" and the "conventional motorcyclist" in the 1960s' (1998, p. 384). Similarly, argues McDonald-Walker, Willis's schema 'of motorbike/male/working-class/violence is [now] problematic' given the more heterogeneous nature of motorbike culture including the involvement of many middle-class professionals whose knowledge of the motorbike and expertise in riding is in every respect comparable to that of working-class bikers (ibid.). Indeed, it is arguable that contemporary bike culture, rather than orientating around class identification, comprises like-minded enthusiasts for whom an avid interest in all aspects of the motorcycle is of primary importance.

McDonald-Walker's study offers an important revision of the socio-economic composition of biker culture and attendant significance of the motorbike presented in Willis's account. There is, however, a further way in which the biker culture of the late 1990s differs quite considerably from that researched by Willis in the early 1970s. This difference has to do with the shifting musical tastes of 'bikers' during the 1970s and the continuing influence of this shift on the musical tastes of biker culture today. The early 1970s saw the appearance of a new style of music that became known as heavy metal. Pioneered by British groups, such as Black Sabbath, whose music and stage presentation influenced a generation of US groups, notably Kiss and Van Halen (see Walser: 1993; Arnett: 1995), heavy metal was characterised by a 'musical and cultural style' that, according to Chambers, had 'been forged in the very heartlands of progressive music' (1985, p. 124).

If heavy metal incorporated the 'technological effect[s] and instrumental virtuosity' associated with the progressive rock, then the music's harder edge and added volume was in turn highly influential upon the development of progressive rock during the early 1970s (Straw: 1983, p. 97). Indeed, it could be argued that the harder progressive rock style developed in the wake of heavy metal, of which the later Pink Floyd is a prime example, was in many ways directly inspired by heavy metal's experimentations with volume and the more dramatic dynamics of sound manipulation which such volume facilitated. Indeed, as Martin observes, 'despite the qualitative developments that led to progressive rock, it is not as though this music was as disconnected from the rest of rock music as some critics and historians now seem to think' (1998, p. 167). Certainly a number of the more musically accomplished heavy metal groups, such as Led Zeppelin, were able to crossover into progressive rock, retaining a foothold in each market for much of their careers (ibid., pp. 166–7). In fact the fan base for heavy metal and progressive rock was essentially the same audience, largely comprising hippies and bikers. Indeed, by this time the sixties style 'rocker' version of motorbike culture, with its attachment to fifties rock 'n' roll, had all but disappeared and been replaced by a new type of biker whose endorsement of the hippie lifestyle was unmistakable. The greasy hairstyle of the sixties had been replaced by long flowing hair and concomitant hippie sensibilities such as burning incense and smoking marijuana. Similarly, the new-style biker was often to be seen at outdoor weekend festivals which, in the wake of the 1969 Woodstock event, became increasingly popular (McKay: 1996). At such festivals the dramatic blurring of the boundaries between the various rock genres was strikingly apparent, heavy metal bands, progressive rock artists and 'blues rock' bands, such as Ten Years After, Free and Taste, often sharing the same billing.

It is within the context of this more eclectic rock sensibility that current biker groups such as the Dopeskis need to be understood. The Dopeski lifestyle is one in which the central tenets of 'motorbike' culture, such as the skill in riding and maintaining a motorbike, knowledge of different makes of motorbike and the various features found on individual models, have become inseparable from a form of hippie lifestyle. The Dopeskis place a great deal of emphasis on being together. During the weekends they live an essentially communal life in which the rhythm of the day is entirely restructured using a combination of drugs, alcohol and music. The very first time I met the Dopeskis I was asked back to a specially arranged 'lock-in' at a pub in Consett and invited to stay the night at Dopeski member Tucker's house on the condition that, to use his words, 'you don't mind sharing the floor with this lot'. Such 'lock-ins', I was told, occurred on a regular basis. Indeed it was during one of these late night drinking and 'smoking' sessions that the group had apparently acquired its name. Thus, as Ben, another member of the Dopeskis explained to me: 'We were all sitting around in the pub one night pissed and stoned and Jill got up on the table and sat there cross-legged. An' I said to her "you look like a Pixie" and she said [puts on slurred voice] "I'm not a pixie, I'm a Dopeski man". And that was it, the name's stuck ever since.' Indeed, the term 'Dopeski' has become an increasingly important marker of group solidarity to the extent that members of the Dopeskis now wear specially made T-shirts featuring the name together with a self-designed Dopeski logo.

In addition to such visual markers of group identity, the Dopeskis also frequently engage in a process of what could be termed collective 'memory-making'. Moreover, if the wearing of Dopeski T-shirts is, to some extent at least, intended to draw the attention of others to the group's existence and felt sense of unity, collective memory-making is a rather more intimate celebration of group identity. Such memories are based upon the Dopeskis' collective experiences, typically those that relate in some way to the consumption of music, the group regularly undertaking long-distance trips to concerts and festivals. Such outings are subsequently 'relived' during informal get-togethers. In relating intricate details of these outings, for example, funny incidents or the antics of a particular group member, the Dopeskis in turn confirm their sense of collective identity to each other. Moore has noted the centrality of similar processes in the formulation of a coherent group identity in his empirical study of skinheads in Australia. Thus, he argues:

> Stories about events become the subject of memories to be relived and embellished in the future... The telling of stories usually occurs in a group context. Several skinheads may be sitting in a pub or at someone's house or flat, drinking. Inevitably, conversation turns to past good nights or good laughs. The history of consociation is invested in these memories (1994, p. 142).

The Dopeskis display a seemingly inexhaustible capacity for telling stories gathered together from the group's own history of partying, concert-going and general socialising. Such collective memories function as a mental catalogue of shared experiences and events, sequences of which are played back each time the group meet. Moreover, in much the same way that an album of family photographs is often used as a means of familiarising new friends and acquaintances with the members of that family and the traits and characteristics that distinguish one member from another, so the collective memories that have built up around each particular Dopeski are used by the group as a way of collectively introducing themselves to others. During my first meeting with the Dopeskis, I was introduced to each of them via this method of collective story telling as the following extract from that meeting illustrates:

Mae: That's Jill over there. She just loves to travel. She can't settle
          down, always wants to be somewhere else. That's right isn't it?
Jill: Aye [grins].
Mae: It's like, she'll clear off an' you won't see her for days. Do you
          remember that time Jill, you phones us up an' I said 'where the
          'ell are you this time' an' you says 'I'm in Wales'?
Jill: Yeah, but it never lasts like, 'cause a' get homesick [laughs].
Tucker: Aye that's right she's always gonna come back...
Jill: 'Cause she just loves us really don't ya like!

Another collective memory, which the Dopeskis particularly enjoy
reliving, relates to the first time they attended a Benwell Floyd performance and the events that led up to this. The following story was told
to me by various members of the Dopeskis, but most graphically by
Ben, whose account I include here:

> We'd been to see Pink Floyd in Amsterdam and then the following week at
> Earl's Court [in London]. More or less straight after that we found out that
> the Benwell Floyd were going to play at our local [pub]. You can imagine
> how we reacted... it was like 'well they'd better be good'. We'd just been to
> see Pink Floyd like and they'd totally blown us away. Anyway on the night
> we were all sitting around stony faced thinking 'who are this lot... they'd
> better be good or they're for it'. So they started with 'Shine On' and one by
> one our faces lit up. And then we were all saying 'this is all right'. I mean,
> we're all crazy about Pink Floyd, so they had to impress us. Since then
> we've seen 'em develop, and we've got to know them all too. Rob's become
> a lot more confident on the guitar, he's really going for some of those
> Gilmour[10] licks[11] now. Mike's a real worrier and a perfectionist and Pat is
> like so laid back, but a great drummer.

In charting the Dopeskis' initial and subsequent encounters with the
Benwell Floyd in this way, Ben's account not only serves to reconfirm
the group's version of these events, constant reconfirmation of the 'facts'
being a vital aspect of the collective storytelling in which the group
engages, but also supplies an important insight into the Dopeskis'
developing relationship with the Benwell Floyd. Thus, the Benwell
Floyd are seen to transgress from 'outsiders' infringing upon the
Dopeskis' memories of good times had at Pink Floyd concerts to close
friends whose performances become themselves the subject of such
collective memory-making. I have already noted that the Benwell Floyd
particularly enjoyed playing in Consett because of the hospitality
offered to them by the Dopeskis. Indeed, there was something of a

received wisdom among members of the band that a gig in Consett was simply the opening feature of a night, or indeed a weekend, of partying. This form of extra-musical sociality, however, also had a reciprocal effect in that, by entering into the Dopeskis' own weekend rhythm and taking part in their activities, the Benwell Floyd offered new ways in which the Dopeskis' memories of good times could be weaved into the collective experience of listening to Pink Floyd music. Thus, for example, as Tucker explained to me:

> When they play in Consett they often come back to ours afterwards for parties... and always end up stayin' the night. I mean, that's how we spend our weekends. There's always about six people sleeping over at our place. An' sometimes they play for us too... like last month. We had a barbecue and we got them to come over and play for us. We sorted out a little marquee for them and they played in the garden.

Moreover, as the bond of friendship between the Dopeskis and the Benwell Floyd became stronger the Dopeskis were able to devise other ways of both consolidating and displaying their collective sense of identity through their association with the band. On one particular occasion the Benwell Floyd had been booked to play a working men's club in west Newcastle. The band had agreed to perform at the club as the event was to be in aid of charity. Nevertheless, the individual Benwell Floyd members were not particularly enthusiastic at the prospect of performing in front of an audience who they knew were more used to playing bingo and listening to the type of 'golden oldie' bands who frequent such clubs (see, for example, Finnegan: 1989; Beattie: 1990; Bennett: 1997). Consequently, the Dopeskis had agreed to go along to the club to cheer the Benwell Floyd on and give them some support. On the evening of the performance I arrived at the club to find the Dopeskis standing outside the building having being refused entry on the grounds that they were not members. After some deliberation on the part of Steve with the club's officials, the Dopeskis were eventually allowed in, much to the surprise of the regular patrons who were obviously not used to their club being visited by men in customised leather jackets and hobnail boots and women with long flowing hair, cheesecloth smocks and beads.

Initially the Dopeskis sat quietly in a corner but as the Benwell Floyd came onto the stage they began to cheer loudly moving into the space left by the regulars who, in anticipation of the loud volume, had moved back from the stage area. Some of the Dopeskis then began to dance in front of the stage, occasionally climbing onto it and grinning at the members of the band who grinned back, obviously finding all of this very amusing. Other Dopeskis sat cross-legged on the floor gently swaying from side to side in time with the music. Occasionally a Dopeski would pick up a beer mat, tear off the front to reveal the plain white card underneath and write down a Pink Floyd request, this being subsequently placed on the stage directly in front of Steve. In between songs Steve would survey the requests, attempting to guess who had made each of them. If the group was able to play a requested song Steve would tell the Dopeskis in advance. Alternatively he would promise to 'get that one sorted out for next time'.

During the performance intermission, a regulation stipulated by the club in order that the club members could play bingo, the Dopeskis became restless and began to call out derogatory remarks. At first these were just mumbled comments such as 'bloody boring this'. However, the longer the bingo went on, the more vocal the Dopeskis became, eventually resorting to shouts of 'get off', 'let's have some more music' and 'we want the Benwell Floyd back on'. When the Benwell Floyd did reappear to perform their second set, there occurred a brief exchange that served to consolidate the bond between the band and their specially imported following. Thus, Steve called out over microphone that Mae, Tucker's wife, should 'get herself on-stage'. As she did so, Steve produced a bouquet of flowers, announcing to the audience, 'it's their wedding anniversary today an' her old man asked me to hide these flowers for him so he could surprise her'.

Thus far, I have been concerned to examine several ways in which the Benwell Floyd, as a local live performing group, facilitate forms of sociality that, in turn, have a considerable bearing upon the meaning and significance that the group's audience attach to the consumption of Pink Floyd music. One such form of sociality, I have suggested, results from the band's own attempts to involve the audience in the show. I have further suggested that friends and relatives of the Benwell Floyd, who as I have shown regularly make up a large part of the band's audience, engage in what I have called forms of 'extra-musical sociality' which are staged around the actual musical performance. There is, however, a further sense in which Benwell Floyd performances may be said to imbue the music of Pink Floyd with a strong sense of locally mediated significance, one that relates to the images and sensibilities of regional identity that are traded between band and audience during such performances.

A tribute to the North East

As I pointed out earlier, the Benwell Floyd are a Pink Floyd 'tribute' band. Although the tribute band is a relatively recent phenomenon, it is a trend that is quickly gaining popularity in many parts of the developed world. Other examples of tribute bands include the internationally acclaimed British quartet, the Bootleg Beatles, the Australian Doors, the Frankfurt ACDC tribute band, ABCD, and Sticky Fingers, a Rolling Stones tribute band from New York featuring Dick Swagger and Keef Ripoff (Evans: 1998, p. 49). Jourard suggests that: 'Tribute bands fill a useful niche in the concert scene by bringing an "amazing simulation" to fans who can't otherwise experience their favourite stars in action', Jourard's observation resting upon the fact that the majority of tribute acts play the music of bands that are now defunct or who tour very infrequently (1998, p. 60). Similarly, Oakes has suggested that: 'Tribute bands aspire to more than just covering a well-known rock band's material, they also try to capture that band's essence, however, elusive and open to interpretation that concept may be' (1995, p. 1). In the case of the Benwell Floyd, however, it seems to me that it is not simply the essence of Pink Floyd and their music that is being celebrated. Rather, the Benwell Floyd also capture in their performances what many members of the audience consider to be essential aspects of the local culture of the North East region. Certainly, the Benwell Floyd's chosen musical text and their interpretation of it is a major factor in their regional success. At the same time, however, such appeal could also be argued to stem from the band's strong regional sense of place and their decision to articulate this during live performances. Similarly, although the Benwell Floyd, in performing Pink Floyd songs, incorporate associated visual icons such as the 'wall' and 'inflatable pig'[12] imagery into their stage show, they also imbue their performances with a range of visual and oral knowledges and sensibilities that derive directly from the North East region and its culture. These 'tributes' to the North East manifest themselves in a number of ways during Benwell Floyd performances.

To begin with, the Benwell Floyd make no attempt to disguise their Newcastle roots. Steve's on-stage banter between songs is delivered in a thick Geordie accent and makes use of a range of mannerisms and colloquialisms that are frequently incomprehensible to audience members from outside the North East region. I suggested earlier that in the context of local pub venues, where the majority of Benwell Floyd performances take place, ready-made channels exist for the exchange of such localised forms of address between musicians and their audiences. Moreover, it is not merely local dialect and locally inscribed forms of expression that are exchanged at Benwell Floyd gigs. The intimacy of the pub venue environment, combined with its accepted role as a site for gossip, small talk and camaraderie, facilitates the articulation of a whole stock of local knowledges and sensibilities. This quality of the local pub venue is clearly in evidence each time the Benwell Floyd take to the stage. During performances, the Benwell Floyd and their audience perpetually engage in a form of dialogue, including in-jokes, story telling and collectively held statements of 'fact', which are often uniquely particular to the North East region. Such forms of localised dialogue are often heard in pub venues. As a student at Hull University, I regularly depped[13] with local pub bands who engaged in similar forms of dialogue with audiences in which past and present aspects of the city's local culture, for example the fishing industry, rugby and annual events such as Hull Fair, were regular talking points.

A local theme with which the Benwell Floyd and their audience regularly engage is the intense rivalry that exists between two of the region's principle football teams, Newcastle United and Sunderland United. It should perhaps be pointed out that such rivalry is not merely a masculine sensibility, football in the North East, as in other regions, having become very much a 'family' game during the 1980s and 90s (see Redhead: 1997; King: 1997). Similarly, increasing numbers of women are becoming actively involved in football with the formation of all-women teams (Haynes: 1993). Such aspects of football and football fandom, as manifested at the local level, are often very much in evidence during Benwell Floyd performances. During the summer of 1995 at a performance in Peterlee, a small town in County Durham with a strong Sunderland United following, Steve, an ardent Newcastle supporter, appeared on stage for the Benwell Floyd's second spot wearing a Newcastle United football shirt. He was immediately greeted with shouts of 'get a life' by a group of women sitting at the back of the pub. Steve's playful response to this anticipated reaction was succinct: 'What's that you just said, "get a life"? Just enjoy the music man.' Immediately a man near the front jumped to his feet and shouted out 'aye your music's great man, no worries. But that top stinks', which resulted in much laughter from the group of women who had initially remarked on Steve's wearing of a Newcastle shirt. Again, however, the Benwell Floyd were ready with their response. As the band moved into the lengthy closing sequence of the Pink Floyd song 'Fearless', Jim, the Benwell Floyd's sound engineer, played a tape of crowd noises through the mixing desk. At the end of the song Steve informed the audience that the crowd sounds had been taped during a Newcastle United match at St James' Park (the team's home ground), adding, 'every time I hear that sound I just close me eyes and imagine the goals goin' in'. Similarly, after the band had played their final song of the evening, Steve decided to make a final joke in relation to the audience's support for Sunderland United. As the cheers and cries for more began to die out, he grinned, raised his hand and said 'good night, thanks for having us and I hope your team does better next year!'

This preoccupation of the band and audience with issues relating to North East football culture is typical of the forms of locally circum-scribed meta-dialogue that often augment the musical content of Benwell Floyd performances. As such, each of the group's performances becomes simultaneously a celebration of musical taste and a celebration of regional place, vernacular and musical discourses being seamlessly interwoven. Similarly, the name of the band itself constitutes a dually articulated cultural statement combining as it does a statement of musical taste with one of regional identity. As I noted earlier, Benwell is a district in west Newcastle from which most of the band originate. A heavily depressed area, which has in recent years become the target for a number of urban regeneration schemes, Benwell has a high incidence of theft and drug related crimes. Indeed, among students and other individuals who have moved to Newcastle from regions outside the North East, the band's name has become something of a source for amusement. As the drummer from a Newcastle student-band put it when I asked him if he had heard of the Benwell Floyd: 'The Benwell Floyd! What a bizarre name. I don't like Pink Floyd that much and I definitely don't like Benwell, so I won't be going to see them.' Neverthe-less, the Benwell Floyd remain undividedly passionate about this choice of name. As one of the band members recently explained to me:

> We've had all sorts of comments from outsiders about our name. Now let me think what was the last one. Oh aye I remember now. It was just the other day like. This promoter comes up and says to me 'how are you going to approach management companies and the like with a name like the Benwell Floyd?' An' I turns round an' says to him 'package up an inflatable pig and send it to 'em' [laughs]. But seriously, I mean we all live and work in Benwell and we play Pink Floyd music, so to me the name 'The Benwell Floyd' is the obvious bloody choice.

Such pride on the part of the Benwell Floyd in their home district and the decision to reflect this pride in the name of the band is, in turn, acknowledged by other Benwell residents. Indeed, such an acknowledgement is not restricted only to those residents who attend the Benwell Floyd's performances. It is rather the case that, owing to the dissemination of information relating to the band via kinship and friendship networks, the Benwell Floyd and their musical achievements have become an aspect of everyday life in Benwell. While collecting fieldwork material for this study, I spent a considerable amount of time talking to people in Benwell and other parts of west Newcastle. Conversations would frequently include references to the Benwell Floyd. Often it would simply be the case that the interviewee happened to know someone in the band, or was going out, or living together, with a relative of a group member. Nevertheless, this was enough to warrant the interviewee forming a bond with the group.

In many respects, the regional success of the Benwell Floyd provides a vehicle via which those who live in the Benwell district are able to re-invest an element of pride in their neighbourhood. As such, the name 'Benwell Floyd' has become a celebrated local icon, while the band members themselves enjoy a form of local star status. Robbie, the group's guitarist, once talked to me about how often residents of Benwell came up to him in the street and congratulated him on showing people that 'something good could come out of Benwell after all'. Thus he said: 'It's absolutely amazing who wants to talk to you, people from sixteen to sixty. And big menacing looking blokes who wouldn't normally think about talking to you and you wouldn't want to talk to them.' It is clear from such accounts that the Benwell Floyd's musicalised celebration of their local identity has, in turn, led to the group itself becoming a form of local 'resource' via which the sections of the population of Benwell are able to symbolically mark themselves out from other districts and communities within Newcastle. During one particular conversation with Steve, he told me of his admiration for former Newcastle United football star Peter Beardsley. It seems to me that a similar, if more loosely understood, version of 'local' hero worship can, in turn, be applied to the Benwell Floyd. Thus, as one Benwell resident explained to me:

> What I really like about them [the Benwell Floyd] apart from the fact that they're shit hot on the old Floyd stuff, is that they're not afraid to say where they're comin' from like. I'm really proud on 'em for that like. It's like every time they play live they put the name o' the place around a bit... an' if people aren't sure about what it means then Steve or one of 'em 'll explain it like. An' like sometimes you'll be out on the toon or somethin' an'

someone'll ask you where you're from, an' when you say Benwell they'll say 'ah right, Benwell Floyd, fuckin' excellent man, 'am bang into them'.

Significantly, such forms of local pride are also attached to local bands and musicians who have become internationally established artists and rarely, if ever, return to their original locality. While playing with a Hull-based rock band during my early twenties, I continually met older rock musicians who claimed to have been in bands with members of the Rats, a local heavy rock band who went on to become the Spiders From Mars, David Bowie's backing band during his Ziggy Stardust period in the early 1970s. Clearly, however, such local pride was not purely a one-way process. Former Spiders From Mars guitarist Mick Ronson's final solo album, released posthumously after his death from liver cancer in April 1993, was entitled *Heaven and Hull* and featured on its cover a picture of the Humber Bridge, a suspension bridge spanning the River Humber which flows past Hull (Fisher: 1997).

In this chapter I have turned my attention to the issue of local music-making and live performance in an attempt to ascertain how the latter, together with the various forms of mutual affinity that exist or become established between local musicians and their audiences, can contribute a further dimension to our understanding of the way in which musical meanings take on highly particularised, local inflections. As the case study presented in this chapter has hopefully served to demonstrate, live music performances offer local musicians and their audiences the opportunity to engage in particularised forms of sociality in which common kinship and friendship ties give rise to contextually unique instances of musicalised dialogue. Similarly, the commonality of local social experience, which bonds local musicians and their audiences, ensures that local live music events are on each occasion characterised by an interplay of musical and vernacular discourses, which are both regionally and situationally specific, such discourses in turn having a direct bearing on the forms of significance that local musicians and their audiences read into particular musical texts.

NOTES

1. My reference to 'pub venues' should not be confused with 'pub rock'. 'Pub rock' was a term coined by music journalists during the early 1970s to describe the rhythm and blues-based music of London pub bands such as Ducks DeLuxe and Kilburn and the Highroads. Such music

represented a backlash against the increasingly elitist sensibility of stadium-orientated progressive rock bands of the time such as Yes, Genesis and, somewhat ironically in the context of this chapter, Pink Floyd (See Laing: 1985, p. 8).

2. In musical terms a 'spot' refers to the amount of time that an artist is permitted to perform for. A 'spot' is different from a concert in that, whereas the latter describes an uninterrupted period of live musical performance, the former suggests that a musical event will be broken into shorter segments of time, or 'spots', spread out over the course of an evening.

3. From the album *No Secrets* released in 1972 on the Elektra label.

4. From the album *Blondes Have More Fun* released in 1978 on the Warner Brothers label.

5. 'Cover' or 'cover version', to use the full term, describes the art of playing or 'covering' a version of another group or artist's song.

6. 'Keyboard' is the term given to any piano-like instrument that requires the player to press a series of keys with the fingers in order to produce music. In its application to popular music the term is more typically used to describe electronic keyboard instruments such as the synthesiser and organ.

7. 'Roadie' is the short term for 'roadcrew member'. When a pop group is touring, the 'roadies' act as a support team, transporting the group's equipment from venue to venue and assembling and dismantling the equipment before and after each performance.

8. *Pink Floyd: The Wall*, the film's official title, was released in 1982. Starring former Boomtown Rats singer Bob Geldof in his first acting role, *The Wall* is a sparsely scripted, visual account of the themes explored on the album of the same name, the latter providing a musical soundtrack throughout the film.

9. Howden is a small town in the county of East Yorkshire where I grew up.

10. The interviewee is referring to David Gilmour who replaced original Pink Floyd guitarist and vocalist Syd Barratt in 1969.

11. A 'lick' is the term used to describe a short musical phrase played on a rock instrument, most commonly the electric guitar.

12. A specially commissioned picture of a large inflatable pig suspended above Battersea power station in London was used on the cover of Pink Floyd's 1977 album *Animals* (see Thorgesen and Curzon: 1997, pp. 84–90).

13. 'Depping' is a term used by musicians which means to 'stand in' for or temporarily replace a member of a band who is ill, on holiday or otherwise engaged.

Chapter 8

Conclusion: Youth Culture and Popular Music

This study has examined the collective use of popular music by young people in a local context. Through ethnographic documentation and analysis of a number of different musicalised activities engaged in by young people on a day to day basis, I have considered the role of music in relation to the local settings in which it is consumed and inscribed with cultural meaning. I have suggested that the relationship between music, the 'local' and the construction of local identities is a dynamic process. On the one hand, music informs ways of *being* in particular social spaces; on the other hand, music functions as a resource whereby individuals are able to actively *construct* those spaces in which they live. Thus, in a very real sense, music not only informs the construction of the self, but also the social world in which the self operates. This aspect of music's cultural significance has been illustrated in relation to two distinctive urban locations, Newcastle upon Tyne, England, and Frankfurt am Main, Germany. During Part II of this study, I have been concerned to examine how Newcastle and Frankfurt are experienced and constructed in musicalised terms. In the four ethnographic studies presented here, I have demonstrated how music plays a role in the construction of different urban narratives which draw on the same essential local knowledges of place but complete such knowledges in accordance with ways of thinking derived from the appropriation of musical and stylistic resources.

I am aware that the related concepts of 'locality' and 'local identity', as I have used them throughout this study, are beginning to attract criticism on the grounds that, in an age of media representation, there can in effect be no such thing as a *bounded local* (see, for example, Thornton: 1995, pp. 120–1). In response to this, a number of theorists have begun to readdress the relationship between the global and the local using a range of terms designed to recast the parameters of the collective appropriations and localised innovations that take place within a stream of globally available media products and information. Slobin, for example, employs the term *trans-regionalism* as a means of illustrating how such appropriations and innovations, as these relate to music, may occur simultaneously across a range of globally diffuse sites. Thus, argues Slobin:

> Transregional musics have a very high energy that spills across regional boundaries, perhaps even becoming global. This category of musics is increasing rapidly due to the mediascape, which at any moment can push a music forward so that a large number of audiences can make the choice of domesticating it (1993, p. 19).

Relating such issues more specifically to youth-orientated musics and attendant styles, Kruse (1993) uses the term *trans-local subculture*, the sense of which relates to how young people appropriate music and stylistic resources in local contexts while still retaining a sense of their connectedness with parallel expressions of musical taste and stylistic preference occurring in other regions, countries and continents. It seems to me, however, that the related concepts of *trans-regionalism* and *trans-locality*, while perhaps throwing new light on the cultural mobility of music, style and even basic sensibilities of consumption, are at the same time serving to obscure fundamental features of the local, which need to be acknowledged in any discussion of how music, style and other forms of mass culture are appropriated by individuals and 'used' in the context of their everyday lives. Clearly, it is *not* possible to speak in terms of a *bounded local* that dominates social reality to such a degree that any other source of information concerning the social world is blocked. Nor has it been my intention to suggest that this might be so. None of the examples of local musical life examined in this study can be realistically described as *locally bounded* in the sense that they are totally *distinct* from musical life in a wider context. Thus, for example, many of the Newcastle dance music fans I spoke to referred to their experience of dance music clubs in other areas of the UK. Such fans were also aware of dance music's global popularity and the comparisons between their own understanding of the genre's cultural significance and that of young people in different parts of the world. Similarly, the young Newcastle Asians I interviewed made reference to bhangra scenes in London and Birmingham and talked about internationally established Asian dance music artists such as Bali Sagoo and Apache Indian. A number of Newcastle hip hoppers were adamant about the cultural linkage between their own white working-class experiences and the experiences of African-American youth. Similarly, other hip hop fans in

Newcastle were very interested to hear my accounts of the local hip hop scene in Frankfurt and expressed a desire to see some of the German rap groups I talked about.

At the same time, however, when discussing the meanings that music had for *them*, young people invariably used the local as a central point of reference. For example, a particular club, the people who went there and, equally importantly, those who didn't, all become important focal points as interviewees mapped out and explained to me the role and significance of music in their daily lives. In effect, there seemed to be two different ways in which interviewees *talked* about music, one that encapsulated more general notions of 'like' and 'dislike' in relation to particular genres, artists and songs, within which global references were commonly used, and another that involved a deeper reflection on music's role in everyday life, in which more locally centred points of reference were used. A general conclusion, which I draw from this observation, is that, in seeking to justify particular tastes in music and style on a more personal level, individuals invariably draw upon a range of locally embedded images, discourses and social sensibilities centred around the *familiar*, the *accessible*, the *easily recognisable*.

To return to my original point then, the physical realisation of musical and stylistic resources appropriated from the global culture industries, while this may at one level evoke broadly similar responses among regionally diffuse youth cultures, also involves the use of such resources in the articulation of collective sensibilities, which are both constructed and subsequently acted out in response to given sets of circumstances encountered in the everyday lives of particular groups and individuals. As the physical territory of everyday life, it is the 'local' that serves both as a basis for social action and for the collective identities forged as a result of particular forms of social action. Consequently aspects of popular culture, such as music and style, in addition to being understood as global cultural forms, assume particularised 'everyday' meanings which respond to the differing local contexts in which they are appropriated and which frame their incorporation into forms of social action.

I would like to leave the reader with one final example of this relationship between musical taste and local everyday experience. In the summer of 1994 I was invited by a German-Romanian friend named Eddy, with whom I had played in a blues band during my time in Frankfurt, to spend two weeks in Sighisoara, the small Romanian town where Eddy was born. While staying in Sighisoara, I was introduced to Kris and Alex, two of Eddy's childhood friends. Not being used to visitors from the west, Kris and Alex were very keen to relate stories about how western popular music had influenced them during their teens and early twenties (Eddy, Kris and Alex are now all in their early forties) and how they had kept up with musical events and developments in the west through magazines and records acquired from black-market traders. During the second week of the holiday, Eddy and I, together with Kris, Alex and their wives and children, spent several days in the east of Romania in a rented house. One evening a guitar was presented before me and I was asked to play Beatles songs, which everyone began to sing along to. A little while later Kris and Alex began to speak with each other and then to laugh uncontrollably. As they were speaking in Romanian Eddy provided the following translation:

> They're talking about how... about the way they [the Romanian authorities] tried to stop it all, stop the music. And they say it was much harder in a small town you know, nowhere to run. You can't turn your back... police are everywhere. At the youth club they [Kris and Alex] got this old 4-Track tape recorder and they record Beatles on two tracks and marching music on the other two tracks. Then they listen to Beatles and have someone looking an' if police or anyone come they turn it over to the marching music and everyone think what good boys they are. Every time they hear Beatles music now, they think of that and how what a great laugh it was.

The above account, centring as it does around the understanding, appreciation and sheer enjoyment of music in relation to locally shared circumstances, bears out much of what I have been concerned with in this study. The mapping of musical life onto the features and activities that characterise local settings is, in many respects, a crucial key to understanding popular music's cultural significance. Indeed there is a clear sense in which the cultural significance of popular music is largely synonymous with the latter's local significance. In appropriating forms of popular music, individuals are simultaneously constructing ways of being in the context of their local everyday environments. During the course of this study, I have gone some way towards examining the relationship between musical taste and local everyday life experience. In doing so, I have begun to illustrate the extent to which the everyday circumstances that individuals struggle with and the narratives of space and place that they construct in an attempt to negotiate or resist such circumstances are inherently bound up with musical taste to the extent that expressions of musical taste are inseparable from those everyday settings in which they occur.

Bibliography

Adorno, T.W. (1941) 'On Popular Music' in S. Frith and A. Goodwin (eds) (1990) *On Record: Rock, Pop and the Written Word*, Routledge, London.

Andrews, A. and Fowler, G. (1996) 'Globalisation, Nationalism and the Notion of "Home"; With Reference to South Asians in Scotland', unpublished paper presented at the British Sociological Association Annual Conference, University of Reading.

Ang, I. (1996) *Living Room Wars: Rethinking Audiences for a Postmodern World*, Routledge, London.

Appadurai, A. (1990) 'Disjuncture and Difference in the Global Cultural Economy' in M. Featherstone (ed.) *Global Culture: Nationalism, Globalisation and Modernity*, Sage, London.

Armstrong, N. (1995) 'A Tale of Two Cities' in *The Crack*, October: 4–6.

Arnett, J.J. (1995) *Metal Heads: Heavy Metal Music and Adolescent Alienation*, Westview Press, Oxford.

Attali, J. (1985) *Noise: The Political Economy of Music*, (trans. B. Massumi) Manchester University Press, Manchester.

Back, L. (1993) 'Race, Identity and Nation Within an Adolescent Community in South London' in *New Community*, 19(2): 217–33.

Back, L. (1996a) *New Ethnicities and Urban Culture: Racisms and Multiculture in Young Lives*, UCL Press, London.

Back, L. (1996b) 'X Amount of Sat Siri Akal: Apache Indian, Reggae Music and the Cultural Intermezzo' in *New Formations*, 27: 128–47.

Banerji, S. and Baumann, G. (1990) 'Bhangra 1984–88: Fusion and Professionalisation in a Genre of South Asian Dance Music' in P. Oliver (ed.) *Black Music in Britain: Essays on the Afro-Asian Contribution to Popular Music*, Open University Press, Milton Keynes.

Barthes, R. (1977) 'The Grain of the Voice' in S. Frith and A. Goodwin (eds) (1990) *On Record: Rock, Pop and the Written Word*, Routledge, London.

Baudrillard, J. (1988) *America*, Verso, London.

Baumann, G. (1990) 'The Re-Invention of Bhangra: Social Change and Aesthetic Shifts in a Punjabi Music in Britain' in *Journal of the International Institute for Comparative Music Studies and Documentation*, 32 (2): 81–95.

Baumann, G. (1997) 'Dominant and Demotic Discourses of Culture: Their Relevance to Multi-Ethnic Alliances' in P. Werbner and T. Modood (eds) *Debating Cultural Hybridity: Multi-Cultural Identities and the Politics of Anti-Racism*, Zed Books, London.

Bayton, M. (1988) 'How Women Become Rock Musicians' in S. Frith and A. Goodwin (eds) (1990) *On Record: Rock, Pop and the Written Word*, Routledge, London.

Bayton, M. (1993) 'Feminist Musical Practice: Problems and Contradictions' in T. Bennett, S. Frith, L. Grossberg, J. Shepherd and G. Turner (eds) *Rock and Popular Music: Politics, Policies, Institutions*, Routledge, London.

Beadle, J.J. (1993) *Will Pop Eat Itself?: Pop Music in the Sound Bite Era*, Faber & Faber, London.

Beattie, G. (1990) *England After Dark*, Weidenfeld & Nicolson, London.

Becker, H.S. (1963) *Outsiders: Studies in the Sociology of Deviance*, Free Press, New York.

Bennett, A. (1997) '"Going Down the Pub": The Pub Rock Scene as a Resource for the Consumption of Popular Music' in *Popular Music*, 16(1): 97–108.

Bennett, A. (1998) 'The Frankfurt Rockmobil: A New Insight into the Significance of Music-Making for Young People' in *Youth and Policy*, 60: 16–29.

Bennett, H.S. (1980) 'The Realities of Practice' in S. Frith and A. Goodwin (eds) (1990) *On Record: Rock, Pop and the Written Word*, Routledge, London.

Bennett, T., Martin, G., Mercer, C. and Woollacott, J. (eds) (1981) *Culture, Ideology and Social Process*, Open University Press, London.

Benson, J. (1994) *The Rise of Consumer Society in Britain, 1880–1980*, Longman, London.

Bhachu, P. (1991) 'Culture, Ethnicity and Class Among Punjabi Sikh Women in 1990s Britain' in *New Community*, 17(3): 401–12.

Björnberg, A. and Stockfelt, O. (1996) 'Kristen Klatvask fra Vejle: Danish Pub Music, Mythscapes and "Local Camp"' in *Popular Music*, 15(2): 131–47.

Bjurström, E. (1997) 'The Struggle for Ethnicity: Swedish Youth Styles and the Construction of Ethnic Identities' in *Young: Nordic Journal of Youth Research*, 5(3): 44–58.

Blackman, S.J. (1996) 'Has Drug Culture Become an Inevitable Part of Youth Culture? A Critical Assessment of Drug Education' in *Educational Review*, 48(2): 131–42.

Bocock, R. (1993) *Consumption*, Routledge, London.

Böethius, U. (1995) 'Youth, the Media and Moral Panics' in J. Fornäs and G. Bolin (eds) *Youth Culture in Late Modernity*, Sage, London.

Bottomore, T. (1984) *The Frankfurt School*, Tavistock, London.

Bradley, D. (1992) *Understanding Rock 'n' Roll: Popular Music in Britain 1955–1964*, Open University Press, Buckingham.

Brake, M. (1985) *Comparative Youth Culture: The Sociology of Youth Cultures and Youth Subcultures in America, Britain and Canada*, Routledge & Kegan Paul, London.

Brewer, D.D. and Miller, M.L. (1990) 'Bombing and Burning: The Social Organization and Values of Hip Hop Graffiti Writers and Implications for Policy' in *Deviant Behavior*, 11: 345–69.

Buck-Morss, S. (1989) *The Dialectics of Seeing: Walter Benjamin and the Arcades Project*, MIT Press, Cambridge, MA.

Cashmore, E. (1984) *No Future: Youth and Society*, Heinemann, London.

Castells, M. (1983) *The City and the Grassroots: A Cross-Cultural Theory of Urban Social Movements*, Edward Arnold, London.

Chambers, I. (1976) 'A Strategy for Living: Black Music and White Subcultures' in S. Hall and T. Jefferson (eds) *Resistance Through Rituals: Youth Subcultures in Post-War Britain*, Hutchinson, London.

Chambers, I. (1985) *Urban Rhythms: Pop Music and Popular Culture*, Macmillan, London.

Chambers, I. (1992) 'Cities Without Maps' in J. Bird, B. Curtis, T. Putnam, G. Robertson, and L. Tickner (eds) *Mapping the Futures: Local Cultures, Global Change*, Routledge, London.

Champion, S. (1997) 'Fear and Lothing in Wisconsin' in S. Redhead, D. Wynne, and J. O'Connor (eds) *The Clubcultures Reader: Readings in Popular Cultural Studies*, Blackwell, Oxford.

Chaney, D. (1993) *Fictions of Collective Life: Public Drama in Late Modern Culture*, Routledge, London.

Chaney, D. (1994) *The Cultural Turn: Scene Setting Essays on Contemporary Cultural History*, Routledge, London.

Chaney, D. (1996) *Lifestyles*, Routledge, London.

Ching-Yun Lee, J. (1992) 'All for Freedom: The Rise of Patriotic/Pro-Democratic Popular Music in Hong Kong in Response to the Chinese Student Movement' in R. Garofalo (ed.) *Rockin' the Boat: Mass Music and Mass Movements*, South End Press, Boston, MA.

Clarke, G. (1981) 'Defending Ski-Jumpers: A Critique of Theories of Youth Subcultures' in S. Frith and A. Goodwin (eds) (1990) *On Record: Rock, Pop and the Written Word*, Routledge, London.

Clarke, J. (1976) 'The Skinheads and the Magical Recovery of Community' in S. Hall and T. Jefferson (eds) *Resistance Through Rituals: Youth Subcultures in Post-War Britain*, Hutchinson, London.

Clarke, J., Hall, S., Jefferson, T. and Roberts, B. (1976) 'Subcultures, Cultures and Class: A Theoretical Overview' in S. Hall and T. Jefferson (eds) *Resistance Through Rituals: Youth Subcultures in Post-War Britain*, Hutchinson, London.

Clifford, J. (1986) 'Introduction: Partial Truths' in J. Clifford and G.E. Marcus (eds) *Writing Culture: The Poetics and Politics of Ethnography*, California University Press, Berkeley.

Cobley, P. and Osgerby, W. (1995) '"Peckham Clan Ain't Nothin' to Fuck With": Urban Rap Style in Britain' unpublished paper presented at the Youth 2000 conference, University of Teesside, Middlesborough.

Cohen, P. (1972) 'Subcultural Conflict and Working Class Community' in *Working Papers in Cultural Studies 2*, University of Birmingham.

Cohen, P. (1986) *Rethinking the Youth Question*, Post 16 Education Centre, Institute of Education, London.

Cohen, Stanley (1987) *Folk Devils and Moral Panics: The Creation of the Mods and Rockers*, 3rd edn, Basil Blackwell, Oxford.

Cohen, Sara (1991) *Rock Culture in Liverpool: Popular Music in the Making*, Clarendon Press, Oxford.

Cohen, Sara and McManus, K. (1991) *Harmonious Relations: Popular Music in Family Life on Merseyside*, Liverpool, National Museums and Galleries on Merseyside.

de Cologne, F. (1980) *Rock gegen Rechts: Beiträge zu einer Bewegung*, Weltkreis, Dortmund.

Colls, R. and Lancaster, B. (eds) (1992) *Geordies: Roots of Regionalism*, Edinburgh University Press, Edinburgh.

Condry, I. (1999) 'The Social Production of Difference: Imitation and Authenticity in Japanese Rap Music' in H. Fehrenbach and U. Poiger (eds) *Transactions, Transgressions, Transformations: American Culture in Western Europe and Japan*, Providence, RI, Berghan Books.

Davies, C.L. (1993) 'Aboriginal Rock Music: Space and Place' in T. Bennett, S. Frith, L. Grossberg, J. Shepherd and G. Turner (eds) *Rock and Popular Music: Politics, Policies, Institutions*, Routledge, London.

Decker, J.L. (1994) 'The State of Rap: Time and Place in Hip Hop Nationalism' in A. Ross and T. Rose (eds) *Microphone Fiends: Youth Music and Youth Culture*, Routledge, London.

Denisoff, R.S. and Romanowski, W.D. (1991) *Risky Business: Rock in Film*, Transaction, New Jersey.

Denzin, N.K. (1969) 'Problems in Analyzing Elements of Mass Culture: Notes on the Popular Song and Other Artistic Productions' in *American Journal of Sociology*, 75: 1035–38.

Deppe, J. (1997) *Odem: On the Run – Eine Jugend in der Graffiti-Szene*, Schwarzkopf & Schwarzkopf, Berlin.

DiMaggio, P. (1987) 'Classification in Art' in *American Sociological Review*, 52 (4): 440–55.

Dywer, C. (1998) 'Contested Identities: Challenging Dominant Representations of Young British Muslim Women' in T. Skelton and G. Valentine (eds) *Cool Places: Geographies of Youth Culture*, Routledge, London.

Dyson, M.E. (1996) *Between God and Gangsta Rap: Bearing Witness to Black Culture*, Oxford University Press, New York.

Easton, P. (1989) 'The Rock Music Community' in J. Riordan (ed.) *Soviet Youth Culture*, Indiana University Press, Bloomington and Indianapolis.

Epstein, J.S., Pratto, D.J. and Skipper Jr., J.K. (1990) 'Teenagers, Behavioral Problems, and Preferences for Heavy Metal and Rap Music: A Case Study of a Southern Middle School' in *Deviant Behavior*, **11**: 381–94.

Ehrenreich, B., Hess, E. and Jacobs, G. (1992) 'Beatlemania: Girls Just Want to Have Fun' in L.A. Lewis (ed.) *The Adoring Audience: Fan Culture and Popular Media*, Routledge, London.

Evans, C. (1998) 'How To Build Your Own Tribute Band: Five Easy Steps To Finding Fortune in Other People's Fame' in *Gig Magazine*, November.

The Face (1993) 'A Bluffer's Guide to Dance Music in the 1990s', February.

Farin, K. and Seidel-Pielen, E. (1994) *Skinheads*, Verlag C.H. Beck, München.

Featherstone, M. (1993) 'Global and Local Cultures' in J. Bird, B. Curtis, T. Putnam, G. Robertson, and L. Tickner (eds) *Mapping the Futures: Local Cultures, Global Change*, Routledge, London.

Fekete, L. (1993) 'Inside Racist Europe' in T. Bunyan (ed.) *Statewatching the New Europe: A Handbook on the European State*, Statewatch, London.

Filippa, M. (1986) 'Popular Song and Musical Cultures' in D. Forgacs and R. Lumley (eds) *Italian Cultural Studies: An Introduction*, Oxford University Press, Oxford.

Fine, G.A. and Kleinman, S. (1979) 'Rethinking Subculture: An Interactionist Analysis' in *The American Journal of Sociology*, **85**(1): 1–20.

Finnegan, R. (1989) *The Hidden Musicians: Music-Making in an English Town*, Cambridge University Press, Cambridge.

Fisher, B. (1997) 'But Boy Could He Play Guitar' in *Mojo*, October: 58–71.

Flores, J. (1994) 'Puerto Rican and Proud, Boyee!: Rap Roots and Amnesia' in A. Ross and T. Rose (eds) *Microphone Fiends: Youth Music and Youth Culture*, Routledge, London.

Fonarow, W. (1995) 'The Spatial Organization of the Indie Music Gig' in K. Gelder and S. Thornton (eds) *The Subcultures Reader*, Routledge, London,

Foner, N. (1978) *Jamaica Farewell: Jamaican Migrants in London*, Routledge & Kegan Paul, London.

Fornäs, J., Lindberg, U. and Sernhade, O. (1995) *In Garageland: Rock, Youth and Modernity*, Routledge, London.

Fountain, N. (1988) *Underground: The London Alternative Press 1966–74*, Comedia/Routledge, London.

Fowler, D. (1992) 'Teenage Consumers? Young Wage-Earners and Leisure in Manchester, 1919–1939' in A. Davies and S. Fielding (eds) *Workers' Worlds: Cultures and Communities in Manchester and Salford, 1880–1939*, Manchester University Press, Manchester.

Frith, S. (1981) 'The Magic That Can Set You Free: The Ideology of Folk and the Myth of the Rock Community' in *Popular Music*, **1**: 159–68.

Frith, S. (1983) *Sound Effects: Youth, Leisure and the Politics of Rock*, Constable, London.

Frith, S. (1984) *The Sociology of Youth*, Causeway Press, Ormskirk.

Frith, S. (1987) 'Towards an Aesthetic of Popular Music' in R. Leppert and S. McClary (eds) *Music and Society: The Politics of Composition, Performance and Reception*, Cambridge University Press, Cambridge.

Frith, S. (1988a) *Music for Pleasure: Essays in the Sociology of Pop*, Polity Press, Oxford.

Frith, S. (1988b) 'Video Pop: Picking Up the Pieces' in S. Frith (ed.) (1990) *Facing the Music: Essays on Pop, Rock and Culture*, 2nd edn, Mandarin, London.

Frith, S. and Horne, H. (1987) *Art into Pop*, Methuen, London.

Frith, S. and McRobbie, A. (1978) 'Rock and Sexuality' in S. Frith and A. Goodwin (eds) (1990) *On Record: Rock, Pop and the Written Word*, Routledge, London.

Frith, S. and Street, J. (1992) 'Rock Against Racism and Red Wedge: From Music to Politics, from Politics to Music' in R. Garofalo (ed.) *Rockin' the Boat: Mass Music and Mass Movements*, Southend Press, Boston, MA.

Fryer, P. (1998) 'The "Discovery" and Appropriation of African Music and Dance' in *Race and Class*, **39**(3): 1–20.

Funk-Hennings, E. (1998) 'The Music Scene of Skinheads in East and West Germany Before and After the Reunification' in H. Järviluoma and T. Hautamäki (eds) *Music on Show: Issues of Performance*, Department of Folk Tradition, University of Tampere, Finland.

Gane, M. (ed.) (1993) *Baudrillard Live: Selected Interviews*, Routledge, London.

Garofalo, R. (ed.) (1992a) *Rockin' the Boat: Mass Music and Mass Movements*, South End Press, Boston, MA.

Garofalo, R. (1992b) 'Understanding Mega-Events: If We Are the World, Then How Do We Change It?' in R. Garofalo (ed.) *Rockin' the Boat: Mass Music and Mass Movements*, South End Press, Boston, MA.

Garofalo, R. (1992c) 'Nelson Mandela, The Concerts: Mass Culture as Contested Terrain' in R. Garofalo (ed.) *Rockin' the Boat: Mass Music and Mass Movements*, South End Press, Boston, MA.

Geiling, H. (1995) '"Chaos-Tage" in Hannover: Vom Ereignis zum Mythos' in *Vorgänge: Zeitschrift für Bürgerrechte und Gesellschaftspolitik*, **4**: 1–6.

Geiling, H. (1996) *Das andere Hannover: Jugendkultur zwischen Rebellion und Integration in der Großstadt*, Hannover, Offizin Verlag, Hannover.

Geyrhalter, T. (1996) 'Effeminacy, Camp and Sexual Subversion in Rock: The Cure and Suede' in *Popular Music*, **15**(2): 217–24.

Gillett, C. (1983) *The Sound of the City: The Rise of Rock and Roll*, 2nd edn, Souvenir Press, London.

Gilmore, A. (1995) 'Tuning in to pirate radio in Leicester – underground culture in the urban context', unpublished paper given at the 1995 British Sociological Association Annual Conference, University of Leicester.

Gilroy, P. (1993) *The Black Atlantic: Modernity and Double Consciousness*, Verso, London.

Gilroy, P. and Lawrence, E. (1988) 'Two-Tone Britain: White and Black Youth and the Politics of Anti-Racism' in P. Cohen and H.S. Bains (eds) *Multi-Racist Britain*, Macmillan, Basingstoke.

Gleason, R.J. (1972) 'A Cultural Revolution' in R.S. Denisoff and R.A. Peterson (eds) *The Sounds of Social Change*, Rand McNally and Company, Chicago.

Gottleib, J. and Wald, G. (1994) 'Smells Like Teen Spirit: Riot Grrrls, Revolution and Women in Independent Rock' in A. Ross and T. Rose (eds) *Microphone Fiends: Youth Music and Youth Culture*, Routledge, London.

Grossberg, L. (1994) 'Is Anybody Listening? Does Anybody Care?: On Talking About "The State of Rock"' in A. Ross and T. Rose (eds) *Microphone Fiends: Youth Music and Youth Culture*, Routledge, London.

Hafeneger, B., Stüwe, G. and Weigel, G. (1993) *Punks in der Großstadt Punks in der Provinz: Projektberichte aus der Jugendarbeit*, Leske & Budrich, Opladen.

Hall, S. and Jefferson, T. (eds) (1976) *Resistance Through Rituals: Youth Subcultures in Post-War Britain*, Hutchinson, London.

Hall, S., Critcher, C., Jefferson, T., Clarke J., and Roberts, B. (1978) *Policing the Crisis: Mugging, the State and Law and Order*, Macmillan, London.

Hanna, J.L. (1992) 'Moving Messages: Identity and Desire in Popular Music and Social Dance' in J. Lull (ed.) *Popular Music and Communication*, 2nd edn, Sage, London.

Harpin, L. (1993) 'One Continent Under a Groove' in *ID: The Europe Issue*, 16 May: 58–60.

Harris, D. (1992) *From Class Struggle to the Politics of Pleasure: The Effects of Gramscianism on Cultural Studies*, Routledge, London.

Harron, M. (1988) 'McRock: Pop as a Commodity' in S. Frith (ed.) (1990) *Facing the Music: Essays on Pop, Rock and Culture*, 2nd edn, Mandarin, London.

Haslam, D. (1997) 'DJ Culture' in S. Redhead, D. Wynne and J. O'Connor (eds) *The Clubcultures Reader: Readings in Popular Cultural Studies*, Blackwell, Oxford.

Haynes, R. (1993) 'Every Man(?) A Football Artist: Football Writing and Masculinity' in S. Redhead (ed.) *The Passion and the Fashion: Football Fandom in the New Europe*, Avebury, Aldershot.

Hebdige, D. (1976a) 'The Meaning of Mod' in S. Hall and T. Jefferson (eds) *Resistance Through Rituals: Youth Subcultures in Post-War Britain*, Hutchinson, London.

Hebdige, D. (1976b) 'Reggae, Rastas and Rudies' in S. Hall and T. Jefferson (eds) *Resistance Through Rituals: Youth Subcultures in Post-War Britain*, Hutchinson, London.

Hebdige, D. (1979) *Subculture: The Meaning of Style*, Routledge, London.

Hebdige, D. (1987) *Cut 'n' Mix: Culture, Identity and Caribbean Music*, Routledge, London.

Hebdige, D. (1988) *Hiding in the Light: On Images and Things*, Routledge, London.

Hesmondhalgh, D. (1995) 'Justified and Ancient: Primitivism and Futurism in Contemporary Urban Dance Music', unpublished paper given at the 1995 British Sociological Association Annual Conference, University of Leicester.

Hetherington, K. (1992) 'Stonehenge and its Festival: Spaces of Consumption' in R. Shields (ed.) *Lifestyle Shopping: The Subject of Consumption*, Routledge, London.

Hill, D. (1986) *Designer Boys and Material Girls: Manufacturing the 80s Pop Dream*, Blandford Press, Poole.

Hill, T. (1992) 'The Enemy Within: Censorship in Rock Music in the 1950s' in A. DeCurtis (ed.) *Present Tense: Rock and Roll and Culture*, Duke University Press, Durham, NC.

Hobbs, D. (1988) *Doing the Business: Entrepreneurship, the Working Class, and Detectives in the East-End of London*, Oxford University Press, Oxford.

Hobbs, D. and May, T. (eds) (1993) *Interpreting the Field: Accounts of Ethnography*, Clarendon Press, Oxford.

Hobsbawm, E. (1983) 'Introduction: Inventing Traditions' in E. Hobsbawm and T. Ranger (eds) *The Invention of Tradition*, Cambridge University Press, Cambridge.

Hoggart, R. (1957) *The Uses of Literacy*, Chatto & Windus, London.

Hollands, R. (1995) 'Friday Night, Saturday Night: Youth Cultural Identification in the Post-Industrial City' University of Newcastle, Department of Social Policy Working Paper No.2.

Horak, R. (1995) 'Diaspora Experience, Music and Hybrid Cultures of Young Migrants in Vienna', unpublished paper given at the 1995 British Sociological Association Annual Conference, University of Leicester.

Hosokawa, S. (1984) 'The Walkman Effect' in *Popular Music*, 4: 165–80

Jay, M. (1973) *The Dialectical Imagination: A History of the Frankfurt School and the Institute of Social Research 1923–1950*, Heinemann Educational Books, London.

Jefferson, T. (1976) 'Cultural Responses of the Teds: The Defence of Space and Status' in S. Hall and T. Jefferson (eds) *Resistance Through Rituals: Youth Subcultures in Post-War Britain*, Hutchinson, London.

Jenkins, R. (1983) *Lads, Citizens and Ordinary Kids: Working Class Youth Lifestyles in Belfast*, Routledge & Kegan Paul, London.

Johansson, T. and Miegel, F. (1992) *Do the Right Thing: Lifestyle and Identity in Contemporary Youth Culture*, Almquist & Wiksell, Stockholm.

Johnson, P. (1964) 'The Menace of Beatlism' in *The New Statesman*, 28 February: 326–7.

Jones, S. (1988) *Black Culture, White Youth: The Reggae Tradition from JA to UK*, Macmillan, London.

Jourard, M. (1998) 'Tribute Bands: Close Enough for Rock 'n' Roll' in *Gig Magazine*, November.

Kaplan, E.A. (1987) *Rocking Around the Clock: Music Television, Postmodernism and Consumer Culture*, Methuen, London.

Kaur, R. and Kalra, V.S. (1996) 'New Paths For South Asian Identity and Creativity' in S. Sharma, J. Hutnyk and A. Sharma (eds) *Dis-Orienting Rhythms: The Politics of the New Asian Dance Music*, Zed Books, London.

Keith, M. and Pile, S. (1993) 'The Politics of Place' in M. Keith and S. Pile (eds) *Place and the Politics of Identity*, Routledge, London.

Keyes, C.L. (1991) *Rappin' to the Beat: Rap Music as Street Culture Among African Americans*, Doctoral Thesis published by University Microfilms International, Ann Arbor, Michigan.

King, A. (1997) 'The Lads: Masculinity and the New Consumption of Football' in *Sociology*, **31**(2): 329–46.

Klitgaard Povlsen, K. (1996) 'Global Teen-Soaps Go Local: Beverley Hills 90210 in Denmark' in *Young: Nordic Journal of Youth Research*, **4**(4): 3–20.

Krüger, H.H. (1983) 'Sprachlose Rebellen?: Zur Subkultur der "Halbstarken" in den Fünfziger Jahren' in W. Breyvogel (ed.) *Autonomie und Widerstand: Zur Theorie und Geshichte des Jugendprotestes*, Rigidon, Essen.

Kruse, H. (1993) 'Subcultural Identity in Alternative Music Culture' in *Popular Music*, **12**(1): 31–43.

Lachmann, R. (1988) 'Graffiti as Career and Ideology' in *American Journal of Sociology*, **94**(2): 229–50.

Laing, D. (1971) 'Listen to Me', in S. Frith and A. Goodwin (eds) (1990) *On Record: Rock, Pop and the Written Word*, Routledge, London.

Laing, D. (1985) *One Chord Wonders: Power and Meaning in Punk Rock*, Open University Press, Milton Keynes.

Laing, D. (1997) 'Rock Anxieties and New Music Networks' in A. McRobbie (ed.) *Back to Reality: Social Experience and Cultural Studies*, Manchester University Press, Manchester.

Lancaster, B. (1992) 'Newcastle – Capitol of What?' in R. Colls and B. Lancaster (eds) *Geordies: Roots of Regionalism*, Edinburgh University Press, Edinburgh.

Langlois, T. (1992) 'Can You Feel It?: DJs and House Music Culture in the UK' in *Popular Music*, **11**(2): 229–38.

Lewis, G.H. (1992) 'Who do you love?: The dimensions of musical taste', in J. Lull (ed.) *Popular Music and Communication*, 2nd edn, Sage, London.

Lewis, W.F. (1993) *Soul Rebels: The Rastafari*, Waveland Press, Prospect Heights, IL.

Leys, C. (1983) *Politics in Britain: An Introduction*, Verso, London.

Liechty, M. (1995) 'Media, Markets and Modernization: Youth Identities and the Experience of Modernity in Kathmandu, Nepal' in V. Amit-Talai and H. Wulff (eds) *Youth Cultures: A Cross-Cultural Perspective*, Routledge, London.

Light, A. (1992) 'About a Salary or Reality?: Rap's Recurrent Conflict' in A. DeCurtis (ed.) *Present Tense: Rock and Roll and Culture*, Duke University Press, London.

Lipsitz, G. (1994) *Dangerous Crossroads: Popular Music, Postmodernism and the Poetics of Place*, Verso, London.

Lull, J. (1992) 'Popular Music and Communication: An Introduction' in J. Lull (ed.) *Popular Music and Communication*, 2nd edn, Sage, London.

Lull, J. (1995) *Media, Communication, Culture: A Global Approach*, Polity Press, Cambridge.

MacDonald, D. (1953) 'A Theory of Mass Culture' in B. Rosenberg and D. White (eds) (1957) *Mass Culture: The Popular Arts in America*, Free Press, Glencoe, IL.

MacKinnon, N. (1994) *The British Folk Scene: Musical Performance and Social Identity*, Open University Press, Buckingham.

McDonald-Walker, S. (1998) 'Fighting the Legacy: British Bikers in the 1990s' in *Sociology*, **32**(2): 379–96.

McKay, G. (1996) *Senseless Acts of Beauty: Cultures of Resistance Since the Sixties*, Verso, London.

McReady, J. (1989) 'The Dark Side of the Mersey', in *The Face*, January: 54–9.

McRobbie, A. (1980) 'Settling Accounts with Subcultures: A Feminist Critique' in S. Frith and A. Goodwin (eds) (1990) *On Record: Rock Pop and the Written Word*, Routledge, London.

McRobbie, A. (1984) 'Dance and Social Fantasy' in A. McRobbie and M. Nava (eds) *Gender and Generation*, Macmillan, London.

McRobbie, A. (1994) *Postmodernism and Popular Culture*, Routledge, London.

McRobbie, A. and Garber, J. (1976) 'Girls and Subcultures: An Exploration' in S. Hall and T. Jefferson (eds) *Resistance Through Rituals: Youth Subcultures in Post-War Britain*, Hutchinson, London.

Maan, B. (1992) *The New Scots: The Story of the Asians in Scotland*, John Donald, Edinburgh.

Macan, E. (1997) *Rocking the Classics: English Progressive Rock and the Counterculture*, Oxford University Press, Oxford.

Maffesoli, M. (1996) *The Time of the Tribes: The Decline of Individualism in Mass Society*, (trans. D. Smith) Sage, London.

Malbon, B. (1998) 'Clubbing: Consumption, Identity and the Spatial Practices of Every-Night Life' in T. Skelton and G. Valentine (eds) *Cool Places: Geographies of Youth Culture*, Routledge, London.

Malik, K. (1995) 'What *really* angers young Asians' in *Independent On Sunday*, 25 June: 23.

Manuel, P. (1993) *Cassette Culture: Popular Music and Technology in North India*, University of Chicago Press, London.

Marks, A. (1990) 'Young, Gifted and Black: Afro-American and Afro-Caribbean Music in Britain 1963–88' in P. Oliver (ed.) *Black Music in*

Britain: Essays on the Afro-Asian Contribution to Popular Music, Open University Press, Milton Keynes.

Martin, B. (1998) *Listening to the Future: The Time of Progressive Rock*, Open Court, Chicago.

Martin, G. and Hornsby, J. (1979) *All You Need Is Ears*, Macmillan, London.

Massey, D. (1993) 'Power-Geometry and a Progressive Sense of Place' in J. Bird, B. Curtis, T. Putnam, G. Robertson, and L. Tickner (eds) *Mapping the Futures: Local Cultures, Global Change*, Routledge, London.

Matthesius, B. (1992) *Anti-Sozial-Front: Vom Fußballfan zum Hooligan*, Leske & Budrich, Opladen.

Matza, D. and Sykes, G.M. (1961) 'Juvenile Delinquency and Subterranean Values' in *American Sociological Review*, **26**(5): 712–19.

Maxwell, I. (with Bambrick, N.) (1994) 'Discourses of Culture and Nationalism in Contemporary Sydney Hip Hop' in *Perfect Beat*, **2**(1): 1–19.

May, T. (1993) 'Feelings Matter: Inverting the Hidden Equation' in D. Hobbs and T. May (eds) *Interpreting the Field: Accounts of Ethnography*, Clarendon Press, Oxford.

Mayer, H.C. (1969) *German Recovery and the Marshall Plan, 1948–1952*, Edition Atlantic Forum, New York.

Mays, J.B. (1954) *Growing Up in the City*, Liverpool University Press, Liverpool.

Measham, F., Newcombe, R. and Parker, H. (1994) 'The Normalisation of Recreational Drug Use Amongst Young People in North-West England' in *British Journal of Sociology*, **45**(2): 287–312.

Meinig, U. (1993) 'Von "e-Moll" und "langen Fingernägeln" – eine Mädchen-Rockband in Hamburg-Eidelstadt' in W. Hering, B. Hill, and G. Pleiner (eds) *Praxishandbuch Rockmusik in der Jugendarbeit*, Leske & Budrich, Opladen.

Melechi, A. (1993) 'The Ecstasy of Disappearance' in S. Redhead (ed.) *Rave Off: Politics and Deviance in Contemporary Youth Culture*, Avebury, Aldershot.

Merchant, J. and MacDonald, R. (1994) 'Youth and the Rave Culture, Ecstasy and Health' in *Youth and Policy*, **45**: 16–38.

Merton, R.K. (1957) *Social Theory and Social Structure*, Collier-Macmillan, London.

Middleton, R. (1990) *Studying Popular Music*, Open University Press, Milton Keynes.

Milestone, K. (1997) 'Love Factory: The Sites, Practices and Media Relationships of Northern Soul' in S. Redhead, D. Wynne and J. O'Connor (eds), *The Clubcultures Reader: Readings in Popular Cultural Studies*, Blackwell, Oxford.

Mitchell, T. (1996) *Popular Music and Local Identity: Rock, Pop and Rap in Europe and Oceania*, Leicester University Press, London.

Mitchell, T. (1998) 'Australian hip hop as a "glocal" subculture', Ultimo Series Seminar, UTS 18 March.

Moore, D. (1994) *The Lads in Action: Social Process in an Urban Youth Subculture*, Arena, Aldershot.

Moores, S. (1993) *Interpreting Audiences: The Ethnography of Media Consumption*, Sage, London.

Muggleton, D. (1997) 'The Post-subculturalist', in S. Redhead, D. Wynne and J. O'Connor (eds) *The Clubcultures Reader: Readings in Popular Cultural Studies*, Blackwell, Oxford.

Müller-Wiegand, I. (1990) 'Jugendliche als Punks in einer osthessischen Stadt: Untersuchung zu ihrer Selbstdefinition und Lebenslage' unpublished Diploma thesis (Educational Science), University of Frankfurt, Frankfurt/Main, Germany.

Murdock, G. and McCron, R. (1976) 'Youth and Class: The Career of a Confusion' in G. Mungham and G. Pearson (eds) *Working-Class Youth Culture*, Routledge & Kegan Paul, London.

Mutsaers, L. (1990) 'Indorock: An Early Eurorock Style' in *Popular Music*, 9(3): 307–20.

Negus, K. (1992) *Producing Pop: Culture and Conflict in the Popular Music Industry*, Edward Arnold, London.

Novack, C.J. (1990) *Sharing the Dance: Contact Improvisation and American Culture*, The University of Wisconsin Press, Wisconsin.

Noys, B. (1995) 'Into the "Jungle"' in *Popular Music*, 14(3): 321–32.

Oakes, J. (1995) 'The Song Remains the Same: Tribute Bands Perform the Rock Text', unpublished paper given at the 1995 International Association for the Study of Popular Music International Conference, University of Strathclyde, Glasgow.

Oliver, P. (ed.) (1990), *Black Music in Britain: Essays on the Afro-Asian Contribution to Popular Music*, Open University Press, Milton Keynes.

Parker, H. (1974) *View from the Boys*, David & Charles, London.

Parker, D. (1998) 'Rethinking British Chinese Identities' in T. Skelton and G. Valentine (eds) *Cool Places: Geographies of Youth Culture*, Routledge, London.

Patrick, J. (1973) *The Glasgow Gang Observed*, Eyre Methuen, London.

Pearson, G. (1976) '"Paki-Bashing" in a North East Lancashire Cotton Town: A Case Study and its History' in G. Mungham and G. Pearson (eds) *Working-Class Youth Culture*, Routledge & Kegan Paul, London.

Pearson, G. (1983) *Hooligan: A History of Respectable Fears*, Macmillan, London.

Pearson, G. (1994) 'Youth Crime and Society' in M. Maguire, R. Morgan and R. Reiser (eds) *The Oxford Handbook of Criminology*, Clarendon Press, Oxford.

Peukert, D. (1983) 'Die "Wilden Cliquen" in den zwanziger Jahren' in W. Breyvogel (ed.) *Autonomie und Widerstand: Zur Theorie und Geschichte des Jugendprotestes*, Rigidon, Essen.

Pickering, M. and Green, T. (1987) 'Towards a Cartography of the Vernacular Milieu' in M. Pickering and T. Green (eds) *Everyday Culture: Popular Song and the Vernacular Milieu*, Open University Press, Milton Keynes.

Pilkington, H. (1994) *Russia's Youth and its Culture: A Nation's Constructors and Constructed*, Routledge, London.

Pini, M. (1997) 'Women and the Early British Rave Scene' in A. McRobbie (ed.) *Back to Reality: Social Experience and Cultural Studies*, Manchester University Press, Manchester.

Pohl, M. (1993) 'Mädchen – und Frauenrockbands in der Jugendarbeit' in W. Hering, B. Hill, and G. Pleiner (eds) *Praxishandbuch Rockmusik in der Jugendarbeit*, Leske & Budrich, Opladen.

Polhemus, T. (1997) 'In the Supermarket of Style' in S. Redhead, D. Wynne and J. O'Connor (eds) *The Clubcultures Reader: Readings in Popular Cultural Studies*, Blackwell, Oxford.

Potter, R. (1995) *Spectacular Vernaculars: Hip hop and the Politics of Postmodernism*, State University of New York Press, New York.

Redhead, S. (1990) *The End-of-the-Century Party: Youth and Pop Towards 2000*, Manchester University Press, Manchester.

Redhead, S. (1993a) 'The Politics of Ecstacy' (sic) in S. Redhead (ed.) *Rave Off: Politics and Deviance in Contemporary Youth Culture*, Avebury, Aldershot.

Redhead, S. (1993b) 'The End of the End-of-the-Century Party' in S. Redhead (ed.) *Rave Off: Politics and Deviance in Contemporary Youth Culture*, Avebury, Aldershot.

Redhead, S. (1997) *Post-Fandom and the Millenial Blues: The Transformation of Soccer Culture*, Routledge, London.

Regev, M. (1996) '*Musica mizrakhit*, Israeli rock and national culture in Israel' in *Popular Music*, 15(3): 275–84.

Reimer, B. (1995) 'Youth and Modern Lifestyles' in J. Fornäs and G. Bolin (eds) *Youth Culture in Late Modernity*, Sage, London.

Richard, B. and Kruger, H.H. (1998) 'Ravers' Paradise?: German Youth Cultures in the 1990s' in T. Skelton and G. Valentine (eds) *Cool Places: Geographies of Youth Culture*, Routledge, London.

Rietveld, H. (1993) 'Living the Dream' in S. Redhead (ed.) *Rave Off: Politics and Deviance in Contemporary Youth Culture*, Avebury, Aldershot.

Rietveld, H. (1997) 'The House Sound of Chicago' in S. Redhead, D. Wynne and J. O'Connor (eds) *The Clubcultures Reader: Readings in Popular Cultural Studies*, Blackwell, Oxford.

Ritzer, G. (1993) *The McDonaldization of Society: An Investigation Into the Changing Character of Contemporary Social Life*, Pine Forge Press, London.

Roberts, R. (1971) *The Classic Slum*, Manchester University Press, Manchester.

Robertson, R. (1995) 'Glocalization: Time–Space and Homogeneity–Heterogeneity' in M. Featherstone, S. Lash and R. Robertson (eds) *Global Modernities*, Sage, London.

Rose, T. (1994a) 'A Style Nobody Can Deal With: Politics, Style and the Postindustrial City in Hip Hop', in A. Ross and T. Rose (eds) *Microphone Fiends: Youth Music and Youth Culture*, Routledge, London.

Rose, T. (1994b) *Black Noise: Rap Music and Black Culture in Contemporary America*, Wesleyan University Press, London.

Russell, K. (1993) 'Lysergia Suburbia', in S. Redhead (ed.) *Rave Off: Politics and Deviance in Contemporary Youth Culture*, Avebury, Aldershot.

Sanghera, P. (1994) 'Identity Politics and Young "Asian" People' in *Youth and Policy*, **45**: 39–45.

Sansone, L. (1995) 'The Making of a Black Youth Culture: Lower-Class Young Men of Surinamese Origin in Amsterdam' in V. Amit-Talai and H. Wulff (eds) *Youth Cultures: A Cross-Cultural Perspective*, Routledge, London.

Sapsford, R.J. (1981) 'Individual Deviance: The Search for the Criminal Personality' in M. Fitzgerald, G. McLennan and J. Pawson (eds) *Crime and Society: Readings in History and Theory*, Routledge & Kegan Paul, London.

Saunders, N. (1995) *Ecstasy and the Dance Culture*, Nicholas Saunders/Turnaround and Knockabout, London.

Schade-Poulsen, M. (1995) 'The Power of Love: Raï Music and Youth in Algeria' in V. Amit-Talai and H. Wulff (eds) *Youth Cultures: A Cross-Cultural Perspective*, Routledge, London.

Sexton, A. (1995) 'Don't Believe the Hype: Why Isn't Hip-Hop Criticism Better?' in A. Sexton (ed.) *Rap on Rap: Straight-Up Talk on Hip-Hop Culture*, Delta, New York.

Shank, B. (1994) *Dissonant Identities: The Rock 'n' Roll Scene in Austin, Texas*, Wesleyan University Press, London.

Sharma, A. (1996) 'Sounds Oriental: The (Im)possibility of Theorizing Asian Musical Cultures' in S. Sharma, J. Hutnyk and A. Sharma (eds) *Dis-Orienting Rhythms: The Politics of the New Asian Dance Music*, Zed Books, London.

Sharma, S., Hutnyk, J. and Sharma, A. (eds) (1996) *Dis-Orienting Rhythms: The Politics of the New Asian Dance Music*, Zed Books, London.

Sharma, S. (1996) 'Noisy Asians or "Asian Noise"?' in S. Sharma, J. Hutnyk and A. Sharma (eds) *Dis-Orienting Rhythms: The Politics of the New Asian Dance Music*, Zed Books, London.

Shepherd, J. (1993) 'Value and Power in Music: An English Canadian Perspective' in V. Blundell, J. Shepherd, I. Taylor (eds) *Relocating Cultural Studies: Developments in Theory and Research*, Routledge, London.

Shields, R. (1991) *Places on the Margin: Alternative Geographies of Modernity*, Routledge, London.

Shields, R. (1992) 'The Individual, Consumption Cultures and the Fate of Community' in R. Shields (ed.) *Lifestyle Shopping: The Subject of Consumption*, Routledge, London.

Shumway, D. (1992) 'Rock and Roll as a Cultural Practice', in A. DeCurtis (ed.) *Present Tense: Rock and Roll and Culture*, Duke University Press, Durham, NC.

Shukla, S. (1997) 'Building Diaspora and Nation: The 1991 "Cultural Festival of India"' in *Cultural Studies*, 11(2): 296–315.

Simmel, G. (1903) 'The Metropolis and Mental Life' reprinted in D. Levine (1971) *On Individuality and Social Form*, University Press of Chicago, Chicago.

Slobin, M. (1992) 'Micromusics of the West: A Comparitive Approach' in *Ethnomusicology: Journal of the Society for Ethnomusicology*, 36(1): 1–87.

Slobin, M. (1993) *Subcultural Sounds: Micromusics of the West*, Wesleyan University Press, London.

Smart, B. (1993a) *Postmodernity*, Routledge, London.

Smart, B. (1993b) 'Europe/America: Baudrillard's Fatal Comparison' in C. Rojek and B.S. Turner (eds) *Forget Baudrillard?*, Routledge, London.

Smith, A. (1994) 'Some Like it Kool' in *The Sunday Times*, 10 July: 12–13.

Smith, A. (1995) 'Tribal and Strife' in *Guardian*, 8 May: 8–9.

Smith, F.M. (1998) 'Between East and West: Sites of Resistance in East German Youth Cultures' in T. Skelton and G. Valentine (eds) *Cool Places: Geographies of Youth Culture*, Routledge, London.

Smith, N. and Katz, C. (1993) 'Grounding Metaphor: Towards a Spatialized Politics' in M. Keith and S. Pile (eds) *Place and the Politics of Identity*, Routledge, London.

Smith, R.J. and Maughan, T. (1997) *Youth Culture and the Making of the Post-Fordist Economy: Dance Music in Contemporary Britain*, Occasional Paper, Department of Social Policy and Social Science, Royal Holloway, University of London.

Smith, S.J. (1989) *The Politics of 'Race' and Residence: Citizenship, Segregation and White Supremacy in Britain*, Polity Press, Cambridge.

Solomos, J. and Back, L. (1994) 'Conceptualising Racisms: Social Theory, Politics and Research' in *Sociology*, 28(1): 143–61.

Spillius, A. (1995) 'The Jungle Telegraph' in *Guardian Weekend*, 28 January: 12–17.

Stokes, M. (1994) 'Introduction: Ethnicity, identity and music' in M. Stokes (ed.) *Ethnicity, Identity and Music: The Musical Construction of Place*, Berg, Oxford.

Straw, W. (1983) 'Characterizing Rock Music Culture: The Case of Heavy Metal' in S. Frith and A. Goodwin (eds) (1990) *On Record: Rock Pop and the Written Word*, Routledge, London.

Straw, W. (1991) 'Systems of Articulation, Logics of Change: Communities and Scenes in Popular Music' in *Cultural Studies*, 5(3): 368–88.

Street, J. (1992) 'Shock Waves: The Authoritative Response to Popular Music' in D. Strinati and S. Wagg (eds) *Come on Down?: Popular Media Culture in Post-War Britain*, Routledge, London.

Street, J. (1993) 'Local Differences?: Popular Music and the Local State' in *Popular Music*, **12**(1): 43–54.

Sweeting, A. (1994) 'Wall of Sound' in *Guardian*, 10 October: 8–9.

Szemere, A. (1992) 'The Politics of Marginality: A Rock Musical Subculture in Socialist Hungary in the Early 1980s' in R. Garofalo (ed.) *Rockin' the Boat: Mass Music and Mass Movements*, Southend Press, Boston, MA.

Taylor, I. Walton, P. and Young, J. (1973) *The New Criminology*, Routledge & Kegan Paul, London.

Thompson, J.B. (1995) *The Media and Modernity: A Social Theory of Modernity*, Polity Press, Cambridge.

Thorgesen, S. and Curzon, P. (1997) *Mind Over Matter: The Images of Pink Floyd*, Sanctuary Press, London.

Thornton, S. (1994) 'Moral Panic, the Media and British Rave Culture' in A. Ross and T. Rose (eds) *Microphone Fiends: Youth Music and Youth Culture*, Routledge, London.

Thornton, S. (1995) *Club Cultures: Music, Media and Subcultural Capital*, Polity Press, Cambridge.

Trevor-Roper, H. (1983) 'The Invention of Tradition: The Highland Tradition of Scotland' in E. Hobbsbawm and T. Ranger (eds) *The Invention of Tradition*, Cambridge University Press, Cambridge.

Ullestad, N. (1992) 'Diverse Rock Rebellions Subvert Mass Media Hegemony' in R. Garofalo (ed.) *Rockin' the Boat: Mass Music and Mass Movements*, South End Press, Boston, MA.

Valley, P. (1995) 'What went wrong in Bradford' in *Independent*, 13 June: 2–3.

Veblen, T. (1912/1953) *The Theory of the Leisure Class: An Economic Study of Institutions*, Mentor Books, New York.

Wallis, R. and Malm, K. (1984) *Big Sounds from Small Peoples: The Music Industry in Small Countries*, Constable, London.

Walser, R. (1993) *Running With the Devil: Power, Gender and Madness in Heavy Metal Music*, Wesleyan University Press, London.

Waters, C. (1981) 'Badges of Half-Formed, Inarticulate Radicalism: A Critique of Recent Trends in the Study of Working Class Youth Culture' in *International Labor and Working Class History*, **19**: 23–37.

Watt, P. and Stenson, K. (1998) 'The Street: "It's a Bit Dodgy Around There" – safety, danger, ethnicity and young people's use of public space' in T. Skelton and G. Valentine, (eds) *Cool Places: Geographies of Youth Culture*, Routledge, London.

Weber, M. (1919/1978) 'The Distribution of Power Within the Political Community: Class, Status, Party' in S. Roth and C. Wittich (eds) *Economy and Society: An Outline of Interpretive Sociology*, University of California Press, Berkeley.

Werlen, B. (1993) *Society Action and Space: An Alternative Human Geography*, Routledge, London.

Whiteley, S. (1992) *The Space Between the Notes: Rock and the Counter-Culture*, Routledge, London.

Whyte, W.F. (1943) *Street Corner Society: The Social Structure of an Italian Slum*, Chicago University Press, Chicago.

Wicke, P. (1992) 'The Role of Rock Music in the Political Disintegration of East Germany' in J. Lull (ed.) *Popular Music and Communication*, 2nd edn, Sage, London.

Willet, R. (1989) 'Hot Swing and the Dissolute Life: Youth, Style and Popular Music in Europe 1939–49' in *Popular Music*, 8(2): 157–63.

Williams, R. (1965) *The Long Revolution*, Pelican, London.

Williams, R. (1980) *Problems in Materialism and Culture*, New Left Books/Verso, London.

Willis, P. (1972) 'The Motorbike Within a Subcultural Group' in *Working Papers in Cultural Studies 2*, University of Birmingham.

Willis, P. (1974) 'Symbolism and Practice: A Theory for the Social Meaning of Pop Music', Stencilled Occasional Paper: Birmingham Centre for Contemporary Cultural Studies, Sub and Popular Culture Series no. 13.

Willis, P. (1977) *Learning to Labour: How Working Class Kids Get Working Class Jobs*, Saxon House, Farnborough.

Willis, P. (1978) *Profane Culture*, Routledge & Kegan Paul, London.

Willis, P. (1990) *Common Culture: Symbolic Work at Play in the Everyday Cultures of the Young*, Open University Press, Milton Keynes.

Willis, T. (1993) 'The Lost Tribes: Rave Culture' in *The Sunday Times*, 18 July: 8–9.

Wittstock, M. (1993) 'Hi-Tech Change Rocks the World of Pop' in *The Times*, 12 October: 10.

Zweig, F. (1961) *The Worker in an Affluent Society: Family Life and Industry*, Heinemann, London.

Additional Sources

'Aa dee it coz aa can' by Ferank (Geordie poet and rapper) (1994).

Criminal Justice and Public Order Act 1994, Chapter 33, HMSO, London.

'Fremd im eigenen Land', music and lyrics by Advanced Chemistry (1993).

Lost in Music (Documentary about German hip hop). Broadcast in March 1993 on ZDF.

Index

A

Aboriginal rock music 42–3
ACDC 189
Achanack 108
acid house 35, 40, 51, 74, 75, 78, 82, 95
active audience 55
Adorno, Theodor 35–8, 51, 55
ADF 152
Advanced Chemistry 8, 143, 144, 165
African-diaspora (and hip hop) 133, 136–7
Afrika Bambaataa 134
ambient 75
America, cinematic image of 149
American Forces Network (AFN) 139
Andrews, Ahmed and Graham Fowler 127
Ang, Ien 55
Animals, the 153
Animals (Pink Floyd) 194
Another Brick in the Wall Part 1 (Pink Floyd) 175
Apache Indian 105, 115, 196
Appadurai, Arjun 66
Arnett, Jeffrey, J. 45, 183
Arrested Development 136
Art School, British 41
Asian *community* 118–20
Asian Dub Foundation 152
Attali, Jacques 40
Australian Doors, the 189

B

'baggy' 114
Back, Les 30, 103, 115–16, 118, 123, 127, 127–8, 152
Banerji, Sabita and Gerd Baumann 105, 131, 144
Barratt, Syd 194
Baudrillard, Jean 149
Baumann, Gerd 111, 118–19, 121
Bayton, Mavis 46, 151
Beach Boys, the 76
Beadle, Jeremy, J. 135
Beardsley, Peter 192
Beatles, the 39–40, 53–4, 56, 76, 198
Beastie Boys, the 135
Beattie, Geoffrey 187
Becker, Howard, S. 15–16
Bennett, Andy 151, 170, 171, 181, 187
Bennett, H. Stith 57
Bennett, Tony and Graham Martin *et al.* 19
Benjamin, Walter 35, 37–8, 51
Berlin Wall, the fall of (the role of music) 42
Bertelsmann Music Group (BMG) 76
Beverly Hills 90210 32
Bhachu, Parminder 112
bhangra 2, 4, 5, 7, 56, 62, 68–9, 101, 103–32, 144, 152, 196
bhangramuffin 115
Bigg Market, the (Newcastle) 86, 102, 123–4
bikers 20, 47, 79, 182–4
Birmingham Centre for Contemporary Cultural Studies (CCCS) 17–24, 26, 46–7, 78
  criticisms of 21–6
Björnberg, Alf and Ola Stockfelt 169–70, 179
Bjurström, Erling 62, 137, 144

Blackman, Shane, J. 174
Black Power Movement 41
Black Sabbath 77, 183
blues 181
Bollywood 121
Bombay Talkie 105
Boston (group) 172
Bowie, David 43, 193
Bradley, Dick 47–8
Bradford riots (June 1995) 113
Brake, Michael 30–1
Br-Asian youth culture 28
breakbeat 134
breakdancing 157
Brewer, Devon D. and Marc L.
    Miller 59
bricolage 62
Brighton Rock (Queen) 182
British folk music 109, 169
Brown, James 41

C
Can 172
Cantopop 42
Cashmore, Ellis 16
Castells, Manuel 96
Celtic Rock (Welsh) 141
Chambers, Iain 26, 28, 62, 152,
    183
Chaney, David 27, 63, 148, 153
Chaos Tage (annual punk event in
    Hannover, Germany) 50
Chemical Brothers, the 79
Chicago house music scene 87,
    90, 96
Chicago School 14–16, 17
Ching-Yun-Lee, Joanna 42
Clarke, Gary 23, 24
Clarke, John 19
Clash, the 79, 173
classless society thesis 18
Clifford, James 67
Cobley, Paul and William Osgerby
    136, 151, 156–7

Cohen, Phil 18–19
Cohen, Sara 5, 56–7, 67, 151,
    167, 180
    and Kevin McManus 180
Cohen, Stanley 15, 22
de Cologne, Floh 165
community discourse 30
Condry, Ian 137
counter-culture 173
counter-school culture 16–17
Country Joe and the Fish 41
Cowboy Song (Texan) 168
Criminal Justice and Public Order
    Act 1994 73, 75, 84
criminal personality 14
cultural intermezzo 115–16, 123
cultural relocation 61–2, 103
cultural reterritorialisation 54, 138
Cure, the 44

D
dance music 4, 6, 56, 68, 70,
    73–102, 163, 196
dance, theories of 21–2, 92–3
Dark Side of the Moon, The (Pink
    Floyd) 177, 179
Davies, Chris Lawe 42
Dean, Roger 173
Decker, Jeffrey Louis 136
deflected racism 156–7
Denzin, Norman K. 140
Deppe, Jürgen 164
'Deutsch-rock' 145
deviance, amplification of 15
    normalisation of 14–15, 17–18
dholak 104, 131
dholki 104, 131
digital recording 77–8, 81,
    99–100
Dimaggio, Paul 92
disco 73, 86, 91, 105
Division Bell, The (Pink Floyd)
    180

DJs
  dance music 74, 76, 81, 82, 85,
    89–90, 98, 100
  bhangra 107, 108, 125
  rap 129, 134–5, 157
Ducks Deluxe 193
Dudley, Anne 81
Dylan, Bob 44
Dyson, Michael Eric 135
Dywer, Claire 113

E

Eastern bloc, significance of
  pop/rock in 141
East Germany
  youth culture in 31
  dance music in 86–7
Easton, Paul 42
Ecstasy 75, 101
Eno, Brian 76
Ehrenreich, Barbara 39
Emerson, Lake and Palmer 172
Entertainments (Increased
  Penalities) Act 1991 (Graham
  Bright MP) 75
Epstein, Jonathon S. 135
ethnography 2–3, 14
ethnoscapes 66
Eurythmics, the 45

F

Face, The (magazine) 75, 173
Fantastischen Vier, Die 165
Farin, Klaus and Eberhard Seidel-
  Pielen 62, 165
Farm Aid 43
Faust 172
Featherstone, Mike 52
Fillipa, Marcelle 137
Fine, Gary Alan and Sheryl
  Kleinman 24
Finnegan, Ruth 57–8, 167–8,
  171, 180, 187
Flores, Juan 135

Focus 172
Fonarow, Wendy 168
Foner, N. 136
Fornäs, Johan 57
football hooligans 78
Fowler, David 13
Frankfurt Rockmobil Project, the
  4–5, 7, 181
Frankfurt School 35–6
Free 184
Fremd in eigenen Land (Advanced
  Chemistry) 143
Frith, Simon 37, 43, 44, 73, 76,
  78
  and Howard Horne 41–2
  and Angela McRobbie 44
Fryer, Peter 165
Fun Da Mental 152
Funk-Hennings, Erica 62

G

Gabriel, Peter 75, 126
Gane, Mike 149
gang studies 13, 14–15, 17
garage 75
Garofalo, Reebee 40
Gastarbeiter (guest worker) 5, 139,
  142, 164
Geiling, Heiko 50
Geldof, Bob 194
Genesis 172, 194
Geordie
  definition of 3
  identity 3–4, 166, 123–4,
    159–63
Geyrhalter, Thomas 44
Gillett, Charlie 38
Gilmore, Abigail 125
Gilmour, David 186, 194
Gilroy, Paul 61, 136–7
  and E. Lawrence 126
glasnost 1
Gleason, Ralph, J. 41

glocality 138, 146
  and hip hop 5, 138
globalisation 52, 53–5
God Save The Queen (the Sex
  Pistols) 48–9
Gottlieb, Joanne and Gayle Wald
  46
graffiti, hip hop 59, 134
Gramsci, Antonio 19
Grossberg, Lawrence 40

H
Hafeneger, Bruno 50
Haley, Bill (and the Comets) 34
Hall, Stuart and Chas Critcher 16
  and Tony Jefferson, 18
Hanna, Judith L. 92
Harpin, Lee 137, 143
Harris, David 22
Harron, Mary 41
Haslam, Dave 89
heavy metal 45, 79, 81, 183–4
  female exscription in 45
Hebdige, Dick 13, 20, 22, 23,
  23–4, 28, 29, 47, 48, 53, 62,
  103, 127, 136, 153
hegemony 19
Hendrix, Jimi 79
Hesmondhalgh, David 80
Hetherington, Kevin 65, 69, 80–1
Hill, Dave 44–5
hip hop 2, 5, 6, 7, 59, 69, 83,
  100, 104, 131, 133–65, 196–7
hippies 41, 47, 51, 172, 173, 184
Hobsbawm, Eric 109
Hobbs, Dick 3, 14
Hoggart, Richard 53, 55
Hollands, Robert 3, 86, 106, 123,
  124
homology 20, 22, 78
Horak, Roman 112
Hosokawa, Shuhei 34
house (music) 68, 73, 74–5, 83,
  85, 90, 105, 126, 156

house parties 68, 73, 86, 88,
  95–101

I
Ibiza (role in development of
  house) 75
independent, specialist record
  shops 100, 154–6
Indie music venues 168–9
Indobands 39
inner-city riots, British (early
  1980s) 16
invented tradition 103, 109–12
Isle of Wight Festival 173

J
Jackson, Michael 82, 102
Jam, the 173
Jefferson, Tony 19
Jenkins, Richard 25–6
Jibaro 75
Johansson, Thomas and Fredrik
  Miegel 26
John, Elton 43
Johnson, Paul 53–4, 55
Johnson, Robert 153
Jones, Simon 29–30, 62, 153, 156
Jourard, Marty 189
Joy Division 173
jungle 68, 75, 98, 100–1, 125

K
Kansas (group) 172
Kaplan, E. Anne 44
Kaur, Raminder and Virinder S.
  Kalra 28
Keith, Michael and Steve Pile 63
Keyes, Cheryl L. 134
Kilburn and the High Roads 193
King, Anthony 190
Kiss 183
Klitgaard Povlsen, Karen 32
Kraftwerk 76

Krüger, Heinz-Hermann, 34
  and Birgit Richard 96
Kruse, Holly 196

L
labelling theory 15–16
Lachmann, Richard 59
Laing, Dave 47, 48, 73, 140, 194
Lancaster, Bill 123
  and Robert Colls 3
Langlois, Tony 89
Led Zeppelin 79, 184
Leftfield 79
Lennon, John 41
Lennox, Annie 45
Levellers, the 81
Lewis, George, H. 50
Lewis, William F. 29
Liechty, Mark 31–2
lifestyle 25–7, 80, 111, 112, 130,
  153
Light, Alan 135
Lipsitz, George 61, 105
Live Aid 43
Lombroso, Caesere 14
London apprentices, the 12–13
Loop Guru 80
Love Parade, the (Berlin) 96
LSD 47, 51
Lull, James 54, 55, 138

M
MacDonald, Dwight 36, 55
MacKinnon, Niall 109, 169
'McDonaldization' 138
McDonald-Walker, Suzanne 183
McReady, John 173
McRobbie, Angela 21–2
  and Simon Frith 44
  and Jenny Garber 21
Maan, Bashir 132
Macan, Edward 172, 173
Madonna 44
Maffesoli, Michel 74, 80, 81, 111

Magazine (group) 173
Malbon, Ben 87
Malik, Kenan 127
Mandela, Nelson (concerts) 43
Manuel, Peter 121
marijuana 174, 184
Marshall Plan, the 148
Marks, Anthony 156
Marley, Bob 29, 82
Martin, Bill 184
Martin, George and Jeremy
  Hornsby 102
Martinez, Tony 34
Massey, Doreen 65–6, 69
Matthesius, Beate 62
Matza, David and Graham Sykes
  16
Maxwell, Ian 159
May, Tim 3, 14
Mays, John B. 17
MC Solar 144
Measham, Fiona 174
Meddle (Pink Floyd) 176
mediascape 196
'mega-events' 43
Meinig, Ute 151
Mela 7, 8, 105, 108–9, 111, 132
Melechi, Antonio 75
Merchant, Jacqueline and Rob
  MacDonald 101
Merton, Robert K. 16
Merseybeat 39
MIDI (Musical Instrument Digital
  Interface) 77
Middleton, Richard 34, 37–8
Milestone, Katie 153
misogyny
  in heavy metal 45
  in rap 143
Mitchell, Tony 135, 137, 141,
  144, 146
mods 15–16, 17, 20, 46, 153
Moore, David 19, 185

moral panics
    mods and rockers 15–16
    mugging 16
    rap 135
    rave 75
Moroder, Giorgio 76
MTV 43, 44, 149
Muggleton, David 78
Müller-Wiegend, I. 50
Murdock, Graham and Robin
    McCron 24, 172
music industry 38–41, 44–5, 46,
    76, 104
    and post-Fordism 100
Mutsaers, Lutgard 39

N
National Association for the Care
    and Resettlement of Offenders
    (NACRO) 6–7, 8
Negus, Keith 41, 43–4, 45, 74, 77
neighbourhood nationalism 127–8
neo-fascism 142, 144, 165
    neo-fascist rock groups 62
neo-tribes 81, 83–4, 87, 99
Nepali youth culture 31–2
New Age hippies 76
new criminology, the 18
Newcastle United 190–1, 192
northern rock (bhangra) 105
Northern Scuttlers, the 13
Northern Soul 153
Novak, Cynthia J. 93
Noys, Benjamin 100–1

O
Oaks, Jason 189
Oliver, Paul 165
Orbital 79

P
Papa Dee 144
Parents Music Resource Center
    (PMRC) 135

Parker, David 29
Parker, Howard 17
Patrick, James 17
Pearson, Geoff 12–13, 126
personal stereo 34
Pet Sounds (the Beach Boys) 76
Peukert, Detlev 13
Pickering, Michael and Tony
    Green 67–8
Pilkington, Hilary 31
Pini, Maria 94
Pink Floyd 69, 169, 171, 172,
    173, 173–4, 175–81, 183,
    186–93
Platters, the 34
Pohl, Manuela 151
Polhemus, Ted 82
polysemy 20, 22, 121
postmodernism 82
Potter, Russell A. 135–6
Presley, Elvis 39, 183
Preston, John 76
Primal Scream 79
progressive rock 44, 47, 56, 73,
    172–3, 183–4
Prohibition (in the US) 15
pub bands 4, 166, 180
pub rock scene (London) 193–4
pub venues 169–71, 181, 182,
    189–90
Public Enemy 44, 75
Punjab, the 104, 111, 115, 121–2
punk 20, 22, 23, 23–4, 35, 40,
    49, 50, 62, 73, 76, 79, 135
    in Germany 31, 50
    in Hungary 49
    in the US 168
    punk rock 47, 48–9, 81, 181
psychedelia 35, 75

Q
Queen 43, 182

R

radio, community 125–31
    pirate 125
raï music 59–60
ragga 105, 126
rap 6, 8, 56, 59, 114–15, 116,
    125, 126, 133–65
    freestyle rap 162–3
    gansta rap 135, 147–8, 164
    Geordie rap 159–63
Rastafarianism 29
rave 74, 75, 78, 82, 86
Recordiau Sain 58
Redhead, Steve 24, 73, 190
reggae 29–30, 61, 104, 105,
    114–15, 116, 126, 130–1
Regev, Motti 58
Reimer, Bo 25, 26
Richard, Birgit and Heinz-
    Hermann Krüger 96
Rietveld, Hillegonda 87, 88, 90,
    96
Ritzer, George 138
Roberts, Robert 13
Robertson, Roland 138, 146
Rock Against Racism 49 (*see also*
    Rock gegen Rechts)
Rock Around the Clock (film) 34–5
rockers 15–16, 17, 46, 76, 184
Rock gegen Rechts 142, 165
rock 'n' roll 34–5, 38–40, 41, 47,
    51, 78, 183
Rolling Stones, the 102, 189
Ronson, Mick 193
Rose, Tricia 59
Russell, Kristian 91
Russia, youth culture in 31

S

Sagoo, Bali 105, 196
sampling 77, 102
Sanghera, Paviter 113
Sansone, Livio 113
Saunders, Nicholas 101
Scary Eire 137

Schade-Poulsen, Marc 59–60
scratching (in rap music) 134–5
'Second' Summer of Love 74, 101
*Sergeant Pepper's Lonely Heart's
    Club Band* (the Beatles) 76,
    102
Sex Pistols, the 48
Sexton, Adam 135
Shank, Barry 64, 154, 168, 174
Sharma, Ashwani 121, 132, 152
Sharma, Sanjay 105, 107
Sheer Heart Attack (Queen) 182
Shepherd, John 60–1
Shields, Rob 63, 80–1, 84
Shine On You Crazy Diamond
    (Pink Floyd) 175, 186
Shumway, David 39
Simmel, Georg 25
Simon, Carly 171
skinheads 17, 19, 46, 127, 137,
    153
    in Australia 19, 185
    in Germany 31, 142, 165
Slobin, Mark 64, 69, 196
Smart, Barry 66, 149
Smith, Andrew 105
Smith, Fiona M. 31
Smith, Neil and Cindi Katz 63
Smith, Richard J. and Tim
    Maughan 100
Smith, Susan J. 127
sociality 57, 117, 169, 171, 174
    extra-musical 58, 167, 177–88
social geography 63
Solomos, John 118
Southall Beat (bhangra) 104–5,
    119
Spiders From Mars, the 193
Spiral Tribe 80
Stanley Blues Festival (County
    Durham) 153
Stewart, Rod 171
Stokes, Martin 61
Stonehenge, Festival 65
    heritage site 65

Straw, Will 64, 69, 84
Street, John 168
Styx 172
subcultural theory 11, 15, 17–20,
  47, 48, 78, 172
  critiques of 21–5
  feminist critiques of 21–2
Suede 44
Summer, Donna 79
Sunderland United 190–1
supercultures 64
'Swing Jugend' (swing kids) 13–14
Szemere, Anna 49

T
Tangerine Dream 76
Taste (group) 184
Taylor, Ian 18
techno 68, 73, 75, 84, 85, 86, 95,
  105
teddy boys 17, 19–20, 46
Tel Quel group, the 20, 33
Ten Years After 184
teeny bopper culture 21
Thin Lizzy 79
Third Reich, the 14
Thompson, John B. 54–5
Thorgesen, Storm and Peter
  Curzon 194
Thornton, Sarah 24–5, 73, 90,
  195
Tiananmen Square (student
  uprising in) 42
Tin Pan Alley 34
Tolkien, J.R.R. 173
Top of the Pops 48
townies 4, 69, 90, 94, 102
Toten Hosen, Die 50
trans-local subculture 196
trans-regionalism 196
Trevor-Roper, Hugh 109
tribus (tribes) 74, 80, 111 (*see also*
  neo-tribes)
tribute bands 69, 166, 171–2, 189
Turkish hip hop 144–5

U
UK Tribal Gathering '95 80

V
Van Halen 183
Vangelis 76
Veblen, Thorstein 25
Vietnam War, movement against
  41

W
Wall, The (Pink Floyd)
  album 175, 194
  film 180, 194
Wallis, Roger and Krister Malm
  58
Walser, Robert 45, 183
Waters, Chris 23
Waters, Roger 175
Watt, Paul and Kevin Stenson 128
Weber, Max 25
Werlen, Benno 65
Whiteley, Sheila 173, 176
Whyte, William F. 14–15
Wicke, Peter 42
Willet, Ralph 13–14
Williams, Raymond 54
Willis, Paul 16–17, 20, 22, 26, 47,
  172, 182–3
wiggers 156–7
Wish You Were Here (Pink Floyd)
  175, 181
Woodentops, the 75
Woodstock Festival 184

Y
Yes 172

Z
Ziggy Stardust 193
Zoo (record label) 173
Zulu Nation 134
Zweig, Ferdynand 18